Respectable Killing

The New Abortion Imperative

"I claimed thee for my own before ever I fashioned thee in thy mother's womb; before ever thou camest to birth, I set thee apart for myself."
—*Jeremiah* 1:4–5

"We hold these truths to be self-evident, that all men are created equal, that they are endowed by their Creator with certain unalienable Rights, that among these are life . . ."
—The Declaration of Independence

"Nor shall any State deprive any person of life . . . without due process of law; nor deny to any person within its jurisdiction the equal protection of the laws."
—Amendment XIV, The Constitution of the United States

Respectable Killing

the

New Abortion Imperative

by
K. D. WHITEHEAD

Catholics United for the Faith, Inc.
222 North Avenue
New Rochelle, New York 10801

Nihil Obstat:
Rev. Msgr. Donald D. Duggan
Censor Deputatus

Imprimatur:
Patrick Cardinal O'Boyle
Archbishop of Washington

April 26, 1972

TO

Paul, Steven, Matthew, David

Contents

Foreword

IT so happened that the manuscript of Mr. Whitehead's work came to my attention when I was deeply involved in an effort to prevent "The New Abortion Imperative" from achieving the total repeal of our Massachusetts abortion laws. It was most welcome. This year, I have observed that the mass of current material pertinent to this topic has increased substantially. One feels like Webster's storm-tossed mariner, anxious for a lull in the tempest in order to consult a compass and obtain one's bearings.

Mr. Whitehead's book admirably serves this directional purpose. It goes to the core issues directly and succinctly. The author has mastered a plethora of material from diverse disciplines, and in an orderly synthesis evaluated the significance of relevant religious, moral, legal, medical, scientific and sociological considerations. The result, however, is not a heavy or technical book. It is a lucid, logical and understandable exposition of the rights of unborn humanity. Moreover, this work performs an additional and unique service. It probes the genesis, the motivation and the strategy of "The New Abortion Imperative", the author's apt term to describe that strong unreasoning propulsion to abortion for convenience and on demand, a movement now without even the pretext of interest in protecting the life or health of the mother.

For several years I have observed the phenomenon of "The New Abortion Imperative" firsthand. Only two years ago, debates before the appropriate legislative committee in Massachusetts centered upon the pros and cons of therapeutic and eugenic abortions. This conditioning procedure of proposing to "liberalize" our statute was duly completed—essentially an exercise in propaganda because our statute, as judicially construed, was "liberal" in any event. Then there was a radical change in the direction of the debate. The New Abortion Imperative slipped

9

from the moorings of the restricted types of abortion previously urged. No longer were there pleas for therapeutic or eugenic abortion. Abortion for convenience became the issue. Thus, last year and again this year, the repeal of the abortion law was sought as a means of vindicating the alleged untrammelled right of a woman to control her own body and when her contraceptive fails, to make her womb a tomb.

The author demonstrates that this ultimate position represents the confluence of two major currents in contemporary life: Hedonism, which makes pleasure the exclusive function of sex, and Totalitarianism, which subordinates the right to life to the power of an élite core of social engineers to prescribe its "quality". He demonstrates the intellectual bankruptcy of previous pleas for "liberalized" abortion laws, and wisely suggests that there is wisdom in not permitting the pro-abortion cabal to forget some of these now demolished arguments which were advanced to condition our people to accept abortion-on-demand, and have left their residual of confusion in the public consciousness. He depicts the spiritual arrogance and malaise of the new false humanism that excludes God from His creation, and purports to sanction direct evil that good may come of it.

When sex gratification without discipline or responsibility, and callous expediency under the guise of social engineering, join forces in The New Abortion Imperative, the movement has strong momentum. Mr. Whitehead has interposed right reason in its path. Meeting this obstacle, The New Abortion Imperative is not an irresistible force. At this writing one may hope that the decisions of pending cases in the United States Supreme Court do not give it further propulsion through judicial discovery or sanction of a new alleged constitutional "right" of a woman to terminate her pregnancy for any reason.

I can testify from involvement in the crucible of the abortion controversy that this book not only clearly presents the basic issues, but also cogently evaluates a movement which is a malign threat to the traditional values of western civilization.

EDWARD B. HANIFY

Boston
February 29, 1972

Introductory Note

It should be stated at the outset that this book on the varied phenomena surrounding today's "abortion explosion" has been written by a Catholic. A regular tactic of those who are promoting the legalization of abortion today is to claim that all opposition to the practice is Catholic in origin. The suggestion that only Catholics oppose the killing of the innocent by abortion, however, happens not to be true. As the following pages will reveal, Catholics have no monopoly on respect for the sanctity of human life.

Almost all the admirable "right-to-life" groups which have been springing up around the country, for example, are officially non-sectarian; these groups have accomplished most of the real work that has been done in opposing today's trend towards permissive abortion. Indeed it seems to the writer—and this viewpoint will be reflected in what follows—that the Constitution of the United States, by itself, and without regard to any religion, provides basic principles sufficient to safeguard the right to life of the unborn; and the unborn's right to the equal protection of the laws. It is astonishing, for example, how the current American debate about whether we are justified in destroying the lives of the unborn or not is carried on in a kind of moral and legal vacuum—as if we did not already live under a Constitution and the rule of law here in America! The same unreality pervades the talk of certain élites in our society who pretend to speak, however sadly and reluctantly, of the "need" for population "control" measures. Who has decided that anyone has the *right,* under the American system, to impose population "controls" on a free people?

Similarly, the data that the writer has assembled here on the abortion issue will scarcely fit any unprejudiced person's definition of "sectarian." Nor do the general principles on which the book's examination and rejection of the arguments for abortion are based proceed from any exclusively Catholic source; they are principles which are almost surely accepted by the vast majority of Americans.

Although the book is written from a Catholic point of view, then—the writer would have been hard pressed to deal honestly with the issue of abortion from any viewpoint other than the Catholic one which he in fact holds —it is nevertheless to be hoped that the book's treatment of the subject is sufficiently general and timely so that it will be of some interest to anyone concerned about America's slide into permissive killing by abortion, regardless of his particular religious affiliation or lack of one.

Moreover, precisely *because* alleged exclusive Catholic opposition to abortion is the favorite straw-man of the pro-abortionists, it might be of some interest for the general public to have the chance to examine what a contemporary Catholic viewpoint on the abortion issue really does involve; and to judge whether such a frankly Catholic viewpoint does in fact contain anything contrary to the American spirit or to the "separation of church and state."

Apart from whatever general interest it may have, however, it is true that this book is addressed to Catholic readers in a particular way. As will be seen, it is the conviction of the writer that Catholics, both as individuals and in the mass, have too often failed to face the crisis of legalized abortion in America with anything like the consistency and resoluteness demanded by the principles which their Church holds in common with the Judeo-Christian, European and American traditions. We are even witnessing at the present moment Catholics prepared to sacrifice principles—and the rights of the unborn who cannot defend themselves—to the supposed demands of ecumenism, pluralism, "democracy," or whatever. Some of today's revisionist "Catholic" views on abortion are critically examined in these pages, and the writer makes no apology for washing such dirty "Catholic" linen, for, in one sense, this book is intended to be a special plea to the author's fellow Catholics to go firmly back to and act on the traditional Catholic teaching about the inviolability of innocent life from conception through natural death.

For—if only because the teaching of the Catholic Church on abortion has been so unmistakable—it seems particularly incumbent upon Catholic Americans to join in the defense of society's most innocent and defenseless members—the unborn.

The Catholic moral condemnation of abortion as a violation of the divine commandment "Thou shalt not kill" has been clear and consistent from the 1st Century until the present day. The moral wrong of deliberately procured abortion should be simply beyond dispute for any Catholic.

Also, a study which frankly adopts the Catholic moral teaching on abortion as the most reasonable and right position on this controversial contemporary issue may not be without interest for the general public in an era which often wrongly assumes all opposition to legalized abortion to be Catholic and which regularly gets a distorted version of what the Catholic position on the issue is.

The term "abortion," as used in this book, means the direct, willed destruction by medical means of an unborn child at any time between conception and birth. Doctors sometimes use the term "abortion" to refer to any interruption of a woman's pregnancy, natural or induced, which occurs before the child is viable—able to survive on his own outside the womb. Any delivery after the normal time of viability but before full term becomes, in this medical usage, a "premature delivery." This medical usage may have made sense in past days when "birth" was accepted as the natural, normal, and desirable "termination" of a human pregnancy, and when "abortions" were either spontaneous or were only induced by doctors for what were believed to be serious and necessary medical reasons. Now that more and more doctors are resorting to abortion for no other reason than to cause the *death* of the child—formerly the practice only of "criminal" abortionists—it no longer makes sense to blur the distinction between "abortions" which occur naturally and those which are *caused.*

Thus a woman doctor representing something called the Woman's National Abortion Action Coalition has maintained on national television that abortions after viability are "induced deliveries," not "abortions"—without going on to mention that the death of the child is nevertheless the aim of such so-called induced deliveries. The pro-abortionist jurist, Dr. Glanville Williams, in his well-known book *The Sanctity of Life and the Criminal Law,* is more honest when he defines abortion as "any untimely delivery procured with intent to destroy the fetus." In the abortion debate today it is important to maintain a definition that understands abortion as the result of intentional human actions. Natural interruptions of pregnancy which result in the child's death should be called "miscarriages" or "stillbirths."

Similarly, the distinction in Catholic moral teaching between "direct" and "indirect" causes for the interruption of a pregnancy is another crucial distinction which must be maintained. Valid medical procedures which are employed to save a woman's life, which do not aim at the death of the child, and which do not involve any direct assault on his person, are not, morally speaking, abortions at all—though the child's death may indirectly result. Remote as a fine distinction such as this may seem in an era given over to abortions for convenience, it remains an essential distinction, unless there would be no moral difference between deliberately blocking a mine shaft in order to trap the miners inside; and unavoidably trapping miners in one shaft as the only way to rescue those in another.

Portions of this book originally appeared in the *Catholic Standard,* Weekly Newspaper of the Archdiocese of Washington. Thanks are due to the Editor, Msgr. William F. O'Donnell, for permission to include them in this more extended essay. Parts of Appendix I, as well as the article on one modern "Catholic" view of abortion reprinted as Appendix II, originally appeared in *The Wanderer,* and thanks are due to the editors, Alphonse J. Matt, Sr., and A. J. Matt, Jr., for allowing this material to be included here. Grateful thanks are especially due to those who have read and commented on the manuscript: William F. Colliton, Jr., M.D., an obstetrician-gynecologist; Mr. Paul Haring and Mr. Victor H. Negron, attornies who have been concerned with the phenomenon of abortion; Msgr. Donald Duggan, Head of the Family Life Bureau, Archdiocese of Washington; Professor William A. Marra of Fordham University. Professor James Likoudis is especially to be thanked for his careful substantive and editorial comments. Mrs. Margaret Suddath is to be thanked for typing the manuscript. Edward J. Connor, William J. Hogan, Sean O'Reilly, and Bernard J. Pisani, M.D.'s all, and Mr. Michael Taylor, Executive Secretary, National Right to Life Committee, are to be thanked for providing considerable valuable background material on abortion. Errors of fact and judgment remain the writer's own. Grateful acknowledgement is also due to H. Lyman Stebbins, President, and Kirby Sheridan, Executive Director, Catholics United for the Faith, for their help, gentle encouragement and, above all, their patience. Lyman Stebbins continued to believe that a contemporary Catholic overview of the question of abortion was indeed timely and necessary at moments when discouragement overcame the writer. Finally, profound gratitude is due my wife, Margaret, who helped me grasp the evil of abortion.

K. D. WHITEHEAD

Good Friday, 1972

I

The Reality of Legalized Abortion

AN Egyptian plague of abortions has descended upon America. The slogan is abortion-on-demand, and events are proving that the demand is all too real. Abortion still remains a repugnant topic for most of us, something far removed from our experience. Few of us willingly think about it, or know very concretely what is involved in an abortion. If we do have some idea what is involved, we may find it hard to understand how anyone could perform an abortion or undergo one, and hence may conclude that the problem of abortion is bound to remain on the margin of our society.

The fact is, that our imagination constantly fails us in trying to take in the reality of abortion today. It is hard to believe how many people apparently see nothing wrong in society's allowing the practice; it is especially hard to believe how many are willing to do or have abortions themselves. And there are those in our society—in the organized pro-abortion movement—who are determined

18

that no legal, medical, moral or practical considerations shall any longer stand in the way of wide-spread, permissive, deliberate destruction of existing unborn human beings. It is no longer possible to remain passive or indifferent in the face of the consequences which legalized abortion is already bringing upon our whole society.

On July 1, 1970, a new statute went into effect in New York State allowing abortion for any reason, or for no reason, prior to the 24th week of pregnancy, or later in case of danger to the mother's life. Within four months, 50,000 abortions had been performed in New York City alone.[1] This amounts to more child victims than there have been American casualty deaths in all the years of the Vietnam war. In these four short months, New York City had witnessed almost as many deaths as occur in a whole year on all of America's notoriously lethal roads and highways; and these abortion deaths were not accidental; they were all deliberately caused. At the end of the first year of legalized abortion the New York City toll had mounted to almost 168,000; at the end of 18 months, it had mounted to 278,122.

This total "body count" averages out at around 460 per day, compared with only 850 performed legally in the city during the entire previous year. More than half these abortions were performed on women less than 24 years of age and almost 80 per cent on women under 30; more than three fourths of them were on white women; abortions on out-of-state women made up about 60.2 per cent of the total.[2] The new state law's lack of any residency requirement brought women seeking abortions flocking into New York City in droves. Many didn't bother to make any arrangements before leaving their homes; from the outset the city's Planned Parenthood organization reported a surprising number of I'm-at-the-airport-where-do-I-go-for-an-abortion calls.[3]

The city's existing hospitals were initially swamped with abortion cases, and beds denied to patients with real illnesses; some hospitals were quickly booked months ahead and some began working seven days a week in order to handle the volume. Before the new law it was not uncommon for a patient to have to wait two to three months for elective surgery.[5] Within weeks after the new abortion law went into effect the bed situation had worsened to the point where the New York Academy of Medicine was urging that scarce beds be allotted to women residing "in New York City or to previous patients of New York City physicians"; the American Medical Association was calling for specialized training courses for physicians unfamiliar with abortion procedures.[6] Meanwhile the activist National Association for Repeal of Abortion Laws (NARAL) was conducting its own symposia to familiarize physicians with abortion techniques.[7] Hospital residents in obstetrics were complaining about the inordinate amount of their training time becoming devoted solely to abortions and more abortions.[8]

The initial shortage of doctors, beds and facilities did not prevent some hospitals and clinics from immediately beginning to solicit abortion cases. The American Medical Association had to denounce hospitals which sent out letters and publicity to doctors across the country. "The establishment of abortion mills must not be permitted," the AMA insisted.[9]

Abortion mills were quickly a reality, however. Clinics performing the "operation" on a mass-production-line basis sprang up to meet the burgeoning demand. Here was the answer to the shortage of hospital facilities: new clinics specializing solely in abortions. One such clinic performed 7000 of them in five months. Women arriving at this particular clinic are met by "sleekly chic" female assistants, as one report describes them; they have all had abortions themselves and they prepare the new women who come in to get theirs. Orange-flowered potholders cover the steel stirrups on the operating table ("Now unveil the colorful potholders," the clinic's operating manual advises the female assistants, "and pause for her laugh"); Muzak is piped in.

The "vacuum aspiration," or "suction curettage," method now widely employed for abortions early in pregnancy is the current specialty of this particular clinic: "Swoosh, and 30 seconds later, it's all over." The tiny child is whisked through a tube into the aspirator like so much trash into a vacuum cleaner. "As they leave, girls are given two pages of instructions, which include taking anti-biotics to prevent infection, and a 'hot-line' phone number to call if they get a temperature.[10]

Almost as soon as it was in business this clinic began negotiating to buy a private hospital that would specialize in the more difficult kinds of abortions performed later in pregnancy.[11] After the twelfth week, two methods are used. The first is a hysterotomy; this is similar to a Caesarean section. An abdominal incision is made and the baby lifted out and left to die in a hospital basin. The second method for later pregnancies, "salting out," involves the injection of a saline solution into the amniotic sac surrounding the baby inside the womb; this saline solution kills the baby, and also induces the normal labor of childbirth by which, within 12 to 36 hours, the dead baby is expelled from the mother's body.

These procedures used later in pregnancy are complicated and fraught with danger for the mother. In Japan, where abortion-on-demand is virtually legal, the "salting-out" method was abandoned years ago as a "hazardous method."[12] In New York, short-term complications from all methods have not been inconsiderable, in fact, running initially at a rate of 12.4 for every 1000 abortions. The complications reported for the short-term included hemorrhage, infection, shock, retained tissue, perforated uterus, lacerated cervix; 13 maternal deaths were reported as a result of the first 70,000 abortions in New York City.[13] Doctors far afield from New York began encountering abortion complications in their own practices after the aborted women returned home; several known maternal deaths have occurred in other states following New York abortions. Many doctors have the impression that not all complications—or, for that matter, all abortions—are reported, particularly where the operation or treatment has been in a doctor's office instead of in a hospital.[14]

By the end of the first year of legalized abortion, however, many of the initial problems were being "solved" with remorseless technical efficiency. Adequate facilities had been found in response to the demand. The maternal complication rate had dropped from 12.4 to 8.7 per 1000 abortions. But we should remember that this rate could only refer to *short-term* complications. Moreover, given the number of out-of-state women and what seems to be the practice of the hospitals and clinics, we can scarcely consider that there has been any degree of *follow-up* which could give us much confidence in the complication rate cited. Only 15 official maternal deaths were recorded in all during the first year in New York.[15] Yet it could hardly be said that abortion had been rendered safe. When the new law was adopted, one New York City health official commented, "We can tolerate three deaths per 100,000 patients. That's fewer than we get from tonsillectomies."[16] (Obviously, he meant "maternal deaths"; he seemed prepared to tolerate an unlimited number of child deaths; the infant mortality rate in successful abortions is, of course, uniformly one hundred per cent.) But the actual incidence of maternal deaths in New York under abortion-on-demand has proved to be about three times higher than was thought "tolerable."

Rarely mentioned in pro-abortion propaganda, then, which prefers to dwell on the dangers of illegal abortions, are these dangers to women having abortions even in the most ideal hospital surroundings. The New York experience has confirmed this. The dangers are in any case well known to informed medical opinion. An article in the *American Journal of Obstetrics and Gynecology,* reviewing the first year of Colorado's experience with a "reformed" law allowing legal abortions only in certain circumstances, found its physician authors "impressed by the spectrum of complications that followed therapeutic abortion procedures," and a later study of abortions in 12 states and the District of Columbia revealed that 10.1 of the women involved suffered one or more complications.[17] The American College of Obstetricians and Gynecologists warned in 1968 that even the medical profession was not fully aware of the dangers inherent in normal abortion procedures.[18]

The British medical journal, *The Lancet,* in its issue of December 4, 1971, revealed that "a review of the methods used and the results obtained in 1182 legal abortions in one teaching hospital confirms that termination of pregnancy, even in the early weeks, is neither simple nor safe. Nearly 17% of patients lost more than 500 ml. of blood and 9.5% required transfusion. Cervical lacerations occurred in 4.2% and the uterus was perforated in 1.2% ... Emergency laparotomy was required for 6 patients and hysterectomy was twice necessary to save life. Pyrexia of 38°C or more persisting for longer than 24 hours occurred in 27%. Peritonitis developed in 14 patients, with paralytic ileus in 7, and 6 others had septicemia." An editorial in the same issue of *The Lancet* concluded that "healthy young women, whose only complaint is that they are pregnant, are entering the hospital and being subjected to procedures that may permanently affect their fertility and occasionally jeopardise their lives."

A San Francisco obstetrician bluntly asserts: "A hysterotomy is a life-threatening operation." He goes on: "In 'salting out,' sudden death can result from the salt injection or the uterus can be ruptured, producing uncontrolled bleeding. Or the patient may suffer water intoxication or septic shock and infection after the procedure. Also, there is about a four per cent failure rate."[19]

By "failure rate," perhaps the doctor is referring to the same thing that has proved to be one of the more shocking results of New York State's "noble experiment" with abortion-on-demand: in mid-December, 1970, it was disclosed that 26 infants had been *born alive* as a result of what we may perhaps call "abortive" abortions. Some of these babies "breathed for only a few minutes and others cried and kicked before finally dying within two days after being artificially expelled from their mothers' wombs," reported the Chicago *Tribune,* the newspaper which broke the story. Although these 26 live births were reported out of the first approximately 70,000 legal abortions, Dr. Robert R. Onorato, an obstetrician-gynecologist from Yonkers, believed that the actual number was "in the hundreds" since the true figure goes unreported.[20] One of the "aborted" twenty six, a little girl, survived, and was put up for adoption.[21]

At the end of a year, 62 live births had been officially reported from New York City abortions. (The Oregon Right To Life Committee has documented no less than 33 cases of infants aborted in that state being born alive; the Oregon abortion law, though liberal, is nevertheless supposed to restrict abortion to certain situations; "Officials Wink At Laws" a leader in the *Oregon Journal* reported.)[22]

Such appalling developments as these are undoubtedly

important factors behind the frequent reports of hospital nurses leaving their jobs in revulsion and disgust, and seeking jobs in hospitals where abortions are not performed. It is to the nurses, of course, that the degrading role is assigned of cleaning up and disposing of the human debris that results from these operations; there is no abortion without a corpse, however tiny.

One nurse has described how she found "throwing away perfectly formed fetuses revolting . . . No matter what anyone tells you and no matter what your religious beliefs," she said, "it's a physically grotesque thing to work at for eight hours a day."

A registered nurse who had just resigned from another hospital said: "I couldn't possibly go on ignoring the live fetuses; or even putting the dead ones in buckets to be sent to the lab. One day when I came on duty, the nurse going off duty pointed to the table on the other side of the room where the fetuses were placed. It was easy to detect all the way across the room a visibly strong heartbeat.

"The other nurse was timid and she asked me to speak to the doctor," this nurse went on. "When I pointed it out to him he said, 'For all intents and purposes it's dead. Leave it there.' I told him I couldn't do it. He could have my job on the line, but I wouldn't do it. This time I was going to take it to the nursery. I knew this fetus would probably die, but I had to give it a chance . . ."

The news report from which the above incidents have been quoted concludes as follows: "In most hospitals each fetus, depending on size, is placed either in an individual carton or in a bucket containing formalin solution and then sent to the lab for pathological examination. Most labs do not remain open on weekends. And according to one nurse, 'you could populate a whole village with the fetuses in cartons lined up on the table on Monday morning.' "[23]

If we have not yet read press reports about the selling of live fetuses for experimental purposes in New York, as happened last year in England, it may be simply because the press has not reported the practice. What is certain is that experimentation—and the use of fetal tissue for medical purposes—is going on right now.[24]

Nurses for Life, a California group, which filed a "friend-of-the-court" brief in an abortion case before that state's Supreme Court, has called attention to such experimental practices (and the other horrors of abortion). In February, 1972, the "Newsletter" of the National Right to Life Committee quoted the Nurses for Life brief as follows: "We believe that if other members of our sex could witness an abortion, if they could see the results of the abortion, if they could see the drowning of the child in amniotic fluid, the experimentation on the living child, the disposal of the dismembered child, the emotional trauma of many women after the abortion, they would, hopefully, not choose to exercise what they term their 'civil right' to an abortion."

Such horrors as these are by no means confined to abortions performed late in pregnancy. Dr. Richard V. Jaynes, a Detroit obstetrician-gynecologist, has graphically described the procedure known as dilation and curettage (D & C), the method traditionally employed for abortions prior to the twelfth week of pregnancy: "A roughly spoon-shaped instrument called the curette, about ten inches long and with sharp edges, is inserted into the uterus. The child inside is cut into pieces and pulled or scooped out limb by limb. In order for the members to be removed, of course, the doctor must stretch the uterine opening. It isn't dilating of its own accord, as it would in normal birth. It can't be stretched too far, however, and in order to pass larger parts like the head, they must be crushed. Some doctors use a ring forceps . . ."[25]

The suction curettage method, which is replacing the D & C in the more streamlined clinics, obviates the need to cut the baby up and scrape him out in pieces; even so, recognizable bits of baby can be discerned in the bloody "product" of the newer method. In any case, the D & C is likely to remain a standard abortion procedure since not all hospitals and clinics will have the new vacuum aspirators. In fact, it is now often estimated that the D & C is performed more frequently than any other surgery.

Nor are these early abortions necessarily free of dangers to the woman. The *New York Times* reported on the death of one 23-year-old Boston woman after a D & C performed in the New York City office of an obstetrician; the doctor who performed the operation later told the city's medical examiner that "she had been unable to find the fetus and concluded that Mrs. Ortega was not pregnant." The autopsy showed, however, "that the curette had plunged completely through the uterine wall . . . The autopsy showed massive internal bleeding and expulsion of the fetus into the abdominal cavity . . ."[26]

Such, then, are some of the realities of legalized abortion. When the New York State Legislature passed the new abortion-on-demand law, the state senator who cast the 29th and deciding vote in favor of it spoke, perhaps more prophetically than he knew, in this vein: "I rise to cast the deciding vote to help move the Empire State toward a new approach to a new society . . . Mr. President, I vote 'Yes'."[27] It seems perfectly clear that what we are now witnessing in New York does represent "a new approach to a new society," but perhaps not in the sense the senator meant. It is a new society erected on the blood and crushed bones of slaughtered babies. New York is well on the way to proving that the curette is mightier than the sword. 215,-453 is the official number of abortions performed in the state as a whole during the first year of the new law.[28] At the Albany Medical Center, in upstate New York, abortions are said to be exceeding live births.[10]

On this scale, abortion has turned out to be nothing else than big business; one of the principal motives behind the drive for "humane" abortion proves to be the old-fashioned profit motive. Legal abortion is not putting the old criminal, "back-alley" abortionist out of business; it is simply affording the opportunity for more people to cut in on the "take"—as well as legalizing for "humane" reasons a racket worthy of the Mafia!

So-called abortion referral services have sprung up in the wake of abortion legalization, offering package deals and advertising their services nationally in publications such as *Look* magazine. College newspapers represent another widely used advertising outlet for these abortion referral agencies. Through these services, it is possible to arrange one's abortion as one might arrange a trip to Europe through a travel agency; indeed some travel agencies went into the business themselves, especially when England was still the center of the abortion bonanza.[29]

New York, however, seems quickly to have outdone everything London had to offer. One of its new referral agencies grossed $150,000 in five months.[30] The New York State Attorney General was soon obliged to open an investigation of the referral firms on the grounds that they were using deceptive advertising and engaging in fee-splitting with hospitals and clinics.[10] The Attorney General was not concerned with the ethics of doing the abortions, only with whether clients were being cheated in the process. A justice of the New York Supreme Court eventually ruled the commercial referral services illegal. A month later, the New York State Assembly confirmed this judgment by passing laws prohibiting fee-splitting and the sale of medical referrals (Planned Parenthood's non-profit referral service promptly doubled its capacity).[31]

The elimination of the commercial referral services, however, has not eliminated the profits for the doctors and clinics. We read of doctors earning as much as $3000 in one afternoon performing abortions. Dr. Byron Gordon, Director of Family Planning Service at the New York Medical College, speaks of "large numbers" of doctors "who are easily making $100,000 to $130,000 extra a year."[32] *Extra!* Competition may have driven the cost per abortion down, but the specialized clinics can still turn a handy profit performing the operation for as little as $150 —for the same reason that Henry Ford got rich selling the Model T—because the thing is organized on an efficient mass-production basis. Most abortions run higher than this, however, and can run as high as $1000 for a hospital abortion on a woman more than 16 weeks pregnant.[10] The journal *Medical Economics* estimates the total worth of the abortion business in New York alone at $80,000,000 a year.[33]

Nor will the "business" be confined to New York state at the pace "abortion reform" is moving. Alaska and Hawaii enacted abortion-on-demand laws at the same time as New York. Alaska's legislature actually overrode a governor's veto to pass its new law. Hawaii's law took effect as soon as enacted (March, 1970). Immediately, officials at Honolulu's major maternity hospital reported they were swamped with applications for abortions; the hospital promised to start performing them as fast as possible but, as a hospital administrator remarked, "We have other surgical procedures going on here, too."[34] Eight months later a survey of Hawaii's hospitals disclosed that there had been one abortion for every five live births since the law went into effect, the majority of them performed on women in their late teens and early twenties.[35]

The State of Washington actually approved abortion-on-demand in a popular referendum, 532,739 votes to 424,875.

Catholics, incidentally, make up only 13 per cent of that state's population; it is perhaps significant that 65 per cent of Washington's population claims no religious affiliation at all.[36] The first available figures indicate that abortions in Washington State are being performed at a rate of about 23 for every 100 live births; in Alaska, in the first year of the new abortion-on-demand law there, about 11 per cent of all the pregnancies which would normally have resulted in the birth of human beings were instead aborted.[37] When more figures are in on Alaska, Hawaii, and Washington, we will be able to compare their experience with New York's frightful record. In Maryland, the General Assembly also passed an abortion-on-demand bill in 1970, but it was later vetoed by the governor. As passed, the bill would simply have eliminated abortion as a concern of the state, and would have obviated the need even to keep a record of the abortions performed. This is undoubtedly the ideal towards which the logic of abortion-on-demand is tending; nobody would ever have to know the extent of the carnage.[38]

But the drive for easy abortions is not confined to lobbying at state legislatures. An equally remarkable manifestation of the veritable frenzy for abortion which seems to be taking America in its grip has been the speed and alacrity with which "public" programs have appeared to "implement" the new abortion-on-demand laws. This has been notably true in New York where health officials ludicrously tripped over each other to insure that abortions at public expense would be available when the new law went into effect.[39] The city which cannot manage to collect its garbage or pay its police force yet managed to allocate a $5-million "contingency fund" to help pay for an estimated 25 to 30 thousand abortions and "help hospitals develop their facilities or to hire the staff to use [existing] facilities at normally underused times—nights and weekends."[40] The Health and Hospital Corps, a city agency, actually instituted a "dial-an-abortion" service,[41] as did, of course, many private hospitals and referral services. The New York State Department of Health and Social Services approved a regulation allowing Medicaid recipients full or partial payment for doctors' fees, hospital-room charges, infant burial, blood transfusions, anesthetists, laboratory and recuperation costs among other charges associated with abortions; the state budget for the following year requested millions to underwrite the costs of this program. New York State Senator James H. Donovan charged that this was taxing people in order to "relieve a woman from accountability for her own acts" and to "permit forfeiture of life without due process."[42] Senator Donovan estimated that the taxpayers spent over $15 million during the first year of legalized abortion in New York.[30]

Thus all citizens, regardless of their views on abortion, are now implicated in the abortion process through the use of their tax monies in those states where abortion-on-demand is a reality. This is a perfectly extraordinary development when we recall that the stated intention of the New York and similar abortion-on-demand legislation was supposedly to make abortion a purely "private" choice between a woman and her physician; this legislation neither required nor, seemingly, *authorized* any public implementation.

Nevertheless, anyone who has followed the abortion reform movement even casually is aware that the proponents of legalized abortion commonly argue out of both sides of their mouths *both* for abortion as a purely private matter between a woman and her doctor *and* for institutionalized abortion at public expense in order to remove the "discrimination" held to be inherent in restrictive laws which tend, in practice, to allow abortion for the rich but not for the poor.

One group of psychiatrists addressing themselves to this topic, for example, is quoted as saying that "those who believe abortion is murder need not avail themselves of it." The same report, however, quotes one of the same psychiatrists to the effect that the eventual answer is government-run abortion clinics: "It's really not enough to get the laws off the books. We need a positive law that would delineate legal procedures, that would empower the public health officer to serve the public . . . to see that the public health officer would not have to take a risk."[43]

Some states have not even waited to "get the laws off the books" before setting up public programs of "charity" abortions. California's "reformed" law, for example, restricts abortion to cases where the mother's life, or physical or mental health is endangered, or to cases of rape or incest. Common sense would suggest that not too many abortions would be required if abortions were truly limited to these circumstances. Yet syndicated columnist James J. Kilpatrick cites an investigation conducted by the California legislature revealing that some 25,000 abortions were performed in the state at public expense during 1970. Each one of these abortions cost the California taxpayer $450. "At least 6000 of these 'free' operations," Mr. Kilpatrick comments, citing the California Legislature's study, "were performed on women who probably had incomes adequate to pay the cost themselves."[44] Total legal abortions in California in 1967, before the passage of the "reformed" law, were no more than 500. With the new law they jumped to 5,030 in 1968, to 15,539 in 1969, and then to an astonishing 62,000 in 1970.[45]

Indeed a skyrocketing abortion rate such as California's seems to be the regular result of any relaxation of the abortion law—even though the law does not allow simple abortion-on-demand. Colorado, which enacted a law similar to California's in 1967, recorded 497 legal abortions in

1968; 946 in 1969; 2,091 in 1970; and 3,759 in 1971. The same phenomenon occurred in Maryland, which liberalized its law in 1968 to allow abortions in accordance with specific "indications." Nevertheless, seemingly without reference to the actual occurrence of these "indications," the abortion rate skyrocketed as in California and Colorado: 2,134 in 1969; 5,530 in 1970; 7,757 in 1971. In Maryland also, a program of state subsidized abortions was begun "quietly" in the spring of 1970 using regular state medical funds. The program surfaced when the Department of Health sought $441,000 to expand the program "fourfold,"[46] again without any change in the law making legal abortions possible under a wider range of circumstances. In this era of rising medical costs and inadequate facilities, it is amazing that public money can nevertheless be made available for abortions—even when their legality is questionable.

In another instance, a *federally* financed program, nationwide in its effect, was established in military hospitals without reference to any abortion legislation whatsoever. In July, 1970, a Deputy Assistant Secretary of Defense issued a purely administrative memorandum allowing abortion at the request of a woman at all U.S. military, naval and air medical facilities, regardless of the local or state law in force where the facility happened to be located. By this action, the U.S. Department of Defense not only directed that the criminal law in many of our states be violated; it began sponsoring and performing abortions at the taxpayers' expense never authorized by any legislation, Congressional or otherwise. The only public rationale which the DOD offered for this clear abuse of authority was that it had the responsibility "to provide medical care to military personnel and their families . . . in accordance with the best medical judgment of military medical personnel."[47]

Shortly afterwards, however, the DOD began authorizing abortions for military personnel and their dependents in *civilian* hospitals even if the military doctors *disagreed!* In other words, the DOD was prepared to pay for the abortion even when *not* "in accordance with the best medical judgment of military medical personnel!"[48]

In the spring of 1971, this DOD abortion program was modified by the intervention of President Nixon himself, who issued an order requiring military hospitals to observe state laws in the matter of abortion, declaring at the same time his own basic opposition to abortion which he said was in conflict "with his belief in the quality and sanctity of life."[49] The President's directive, of course, did not stop the free military abortions in states where the practice is legal. Moreover, according to *Medical World News,* "if a WAF on active duty cannot get an abortion on her base because of restrictive state laws, she can fly via an Air Force plane to a facility in a liberal state."[50]

When not even the President of the United States himself, apparently, can *prevent* an arm of the government which he heads from performing abortions at public expense, without any authorization and often in contravention of existing laws, we may legitimately begin to wonder what sort of insanity is overtaking this country. What we may perhaps call an "Abortion Imperative"—the apparent belief that, whatever other factors may be involved, we must at any rate get on with abortions and ever more abortions at all costs—seems to be rapidly superseding all other possible legal, medical, moral or practical considerations in America today.

The dictates of this new Abortion Imperative have been notably operative in the nation's capital, Washington, D.C., where the courts stepped in to keep the abortion ball rolling, in spite of the existing law. In November, 1969, U.S. District Judge Gerhard A. Gesell declared the District of Columbia statute on abortions invalid. The main thrust of the judge's ruling was that the D.C. law, which allowed abortion not only to preserve the mother's life but to preserve her "health" as well, nevertheless did not make clear under what conditions the mother's health might be endangered by a pregnancy. "The word 'health' is not defined," the judge declared, "and in fact remains so vague in its interpretation and the practice under the act that there is no indication whether it includes varying degrees of physical and mental health."[51] The judge also felt the D.C. law placed upon the physician the burden of proof that a given abortion was indeed performed to preserve the mother's life or health.

While, according to Judge Gesell, there may not have been an "indication" that the law permitted abortions for broad so-called "mental health" reasons, and hence one of the questions before the Court of Appeals seemed to be whether the law did in fact allow abortions on these grounds, nobody bothered to wait to see how a higher court might decide this question. Instead it was rapidly just *assumed* that Judge Gesell's decision throwing out the D.C. law established that abortions henceforth *could* be performed in the nation's capital on broad "mental health" grounds. The judge himself spoke in his decision of the need to provide "uniform medical abortion services" to all segments of the population, "the poor as well as the rich." In other words, since the rich were paying for abortions on mental health grounds, and nobody was being prosecuted under the existing law, then the poor should get abortions on mental health grounds too, *although* what was not clear was whether *anybody* should be permitted to get an abortion on these grounds!

Public "implementation" of this judicial decision came only a little less rapidly than the scramble in New York to implement the Empire State's new law. In February, 1970, a Mayor's Task Force on Health Goals pressed upon the city's Health Department a recommendation that D.C. General Hospital, a public facility, should provide free abortions for *all women requesting them!*[52]

Initially, the hospital declined to accept this recommendation. Overworked and understaffed, and underfunded into the bargain, the hospital was hard put to accomplish its regular medical tasks in service to the community. Even apart from what common sense would judge to be the dubious legality of considering a judicial decision turning upon the definition of "health" as a license for abortion-on-demand, there were practical considerations. D.C. General Hospital depended about equally for its resident staff on the medical schools of Georgetown and Howard Universities; residents from the former, a Catholic university, objected to performing abortions on moral and religious grounds; residents from the latter, a predominantly black university, additionally saw the recommended program of charity abortions at D.C. General as an exercise in "black genocide." The hospital thus had neither the facilities for the recommended program nor the doctors to perform the abortions.

In strict accordance with the Abortion Imperative, however, another U.S. court soon stepped in to force the issue. The American Civil Liberties Union instituted a suit to oblige D.C. General to perform an abortion on an indigent 21-year-old woman on broad mental health grounds. Since this woman, "Mary Doe," was nearing the twelfth week of pregnancy, it was argued that the case must be decided immediately so that the abortion could be promptly performed with greater relative safety. The courts were apparently happy to oblige; one newspaper account spoke of the "race" of this ACLU suit through the normally clogged and lethargic federal judiciary in the District of Columbia. "Somebody is pushing this case faster than normal processes allow," the Medical Director of D.C. General remarked at one point.

The result of all this feverish judicial activity was that this public hospital was in due course *directed* by a U.S. Court of Appeals to perform the abortion on Mary Doe.[53] The same U.S. court officially "reprimanded" D.C. General when time ran out on the woman and the abortion had to be performed at a private hospital. "Our primary concern," wrote Chief Judge David L. Bazelon, "is not the good faith of the city and hospital officials, but the deprivation of medical care suffered by indigent patients." Commenting on the lack of facilities at D.C. General, the court observed that increasing the number of abortions would in all likelihood decrease the number of women coming to the hospital for childbirth![54]

Within a matter of weeks, a full-fledged abortion clinic was established at D.C. General Hospital. Shortly after that, both the hospital's medical director and its chief of obstetrics and gynecology moved on to other positions.[55]

In any other situation, we might have expected some note of caution on this issue. The D.C. law on abortions was not in a kind of legal limbo while the Gesell decision was being appealed to the U.S. Supreme Court, as was widely believed and as the press had reported.[56] The law remained in force. Apparently, however, the demands of the Abortion Imperative are not to be denied on the basis of considerations such as that the law ought to be enforced. The courts themselves directed that the law be violated.

And if the courts were incautious while the status of the D.C. law was believed to be in doubt, physicians and hospitals seemed all too ready to follow their example. The medical establishment began to act pretty much as if abortion-on-demand had already become a reality in the nation's capital as a result of the several court decisions.

Washington, D.C., rapidly became such an abortion mecca that some wags began to say that the initials actually stood for "dilation & curettage." By the spring of 1971, Planned Parenthood of Metropolitan Washington had established one of the now familiar abortion counseling and referral services.[57] The Washington Hospital Center, a private facility, had established an outpatient clinic capable of handling 100 abortions a week.[58]

The clinic was hardly established before the familiar scandals began. As disclosed by Congressman Lawrence J. Hogan (R.-Md.), a baby born alive after an abortion was placed in a refrigerator to be found later still alive by a hospital employee; the responsible physician delivered a second live baby via abortion before the Washington Hospital Center finally revoked his privileges at the hospital, according to Rep. Hogan's office.[59]

At least the Washington Hospital Center continued to pay lip service to legality by going through the motions of having at least two doctors certify that a woman's physical or mental health was indeed being harmed by her pregnancy. In March, 1971, however, a full-fledged "Abortorium," called Preterm, Inc., was opened with a capacity of 300 abortions per week. The extent of this clinic's compliance with the legal fiction that "health" was still somehow involved in the performance of abortions may perhaps be judged by the fact that "13 counselors, all of them young women, [would] determine in private interviews if abortion was appropriate for the patient." No one even attempted to claim that these young women had any strictly medical qualifications. It was reported at the same time that the clinic was "being opened on the expectation" that Judge Gesell's ruling would be "upheld" by the Supreme Court.[60]

It is perhaps typical of the mentality fostered by the Abortion Imperative that when the Supreme Court, in

April, 1971, *reversed* Judge Gesell's decision, ruling that the D.C. law was *not* "unconstitutionally vague" in requiring only the mother's life or health as grounds for abortion, the Preterm clinic, without pausing in its operations, announced that it would simply continue business as usual. "The physicians at Preterm, as in the past, will perform abortions when in their judgment the life or health of the patient so requires," said Harry Levin, a former employee of the Population Council and director of the clinic.[61] In other words, *whatever* a doctor determines becomes *ipso facto* a matter of "health." By this logic a doctor could prescribe arsenic, and it would thereby become medicine.

Lest this idea be thought strange, we should hasten to point out that a Justice of the Supreme Court explicitly endorsed it in this case. Mr. Justice Stewart, dissenting from the majority decision of the court in the Vuitch case, solemnly held that "when a physician has exercised his judgment in favor of performing an abortion, he has, by hypothesis, not violated the statute"![62] Mr. Justice Stewart's opinion, of course, does not have the force of law, but we begin to glimpse the rationale behind the argument that abortion is primarily a "medical" matter; if a man can boast "M.D." after his name, he can *make* it a medical matter.

The defendant in the case, Dr. Milan Vuitch, who has commented that he "has more lawyers than Jimmy Hoffa," celebrated the court's ruling against him by performing eight abortions in his office the very same day.[63] "The guys on the Supreme Court threw the whole mess back to the doctors," was Dr. Vuitch's comment. "I myself as a physician can see that this is correct. It's strictly a medical problem. If they had ruled that an American woman is entitled to decide for herself whether to be pregnant, no doubt about it, that would have meant a further reaching decision. But this way, it can be worked out."[64]

Whatever our views on abortion, we must surely agree that it is indeed a remarkable legal situation when a Dr. Vuitch can tranquilly go on plying his abortionist's trade no matter how the highest court in the land may rule. Judge Gesell throws out the D.C. law and suddenly abortions are considered legal, as the Washington *Post* erroneously reported to the public the day after the Gesell decision. Its leader read: "Abortion Law Here Is Voided. Doctors Free to Operate but Some Voice Caution." A year and a half later, the Supreme Court overrules Judge Gesell's decision, but doctors are *still* free to operate!

Another Washington *Post* article accurately described the abortion situation in the nation's capital shortly after the Supreme Court supposedly upheld the D.C. law, and confirmed how little effect the law had, in the absence of any enforcement: "The U.S. Supreme Court's decision last April 21 cleared up much of the legal haze over the abortion issue that resulted from the ruling by a U.S. District Court judge here that the D.C. abortion law was too vague to be enforced. The Supreme Court upheld the law, but in so doing required that the prosecution prove that the woman's mental or physical health was not at stake in order to prosecute the physician.

"Doctors say that successful prosecution on these grounds will be very difficult, and that the District can, in effect, be considered as legal a place for abortions as Hawaii, Alaska, California [sic], Washington State and New York.

"If Washington is to compete with New York City for a large share of the market, it will have to do so by drawing from the South and Midwest, areas where Washington is more accessible than New York . . ."[65]

In June, 1971, the women's magazine *Redbook* published a "guide" to legal abortion nationally, and, under

"District of Columbia," listed: "On request. No restrictions."[67] Thus, neither existing laws nor Supreme Court decisions seem to avail in the face of the Abortion Imperative. Doctors and hospitals openly perform illegal abortions, but they are not prosecuted.

On January 28, 1972, the Washington *Post* reported that around 20,000 abortions had been performed in the nation's capital during the previous year. The overwhelming majority of these operations could not have been anything but illegal by anybody's common sense definition of what constitutes a threat to the life or health of the mother. Yet nobody seemed to be in the least concerned by this open and widespread violation of the law. Indeed the D.C. City Council was considering a set of guidelines which would "regulate" the illegal practice of abortion!

Nor has it been only in the nation's capital that abortions have been performed regardless of what the law says; or that a U.S. Court has virtually directed that an existing law be violated. In Pennsylvania, between 1968 and 1970, 1,850 abortions were performed at Magee-Women's Hospital in Pittsburgh while the law forbidding them was still in effect.[68] In Illinois a U.S. District Court issued an order forbidding interference with the performance of an abortion on a 16-year-old rape victim, although the Illinois law does not allow the procedure in cases of rape but only to save the life of the mother![69] It is true that the Illinois law has been under challenge, both in the legislature and in the courts; but it is hard to see how a U.S. District Court can presume to anticipate the outcome of these challenges and allow abortions in cases of rape, contrary to the statute. In any event, the court *failed* to anticipate the real outcome in the elected legislature of the State of Illinois. In 1970, an attempt to amend the law —the second in as many years—failed to pass by a margin of more than two to one; in 1971, an attempt to repeal the law failed even to emerge from a House committee.[70]

In the meantime, in February, 1971, a three-judge federal court had overturned the Illinois statute. Immediately, a rash of abortions broke out. Then, 12 days and nearly 100 abortions after the federal court decision, Supreme Court Justice Thurgood Marshall issued a temporary stay order, and Cook County Hospital had to cancel its plans to perform 125 abortions per week![71]

In New York, in 1968, prior to the passage of the current abortion-on-demand statute, another court actually ruled *against* a hospital which refused to perform an abortion on a woman who had had German measles and feared the birth of a "defective" child—although it was then strictly illegal to perform an abortion on any grounds except to save the mother's life! Nevertheless, the woman was awarded $10,000 damages because of the hospital's refusal to perform the abortion. In Virginia, a court refused to allow a college administration to forbid abortion ads in the student newspaper in spite of the fact that solicitations for abortion are prohibited by Virginia law.[72]

When doctors, hospitals, the government and the courts connive to promote abortions in spite of existing laws; and indeed, as in Illinois, in the face of the expressed will of elected legislatures—and when elected legislatures too are found on the abortion bandwagon—we may rightly conclude that the Abortion Imperative has become deeply entrenched in our national thinking. In some quarters a radical anti-life attitude is coming to seem the normal and accepted thing. Abortion is actually preferred to birth. Insurance plans such as Blue Cross-Blue Shield, for example, are now providing for abortions under "single" enrollments—though no benefits are allowed for routine delivery of a baby under "single" enrollments![73] The insurance companies pay to kill a baby; but will not pay to let him be born.

During the year beginning July 1, 1970, it is estimated that some 505,000 legal abortions were performed throughout the country—in those states which had either adopted abortion-on-demand or had "reformed" their laws to permit legal abortions under certain circumstances. This figure should be compared with the figure of 18,000 legal abortions performed in the U. S. during 1968.[74] It is not clear that the estimate of 505,000 "legal" abortions includes those which are *not* in fact "legal", even though they are performed proudly and openly by doctors working in accredited hospitals.

What can we say about this ghastly, headlong race to destroy human lives? Has the awesome gift of procreating new life suddenly become such an intolerable burden as to be cast away with such utter abandon by so many? Truly the abortionists have come, as G.K. Chesterton once remarked of the Manicheans, that we might have death and have it more abundantly. Who would have believed, even two or three years ago, that our country would ever come to this?

No combination of the supposed reasons usually brought forward to justify abortion can possibly explain the frantic scale on which the operation is now being allowed, encouraged, and performed. We have seen what has happened in New York and elsewhere now that abortion has been made legal. We have seen what is taking place in Washington D.C., even though it has *not* been made legal! We have seen what is happening when abortion laws are "reformed." We are clearly no longer talking about women who might have children born without arms, about 14-year-old girls who have been raped, or about women with serious health problems. We are not talking about the girl whose boy friend doesn't want to marry her (or whom *she* doesn't want to marry); or the pregnant mother of six or eight subsisting on welfare; or the forty-two-year-old divorcee, supporting teen-age children, for whom an accidental pregnancy would be "unthinkable."

It is not that, on sound moral grounds, even abortions in these cases would be justifiable. Abortion is the deliberate destruction of an existing, independent, innocent human being, who is no more responsible for his conception than the rest of us, the living, were responsible for ours. Pro-abortion propaganda dwells largely on the kinds of situations where some regard abortion as called for—or, at any rate, where the abortions are desperately wanted—but in the Brave New World of abortion-on-demand, it is no longer necessary even to have these reasons. If the woman does not want to carry to term the child she has conceived, she should be able to arrange to have the child disposed of with no further questions asked. This is where laws legalizing abortion are taking us. Indeed, as we have seen, many are not even waiting for abortion to be legalized before implementing this alleged new woman's right. The Abortion Imperative seems too compelling.

The press and media are already full of stories which depict the utter and frivolous casualness with which abortions are now being demanded and performed. A metropolitan newspaper sympathetically recounts a case from, of all places, *Bride's Magazine:* "Pat got pregnant in April, and their big wedding was two months away. She and Ed knew that if they got married in June and had a baby before Christmas, some Victorian would be sure to count. She and Ed were afraid their parents might be Victorian enough to find this embarrassing. Besides, Ed wanted to go on to graduate school, which meant Pat's working. 'I'm so afraid I would resent the baby, maybe hate it,' Pat said, adding: 'I don't want my first baby to mean that to me.'"[75]

Solution? Kill the baby, of course. Our society is not

merely coming to this. It is important to understand that it has already come to this. Killing by abortion is becoming respectable. To be against this state of affairs is apparently to be labeled "Victorian." In an era of such permissive killing, perhaps this word, like the word "Puritan," now applied to those who object to *anything* on moral grounds, is a word we dare not be afraid of any longer.

Another feature story in a metropolitan newspaper reports favorably on another girl who decided to have an abortion because she could not endure "morning sickness." What the girl called "the glorious idea of having a baby," the newspaper related, "ended after three weeks of being sick 'every two seconds,'" as the girl herself expressed it. "She will take a week to gather the courage to tell her boy friend that she has ended the pregnancy . . . 'We both wanted it, but I was not aware of what it would cost in terms of mental and physical anxiety and pain. I am not ready at 26. Maybe in another two or three years.'"[76]

Still another reason for having an abortion, once again from a sympathetic daily press: "My child's two years old and I'm living in a bad neighborhood and I can't afford to have another before I move." "Swoosh, and 30 seconds later, it's all over." [10]

One New York physician, specializing in the treatment of sterility, wrote in to the *Journal of the American Medical Association* to describe his experience after he had, "by a stroke of chance," found himself and his patients in an office building "sandwiched in between one abortion clinic on the floor above and the other on the floor below . . . Approximately 40,000 abortions were performed in this single location during the past year . . . My office building was unquestionably the largest abortion center in the United States."

This physician, Dr. Abner I. Weisman, described the activities in his building as follows: "The two clinics, each occupying an entire floor, worked incessantly around the clock. One clinic functioned six days a week, while the other took no rest or respite even on Sundays. Abortions started at 8 A.M. each day and ended after 12 or more hours —terminating by 10 P.M. when the building closed for the night. Operating doctors usually rotated to avoid the syndrome of 'abortion fatigue.' Groups of young women, awaiting their turns patiently for their exposure to the 'suckers' were eventually herded by abortion counsellors into an elevator and ushered to their respective floors. The suction techniques, with the patient under paracervical anesthesias, were quick. The average recovery period was two hours. The entire process from beginning to end— laboratory work, history-taking, counseling, operation, recovery, and discharge—was accomplished in three hours. After this, the building's special limousine transported the girls back to the airport for the speedy return trip home.

"The vast majority were unmarried youngsters fresh from college campuses or senior high schools. The largest number came from smaller communities in the Midwest or South. A tiny proportion of these youngsters were from New York state. Most of the girls had arrived at the La Guardia airport with their boyfriends who carried the small overnight bags. Because of the crowding at the center, an additional waiting-room in a basement of a brownstone building around the corner was prepared for the concerned, sympathetic, and loyal boyfriends.

"The main waiting-room was always crowded by the young women awaiting 'their next'—not unlike the salon of the local beauty parlor where women waited their turn. My own patients had a front-row orchestra seat in a theatre, witnessing a play or travesty on human experiences. But this was no play; this was for real!

"It was not long before I got the reactions of my already-frustrated sterile patients to this unusual exposure.

"The replies were not unexpected. Anyone could anticipate their initial reactions. Of course they were hurt by what they saw. Without exception, each sterility patient was shocked with the visualization of the sheer numbers coming for abortions. They were amazed by the youthfulness of the girls. They remarked on how typically American these kids were, in their dress, appearance, and overall mannerisms. My patients were distressed by the apparent lack of concern and calmness which the youngsters portrayed while waiting for the abortions. They would have expected to find some teary-eyed, but they did not. My patients were perplexed, confused, and appalled by the utter routineness and acceptance of 'abortion, production-line style.' "[77]

We have clearly come a long way from being a society which legally allowed abortions only to preserve the life (and, in a few states, also the health) of the mother. This was the legal status of abortion in America up to the year 1966. If, as a society, we can now sanction the slaughter of the unborn, merely because their mothers have decided that they cannot endure morning sickness, we can be chillingly certain that the principle, once established, will be applied to situations other than human pregnancies. Killing other than abortion will also become respectable. We need only think of the suffering inherent in many terminal illnesses. Why should terminal patients have to suffer, either?

And, in actual fact, bills providing for "euthanasia" of the seriously ill have now been introduced into the legislatures of American states. A bill was introduced into the Florida legislature by a physician, Dr. Walter W. Sackett, Jr.; it would not only permit voluntary euthanasia; it would allow three physicians to decree and execute a death sentence, with the approval of a circuit judge, on anybody whose life had become "meaningless," as the bill expresses it.[78] This same Dr. Sackett's idea that the medical profession should "make the death process more comfortable and dignified" received applause from the 3000 delegates to the White House Conference on Aging, in November, 1971.[78] A euthanasia bill has similarly been introduced into the Hawaii legislature—certainly it is not without significance that such a bill would come in the wake of the legalization of abortion-on-demand, already accomplished in that state. Similarly, in Oregon, another state which has "reformed" its abortion law, Governor Tom McCall has said that the state should look into legislation which would allow mercy killing. To be able to choose death, the governor said, is "a need that is so agonizingly overwhelming in the minds of the elderly"; he indicated that he would be calling "seminars" to discuss euthanasia, and would seek advice from "physicians, sociologists, and philosophers."[79]

And in Washington State, which, again, has legalized abortion-on-demand, it is surely not without significance that 46 per cent of medical students polled now favor *positive* euthanasia, i.e., not merely letting the incurably ill patient die but *killing* the patient.[80] With sentiments such as these growing in the medical profession, we need not wait long before other bills will be introduced into our legislatures making euthanasia as concrete a reality as abortion already is. Dr. Sackett's bill in Florida and the one in Hawaii are pointing the way.

Could such bills as Dr. Sackett's or the one in Hawaii ever be enacted into law in the United States of America? Two or three years ago, most of us would have unhesitatingly replied "no", if we had been asked whether a law allowing abortion-on-demand could ever be passed in the United States of America.

II

Is an Unborn Child a Human Being?

WHEN we confront the reality of legalized abortion we immediately see that, unless we are prepared to acquiesce in allowing killing by abortion to be legal and respectable, we are faced with a battle of gigantic proportions. This battle may not be won merely by showing that an unborn child is a human being. There are many who, in response to the modern Abortion Imperative, are apparently prepared to sacrifice the unborn child whether or not he can be shown to be fully human. *At the same time it is obviously essential to the case against abortion that the humanity of the fetus be established,* if only because the American people as a whole will undoubtedly show greater respect for the unborn than certain élites in our society are prepared to show.

Fortunately, the scientific evidence for the full humanity of the fetus from the time of conception is overwhelming. It is now established beyond all doubt that each individual human life begins at conception, i.e., when the

49

sperm cell of the father unites with the egg cell of the mother; with the uniting of these two cells, the genetic inheritance of a new individual is complete; a unique person, different from either parent or from any other possible combination of sperm and egg, has come into being. From the time of conception, the new human person takes only nourishment, and, after birth, respiration from his environment.

We all continue to take nourishment and respiration from our environment throughout our lives: the adult human being is no more "viable" outside the highly specialized environment of the earth's atmosphere than is the early fetus viable outside the highly specialized environment of the womb; this fact has been dramatically brought home to us by all the elaborate paraphernalia which astronauts have to take with them into outer space in order to survive there. To posit "viability" outside the mother as a condition of humanity, as some of the liberalized abortion laws in effect do, is as absurd as denying humanity to adults who temporarily require an oxygen tent or an iron lung in order to survive.

The essential scientific facts about human conception and development can be ascertained from any standard textbook of biology. Dr. Bradley M. Patten, in *Foundations of Embryology,* for example, writes: "Every one of the higher animals starts life as a single cell—the fertilized ovum . . . The union of two such sex cells (male germ cell and female germ cell) to form a zygote constitutes the process of fertilization and initiates the life of a new individual."[1]

Within four weeks after this conception—as soon as a woman can verify the fact that she is pregnant, and hence can even consider having an abortion—*the heart of the new individual inside her is already pumping its own blood!* Within eight weeks after conception—the point at which a great many abortions are actually performed—the new human individual has "a pumping heart with fully deployed blood vessels and has all other internal organs. The face is completely formed, and the arms, legs, hands, feet, toes and fingers are partially formed. The fetus will react to tickling of the mouth or nose, and there is readable electrical activity coming from the brain."[2] To assert, in the face of this scientific evidence, that the fetus is not a living human being would be comparable to asserting that the earth was flat or that the basic components of matter were fire, earth, air and water.

What modern science tells us about the complexity of the single-celled human zygote—already "programmed" to transform itself into the trillions of cells which make up the adult human body—easily persuades us that it is in no sense "rudimentary" or "simple" life; it is as complex and marvelous, as a single cell, as the human organism is at any subsequent stage of its natural development. The zygote, or the blastocyst, or the embryo, or the fetus—names of the same human organism at different stages of a continuous natural development—is, every bit as much as the child or the adult, as the Psalmist says, "fearfully and wonderfully made" (*Psalms* 138:13). Indeed the Psalmist specifically says, "Thou hast covered me in my mother's womb . . ."

The scientific and moral truth of this is too easily lost in a permissive era. The vast, dismal and growing pro-abortion literature rarely even attempts to face up to the overwhelming evidence of the humanity of the unborn child at all stages; rather, *assertions* are often made to cast doubt upon his humanity. These assertions are not accompanied by scientific proof for the simple reason that they *could* not be. It is impossible to "prove" what is in fact not so. Dr. Alan F. Guttmacher, for example, President of Planned Parenthood-World Population and a pioneer and one of the principal leaders of the pro-abortion movement,

feels that "the *fetus,* particularly during its early intrauterine life, is simply a group of specialized cells that do not
differ materially from other cells . . . and I feel that if it is
going to be for the welfare of the adult individual, and for
society in certain instances, we are justified in eliminating
these cells."[3]

This statement establishes something about Dr. Guttmacher's own feelings and attitudes—*all* of us are "simply
a group of specialized cells" from one standpoint. As scientific evidence, however, it is about on the same level as the
statement made by a group of "concerned clergymen"
when setting up an abortion "counseling service": "We
affirm that there is a period during gestation when, although there may be embryo life in the fetus, there is no
living child upon which the crime of murder can be committed."[4]

So they "affirm" it, do they? What kind of evidence is
that? And what in heaven's name is "embryo life"? Can
they perhaps mean *human* embryo life, as we might
speak with equal validity of "adult" human life? Or are
they perhaps referring to the embryo of a fish or a goat?
The second preferred method of denying humanity to the
unborn child, after neglecting to raise the question of his
humanity at all, is to *call* him something else than human.

The fact is, that nobody has been able to suggest, much
less establish, what the new individual conceived might
be, except human. Much less has anybody been able to
show at what point the new individual becomes human, if
not at conception. Laws forbidding abortion after a certain
point in the gestation period are not based on scientific
evidence.

Many proponents of abortion, especially when speaking
outside the immediate context of their advocacy of the
practice, themselves often refer to the moment of conception as the moment when life begins. "The basic fact is

simple," Professor Ashley Montagu of Columbia University informs us. "Life begins, not at birth, but at conception. This means that a developing child is alive not only in the sense that he is composed of living tissue, but also in the sense that from the moment of conception, *things happen to him*, even though he may be only two weeks old, and looks more like a creature from another world than a human being . . . *he reacts*. In spite of his newness and his appearance he is a living, striving being from the very beginning."[5]

Similarly, the British jurist Glanville Williams, whose book *The Sanctity of Life and the Criminal Law* has been highly influential in the drive to remove the control of life from the purview of the criminal law, speaks of "man's beginning in the union of two germinal cells, and his development in the body of his mother."[6] Professor Garrett Hardin, one of the most prominent voices in the American scientific community calling for unrestricted abortions to reduce population growth, nevertheless writes in his college biology textbook: ". . . We may say that the life of a new individual begins when two haploid gametes (an egg and a sperm) unite, forming a fertilized egg or zygote, which is diploid. The zygote, by successive mitoscs [divisions], produces the approximately 10^{14} cells that constitute the adult body."[7]

This impressive testimony in favor of the proposition that human life begins at conception comes, we should bear in mind, from men who publicly favor the legalization of abortion. Professor Montagu has explained, in a letter to the New York *Times,* that by his own statement locating the beginning of human life at conception he actually meant "that from the moment of conception the organism thus brought into being possesses all the potentialities for humanity in its genes and for that reason must be considered human [that *isn't* what he said, of course!]

... but the embryo, fetus and newborn of the human species do not really become functionally human until humanized in the human socialization process ... I have always supported and will continue to support the legalization of abortion."[8]

It will be clear that Professor Montagu's second statement denies none of the scientific evidence about the beginning of life; it merely gives his philosophic interpretation of this scientific data. His belief that human beings must be "humanized" by society would seem to suggest that human rights are conferred only by society. In other words, there are no *inherent* human rights, in Professor Montagu's view. It is significant that he includes "newborn" children in the same category as "unborn" children. In his view, infanticide would seem to be as permissible as abortion. Nor could a helpless cripple, a paralytic, or a man in a coma seemingly qualify as "functionally" human by his definition.

In spite of his own testimony that human life begins at conception, Glanville Williams finds that "it is an abuse of words to call the fertilized ovum, the zygote, which is a microscopic speck of jelly, a child or human being ... the notion of a human being connotes a human intelligence and a defined bodily structure."[9]

If the child were *only* a "microscopic speck of jelly," Glanville Williams would have nothing to worry about. It is precisely because this particular speck is capable of developing into a being with the bodily structure and intelligence of, say, a Glanville Williams, that there is any abortion problem at all, and that the latter is found writing books about it. It is patent that people are calling for abortions *because* a child is involved; nobody is worried about any mere microscopic specks of jelly. Calling the first stage in the development of every human being "jelly" doesn't change anything about the facts of the matter.

Garrett Hardin's device for denying true human dignity to man's embryonic beginnings is simply to look at "life" as one giant "process." "Life, in our experience, never begins", he asserts.[10] By this he seems to mean that the egg and the sperm are "alive" before they unite to form a new individual; the new individual is neither more nor less part of the same life process than any other collection of living cells; everything is reduced to the lowest common denominator of the life process.

But considering life a process in no way removes the distinctions between individual living beings—nor, especially, does it remove the moral value inherent in each individual human being. Even from a strictly scientific point of view it would seem highly questionable to equate the "life" of living cells with the "life" of an integral unique living organism—which a zygote is, but a sperm or egg cell by itself is not. Modern biology itself has developed the definition, available in any dictionary, that life, in the fullest sense of the word, is that "state of a material complex or individual characterized by a capacity to perform certain functional activities including metabolism, growth, and reproduction."[11] We note that these characteristics of "life" are predicated of *individuals*. Components of individuals, however indisputably "alive" themselves, do not have "life" in the same sense that individual living beings do. The fallacy of Garrett Hardin's concepts lies precisely in the assumption that all "life" is essentially on the same level and indistinguishable.

But can Professor Hardin's "haploid gametes" grow, or reproduce, or even continue to live, by themselves? How can they be equated with organisms which can do these things? It is scientific absurdity to blur the distinctions between living beings by amalgamating them in the process by which they are all conceived, born, grow, decline, and die—and then to pretend that the individuals themselves do not count and that it is all "nothing but" a process.

Actually, Ashley Montagu, Glanville Williams, and Garrett Hardin are all dealing in semantics. They are using words in a way which seems to render abortion—the deliberate destruction of living human beings—more acceptable. Nothing they say really alters in the slightest degree the real fact about when each human being comes into existence; they themselves admit the fact; they really differ from us in the *importance* they assign to it. What they are saying belongs to the moral sphere, not to the scientific sphere.

They are saying that man has unfettered control over human life. This is perfectly true in the physical sense, since man can obviously take the life of his fellow man in a variety of ways. Most human cultures, however, especially those considered civilized, have denied that man has control over human life in the moral sense; human life has been protected with strict legal sanctions, and the taking of it circumscribed carefully by all societies. Only in our day have enlightened thinkers appeared to assert that man actually derives his very humanity from society and its "humanizing" process, as Professor Montagu has styled it. If this is so, it really does follow that there are no moral precepts or rules, independent of society, which might forbid resorting to abortion for convenience, for utilitarian motives, for population control, or whatever; it is purely a question of what course of action society determines upon. But it would also follow, if this were true, that there are no moral rules, independent of human decision, which would forbid *anything*.

This is nothing less than a new morality. Man cannot escape the fact that there is a moral dimension to his life. The "ought" is universal in human experience. Ironically, the Abortion Imperative ("We ought to have abortions") is itself an illustration of this. The moral assumptions behind the "scientific" thinking of Montagu, Williams, and Hardin are clearly typical of the new morality which has made the Abortion Imperative possible. This new morality is prepared to sanction the killing of human beings with the full knowledge that they are human beings. Arguments denying the humanity of the unborn child may be devised for popular consumption; but the leaders of the pro-abortion movement know what they are about.

It goes without saying, however, that their new morality is a false morality. No morality based on the idea that moral values exist independently of the human will could ever sanction the tenets of this new morality. The United States of America was not founded on such a morality. Nor is it likely that any community could in fact long endure on the basis of such a morality; its logic leads to the denial of any rights, nor merely the rights of the unborn child. If moral values are simply a product of the human mind, then any values the individual might declare are equally valid with those proclaimed by "society." This is moral anarchy. Ultimately it leads to coercion by those who turn out to be the strongest: might makes right.

Nevertheless, the new morality has apparently found increasing acceptance in our society. In the popular, propagandistic sphere, Professor Paul Ehrlich of Stanford University has been one of the best known exponents of this new moral outlook on human life. Dr. Ehrlich is frankly out to get rid of as many people as he can persuade others to do away with; abortion is a proven technique. Professor Ehrlich doesn't even bother to conceal his belief in the need for coercion in the employment of this technique. The moral question of abortion, he informs us, "results from confusion over what a human being is. A human being is the result of interaction between a genetic code and a physical and cultural environment, particu-

larly the cultural environment. A fetus isn't a human being; it's a *potential* human being. Religious objectors are
confusing the blueprints for a building with the building
itself. Religious objections are based on ignorance."[12]

Though Dr. Ehrlich is said to travel widely these days
preaching his anti-Gospel of zero population growth, we
may doubt whether even he has ever seen a building *made
out of* blueprints. Buildings are made out of bricks and
mortar. It is even more doubtful whether Dr. Ehrlich has
ever seen a blueprint *transform itself* into a building. Dr.
Ehrlich's hopelessly confused analogy is the reflection of
the confusion and shallowness of his thought.

A human embryo not only possesses the "blueprints" for
the adult human being, but its own built-in "factory" to
manufacture the bricks and mortar and to make them into
the finished "building." In accomplishing this marvel, the
embryo takes only the fuel from its environment which
the adult Paul Ehrlich, for example, still requires from *his*
environment. Indeed it is supposedly his concern about his
environment which has set him upon his anti-people
jihad. If the unborn child's dependence upon a specialized
environment for the first nine months of his life truly
diminishes his humanity, then Dr. Ehrlich's humanity in
the highly specialized environment of the earth on which
he depends is similarly diminished.

No: the environment doesn't make the man, any more
than the value of a human being is conferred by society.
Nor are there any "degrees" of humanity. This latter truth
is perfectly expressed by the popular saying that no
woman is ever "a little bit pregnant". She is either pregnant or she is not. If she is, she is carrying a new human
being.[13]

III

What Did We Do
to Deserve Abortion-on-Demand?

ABORTION-on-demand, the notion that abortion should be solely a matter between a woman and her physician, has been discussed for some time in certain more or less specialized medical, legal, humanitarian, or social-worker circles, but it has burst upon the public at large so suddenly that many of us are still trying to adjust to the idea of it; and marveling at the audacity of those who dare to promote it. It has all the boldness and simplicity of a totalitarian "final solution". Why indeed should there be any restrictions on the performance of abortions? The point that abortion kills a human being is studiously avoided.

That the idea has taken hold in America today, however implausible or unacceptable it might once have seemed in any society which professed to respect the sanctity of life, can be seen from the rash of abortion-on-demand bills which, in the past few years, have suddenly appeared in the legislatures of state after state. During 1970, as we have seen, such bills were actually enacted into law in Alaska, Hawaii, New York, and Washington state; during the same year, similar bills were introduced into the legislatures of Arizona, Florida, Georgia, Illinois, Maryland, Massachusetts, Michigan, Ohio, and Rhode Island, but were defeated by a governor's veto or at one stage or another of the legislative process. In 1971, bills to relax restrictions on abortion or to make it a matter of private decision for a woman were introduced in the legislatures of no less than 36 states.[1] Some of them have carried over into the 1972 legislative sessions, and other similiar legislation will undoubtedly continue to be introduced. Since 1970, all of these bills have failed to pass (some remain to be acted upon); in Florida a relaxed law short of abortion-on-demand was adopted in 1972 under pressure from a court decision which would have left the state without any law at all.

It is clear that the drive to reform or repeal existing laws prohibiting or restricting abortion remains nationwide. Senator Robert Packwood (R.-Ore.) has introduced a bill into the U.S. Senate to legalize abortion throughout the country.[2] Although we may hope that the nationwide abortion drive will be slowed as the results of New York's experience begin to sink in, we cannot expect, given the strength of the Abortion Imperative today, that the drive will be stopped by anything less than determined, systematic, and continuous resistance in the political arena.

As a preliminary to any effective action against the legalization of abortion, we must ask ourselves how the abortion debate ever reached its present stage while so many of us were completely unaware of what was happening. At the present time, the question is no longer, "Under what circumstances might an abortion be permissible?" but "Why should there be any restrictions on abortion at all?" When we look carefully at our present situation, we soon see that abortion-on-demand has both its logical and its historical roots in the more moderate abortion "reform" carried out in a number of American states between 1966 and 1972.

Traditionally, the criminal law of all fifty states, of the District of Columbia, and of Puerto Rico allowed medical abortions to save the life of the mother. Five states and the District of Columbia also allowed them either to protect the health of the mother or to protect her from "serious and permanent bodily injury".[3] No abortions were legal unless performed for true medical and "therapeutic" reasons. The idea that a woman should be able to get an abortion merely because she wanted one was undoubtedly never imagined.

The American laws on abortion derived from English law. From the 13th Century, in fact, the Common Law had recognized that legal protection was owed to the unborn. Henry of Brackton (1216–72), in the first mention of abortion in English law, wrote: "If there is anyone who has struck a pregnant woman or given poison to her, whereby he has caused an abortion, if the fetus be already formed or animated, and especially if animated, he commits a homicide."[4] The idea that a child had to be "formed" or "animated" derived from the idea current in the Middle Ages that a child was not fully human until it "quickened." The Church condemned abortion at any stage as a sin; but the English law punished abortion as *homicide* only if the child were "animated" or "quickened."

The first English statute on abortion passed by Parliament dates from the year 1803; among other things, this law eliminated the distinction between a "quickened" and an "unquickened" child, which the science of the Eighteenth Century had already shown to be a false distinction.

Henceforth abortion at any stage in a pregnancy, not merely one after "quickening", was considered a legal *crime*. It is true that abortion has never in English law been considered a legal crime of the same seriousness as murder, with comparable penalties; nevertheless the basic principle was maintained that the unborn child was entitled to the protection of the law. In England itself this principle was not to be fatally compromised until 1967. In that year Parliament passed a new law which became "the most liberal in the Anglo-American legal world"[5] up to that point.

American laws had quite naturally taken over from the consistent English pattern the idea that the unborn child was at least in some senses a legal person. Though they allowed therapeutic abortions on a carefully restricted basis, all the American laws, most of them enacted in the nineteenth century, reflected this belief. In 1966, Mississippi became the first American state to depart from the consistent American pattern of legal protection of the unborn child. Mississippi "reformed" its abortion law in that year to permit the procedure if conception occurred as a result of rape. No longer was the child's life balanced only against the mother's life or health in American law; a new concept entirely was introduced. The child's life could henceforth be sacrificed in circumstances which *society* would decide upon; in this instance, in cases of rape.

By mid-1972, less than six years later, more than a dozen additional American states had revised their laws to permit legal abortions under a variety of circumstances besides rape but without permitting simple abortion-on-demand as in Alaska, Hawaii, New York, and Washington State. The states which merely "reformed" their laws without going all the way were Arkansas, California, Colorado, Delaware, Florida, Georgia, Kansas, Maryland, New Mexico, North Carolina, Oregon, South Carolina, and

Virginia. The new laws in those states were all based more or less on a "model" statute on abortion which the American Law Institute (ALI) had incorporated into its Model Penal Code in the early nineteen sixties. This ALI model abortion law was itself based on concepts and practices which had been codified into law in the Scandinavian countries; it allowed abortions to be performed legally in accordance with certain "indications" believed to call for abortion. Thus, at the outset, abortion reform aimed to allow the procedure in specific cases where it was believed to be justified, as regulated by law. It did not aim at simple repeal of existing restrictions on abortion, nor at removing abortion from the cognizance of the criminal law entirely, as is now advocated, and as has already been done in four states.

The ALI "model" statute on abortion provides that induced abortion prior to the 26th week of pregnancy by a licensed physician in an accredited hospital is legal under the following circumstances (the "indications" for abortion):

—To save the life of the mother.

—If there is substantial risk that continuation of the pregnancy would gravely impair the physical or mental health of the mother.

—If the child might be born with a grave physical or mental defect.

—If the pregnancy resulted from rape, incest, or other felonious intercourse.[6]

The ALI-type laws enacted in thirteen states between 1967 and 1972 follow this pattern with some differences in language and emphasis. The California law omits the defective child grounds; the Arkansas and North Carolina laws omit the "physical and mental health of the mother" as allowable legal grounds. Arkansas, Delaware, Maryland, North Carolina, South Carolina, and Virginia allow abortion only in cases of forcible rape (not in cases of statutory rape). Georgia, Maryland, and New Mexico drop incest as an allowable ground.

These laws also differ among themselves as to whether there are time limits within which an abortion can be performed or whether residence in the state is required of the woman. They differ in such things as the lengths of such time limits or residency requirements, if imposed. They differ further in such things as whether the consent of one or more doctors is required or whether a "conscience clause" is included protecting doctors or hospitals refusing to perform abortions. All of them claim to regulate the practice of abortion, however, and the assumption clearly underlies them that it should be regulated. They represent actual responses to the question: "Under what circumstances may an abortion be legally performed?"[7]

These responses are no sooner embodied in concrete laws, however, than the fact becomes apparent, as we have seen, that the very question has changed, and we are suddenly concerned with the question of why the criminal law has to be involved with abortion at all. At first sight the two questions seem incommensurate. There seems a vast difference between doing abortions for "serious" reasons, and doing them for any reason or for no reason. It cannot be emphasized too often that, with abortion-on-demand, we are dealing with the latter situation.

But the common ground that these "reformed," ALI-type laws do share with abortion-on-demand legislation is that both assume the disposition of human life to be a matter within the competence of the state legislature. Society, through the regularly constituted mechanisms of the state, can determine who shall live and who shall die. By passing an ALI-type law, lawmakers, in effect, delegate to the medical profession the power to terminate fetal life legally under certain conditions. In voting abortion-on-demand laws, the lawmakers allow the woman to make the decision, provided she gets the abortion from a licensed physician in an accredited hospital, as most of the laws are worded.* The question that is unfortunately not always brought up is whether, according to the letter and spirit of the American Constitutional system, any state legislature should have the right to decide arbitrarily who shall live and who shall die.

The fact is that our Constitution and our laws have never recognized that the state—or man himself—can dispose of human life without regard to underlying human rights and generally accepted moral principles. Our Constitution and our laws have always held, and continue to hold, exactly the contrary. In the Declaration of Independence, the first "unalienable" right with which man is said to be endowed by his Creator is the right to life; the reason that governments are instituted among men is to secure this right to life and other rights. The Declaration of Independence may not have the force of positive law, but its spirit and assumptions must surely continue to inform all our laws, if the American system is not to be changed beyond recognition.

The Constitution of the United States, in the Fourteenth Amendment, declares that no state shall deprive any person of life without due process of law; and forbids any state to deny to any person within its jurisdiction the equal protection of the laws. The Fifth Amendment, more general, specifies simply that no person shall be deprived of life without due process of law.

If the right to life is unalienable, how can a state legislature presume to alienate it? If governments are instituted

*In March, 1972, a federal court held "unconstitutional" even the portion of the "reformed" Kansas law requiring the performance of abortions in accredited hospitals, according to the Washington *Post* (March 14, 1972)

to "secure" inherent human rights, what can we say of governments which take it for granted that they *may* pass laws which provide whether and to what extent certain classes of persons even have rights? How can lawmakers in many of our states simply ignore the constitutional guarantees of due process and equal protection when legislating the fate of countless unborn children?

It is true that the rights of a person which are made plain in the Declaration of Independence and the Constitution have not yet been completely recognized in statute and case law as applying to the unborn child. It also took some time before the rights of Americans under the Constitution were fully applied to slaves. The original Constitution considered a slave only three-fifths of a person; but it is doubtful if the unborn child can be considered even one-fifth of a person if the state may arbitrarily decide the circumstances in which he may be killed.

Apart from the question of abortion, the legal trend in America has been consistent until recently in the direction of a greater and greater recognition of the legal rights of the unborn. An unborn child can inherit, for example. A variety of property rights have long been recognized as applying to the unborn. An unborn child can have a guardian appointed. An infant can sue for injuries inflicted upon him as a child in the womb. The leading academic authority on the law of torts (wrongs for which an injured person can sue for damages) has written that "the unborn child in the path of an automobile is as much a person in the street as the mother."[8] The fact that his rights are not fully recognized and spelled out in the fabric of our law is hardly a pretext for denying that he has any rights at all.

ALI-type abortion laws, however, do represent a denial that the unborn child has any inherent rights. His own right to life provides no weight in the balance to offset the consideration that, for example, his mother might be suffering mental distress because of his conception; that he himself might be born defective; that his father was an aggressor or his mother below the age of consent. Whatever right to life he may have is clearly made contingent not only upon his successful avoidance of any of these situations, but upon the whim of the state legislature which might establish by majority vote still other "indications" calling for his destruction.

Moreover, the law abdicates whatever residual responsibilities it may have towards the unborn when it simply delegates to the medical profession the entire question of determining when the accepted "indications" for abortion in fact obtain. It is an evident absurdity, for example, to leave to a physician the essentially legal question of attempting to determine whether rape or incest has actually occurred; it would seem that such a determination about what, after all, are still crimes ought to be made by a court under the legal and constitutional system we learned in school was supposed to prevail in America.

It has been urged in defense of the ALI-type laws that they codify what has become standard medical practice in many non-Catholic hospitals.[9] But that is merely to say that some standard medical practice is indeed questionable if it is to be allowed to develop on its own the practice of destroying life in certain circumstances without regard to existing law or human rights. "Standard practice" is a dubious criterion for any law. It has been well said that no civil rights laws would ever have been passed if they had depended upon existing practices for their inspiration.

In any case, standard practice, in medicine as in other fields, can change. When it changes, there would be no reason why the law shouldn't change too, if law were based on nothing but standard practice. In the case of abortion we seem to be confronted with something very like this. Many have come to believe that abortion is justified on broad socio-economic grounds—or merely on the grounds that the mother wants the abortion. The law doesn't specifically allow this, of course, but it is interpreted broadly so that common practice may prevail, regardless of the law. Even restrictive abortion laws were rarely, in the past, used to prosecute licensed physicians operating in good faith; they were used against illegal abortionists. But in the past the non-enforcement of the laws was perhaps tolerable because doctors didn't perform abortions without what they believed to be serious medical reasons. Today, many of them will perform abortions for non-medical reasons. Today it is notorious how the "mental health" indication in the ALI-type laws, for example, is used to justify practically any abortion requested, as we shall see in a subsequent chapter. Once *this* becomes standard medical practice anything goes. Why, for example, should a woman have to get a psychiatrist to certify that she "needs" the abortion? The psychiatrists themselves have come to admit that they are really only certifying that the abortion is needed because the woman wants it, not because there are any true psychiatric reasons for it.

It is by this logic that liberal ALI-type abortion laws *lead* to abortion-on-demand. This transition is perhaps not inevitable in every case since there are other factors besides the logic of the thing at work; but the logic itself is clear. And the American experience appears to be in the process of verifying it. The four states which have scorned the half-measures of the ALI-type laws and have simply legalized abortion have acted in perfect accord with this logic.

Three years before abortion-on-demand became a reality, while abortion "reform" still aimed at moderate changes in the laws, Fr. Richard A. McCormick, S.J., stated the underlying principle which has seen itself worked out in the transition from limited abortion "reform" to abortion-on-demand: "As soon as one allows direct suppression of innocent human life in any form, he has priced human life. That is, he has subordinated it to some temporal value: economic advantage, physical well-being, the good life, protection of reputation or whatever it may be. Once he has done this, there is nothing *in principle* that prevents his destroying human life at other stages and in other circumstances: the aged, the infirm, the socially or economically burdensome, the crippled, the suffering. It is only a matter of waiting until the going price has been reached."[10]

Even if these other types of killing are not yet sanctioned, it seems perfectly clear that the going price for the unborn has been reached for many, and the price is not very high. While it may still seem shocking to kill rather than suffer morning sickness, there is no reason why, in principle, as Fr. McCormick puts it, we cannot kill also for this reason—if we can kill for the sake of the mother's so-called mental health.

Furthermore, if we can, we will. The demands of the Abortion Imperative are relentless. Once the power to take life has been legally delegated to the medical profession or to individual women, it defies all experience to expect that this power will only be exercised for the "hard" or "pathetic" cases on which the propaganda for abortion likes to dwell. Other women want abortions too, for reasons which may seem valid to them, particularly in a society which has come to view sexuality in terms of personal fulfillment, or pleasure, or achievement of full female "rights"; in such a climate as this, many pregnancies can indeed be considered unwelcome or accidental. For the law to deny the means to terminate these pregnancies, once it has been accepted in principle that abortion is an allowable procedure, comes to seem highly arbitrary.

This is one of the reasons why not even the proponents of liberalized abortion want these ALI-type laws any longer. In California, Colorado, and Maryland, the same legislators who sponsored the current ALI-type laws in these states, Anthony Beilenson, Richard Lamm, and Allen Spector, later became the sponsors of bills to repeal them! They themselves became the severest critics of the laws they had so vigorously fought to get passed only two or three years before. The same development can be observed in the rapidly shifting positions of the many groups and associations, including many churches, which have been endorsing abortion-on-demand the way politicians used to endorse motherhood. Formerly the cry was "reform"; now the cry is "repeal."

Not the least disconcerting thing about the drive for abortion-on-demand has been the variety of organizations which have felt moved to endorse it.[11] We may be resigned to the fact that Women's Liberation wants it, but what can we say when the YWCA comes out for it too? Or when *Glamour* magazine includes the demand for legalized abortion in a spread entitled "What's On The College Girl's Mind?"[12] Or when the newly elected 17-year-old President of Girl's Nation, sponsored by the American Legion Auxiliary, announces at a press conference that "a legal abortion should be available to every woman without parental permission?"[13] Something is drastically wrong with the moral outlook of a nation which fosters and permits such simple-minded immorality to go unchallenged as merely one more "opinion" in an officially pluralistic society.

In retrospect it is perfectly clear what we did to deserve abortion-on-demand: we failed to oppose the earlier abortion "reforms" vigorously enough. We failed to protest loudly enough when the child's right to life seemed only "partially" eroded. But the mentality engendered and encouraged by acceptance of some abortions has led to the impeccably logical question (to mention only the logic of the thing): Why should we stop only with *some* abortions? Why not accept all abortions? As Dr. Lester Breslow, Honorary President of the National Association for Repeal of Abortion Laws, has expressed it in the inimitable jargon of the pro-abortionists, "Modification has overthrown some of the old shibboleths and made life easier for some women, but limited reform has failed to keep desperate women from resorting to illegal abortion and suffering all its harm. Repeal is the position to which logic and health interests compel us."[14]

From the standpoint of effective opposition to legalized abortion, we should recognize that, just as the pro-abortionists no longer want half measures, so for us too the moderate "reform" embodied in the laws of the ALI pattern cannot be either a possible or an acceptable "compromise." If we concede that these laws are acceptable, we have destroyed the ground on which we must stand in order to protect the *right* of the unborn child to life. These laws do not recognize that right; nor do they balance the child's life against any remotely comparable value.

If, as a practical matter, we tell ourselves that "the battle on rape is lost," or that "the American public will no longer accept the idea of carrying defective children to term," or that there really do exist strong "health" reasons for performing abortions, we may be sure that whatever compromise emerges in the political arena will be a highly unstable one; pressures for abortion-on-demand will continue, and our "compromise" will lie somewhere between whatever concessions we have made and abortion-on-demand. Experience has already verified that the abortion lobby will cheerfully accept whatever concessions we wish to make—and then go on from there. For our part, we will already have conceded that unborn children can be destroyed in some circumstances. We can then only oppose the slide to completely permissive abortion on the strength of whatever numbers we can muster, not on principle.

The principle, however, is clear. Even to permit the destruction of a human being to save the life of the mother, as American laws did before the advent of abortion "reform," is an unacceptable principle. In what other situation can we legally take the life of one human being, even to save the life of another? Catholic teaching has been perfectly consistent in forbidding any direct, intended assault on the unborn child, even to save the mother's life. The pertinence of this Catholic moral teaching becomes especially significant when, as we shall see in a subsequent chapter, the advance of medicine has compelled even doctors who favor abortion to admit that it is doubtful if there are any longer any really valid medical conditions which "require" abortion to save a woman's life.

Why *shouldn't* Catholics, as citizens - as well as the large number of non-Catholics who also recoil from this taking of innocent life - why shouldn't we all press in the political arena for abortion legislation which reflects the only logical and consistent conclusion from the demonstrated fact that the unborn child is a human being? If the abortion lobby has the right to make its maximum demands, why should we hang back? Do not we have the political right to work to have our moral convictions embodied in the laws by which Americans are governed? Abortion legislation which fully recognizes the unborn child's right to life may not seem to be a *realistic* possibility in America. But what can be the harm of working to maintain the principle? At least the practical "compromise" finally achieved will be that much more acceptable.

It might be replied that we cannot legislate morality. If Americans now accept abortion, it is alleged, laws will not deter them from resorting to it. We shall see, however, that the average American does not approve of completely un-restricted abortion to anything like the degree suggested by the current "abortion explosion." But even if many are prepared to resort to it, why concede the principle to them? Why acquiesce in making abortion respectable? We will purchase no social peace thereby. Once legal abortion is established on a firm basis the anti-lifers will move on to the next thing, euthanasia, or whatever, and we will then have to fight *that*. A stand *must* be made somewhere. Why not on the principle of the child's right to life?

At the very least, Catholic opposition to legal abortion should be based on the proposition that the traditional American statutes which permit abortion only to save the life of the mother represent the only possible compromise on the whole question; only laws such as these are at all commensurate with the other situations in which civi-lized societies permit the taking of life (in just wars, in self-defense, in the case of capital crimes). Such tradi-tional abortion statutes are still on the books in a majority of American states. Moreover, as we shall see, some of them have recently been declared by a number of state and federal courts to be constitutional in every respect. Though these laws are not strictly in accord with Catholic morality, the life of the mother does represent a certain fixed value against which to balance the life of the child; and it also provides for the medical profession a fixed standard against which medical judgment could be ap-plied in concrete cases without a doctor's being obliged to make legal or sociological-type judgments. But even in the case of a Catholic "compromise" on these traditional laws, it should be clear that it *is* a compromise.

Many who are opposed to abortion will feel that things have gone too far to take a principled stand on the basis of the child's right to life. They will be disposed to favor a more "practical" compromise. Neither the logic nor the history of abortion reform in America will sustain their view. Our contention that the unborn child is a human being, with human rights, is either valid or it is not. If it is valid, it should be presented to the American people on its merits by every means available to us. If we can revitalize in a majority of Americans the belief in the humanity of the unborn child (that at least in some sense has been assumed in this country since its founding), we should not then turn around and say, oh, but we agree that we can kill him anyway in cases of rape, or whatever. We cannot repeat too often: the pro-abortion movement does not hesitate to put forward its maximum demands for acceptance by the American people. The opposition to abortion will be crippled and hesitant to the degree that we ourselves fail to accept and to advocate in all its implications the position that the unborn child is a human being.

IV

Will the Courts Save Us?

A great deal of publicity has surrounded recent court decisions declaring restrictive abortion laws "unconstitutionally vague" or simply "unconstitutional." Decisions to this effect have been rendered by both state and federal courts on the traditional statutes of California, Connecticut, District of Columbia, Florida, Illinois, New Jersey, Pennsylvania, South Dakota, Texas, Vermont and Wisconsin. Even two ALI-type statutes, those of California and of Georgia, have been declared "unconstitutional." The ALI-type law in Kansas has been ruled unconstitutional in part. Most ot these court decisions are in various stages of appeal as of the spring of 1972; it is not at all clear how some of the issues raised by them will be resolved.[1] It is not possible to discuss the fluid abortion situation in the courts without danger of having one's conclusions rendered quickly obsolete by new decisions. What is clear is that the Abortion Imperative has evoked a significant response from our courts, as it has from our state legislatures. We have already mentioned several cases wherein courts have actually demanded that existing laws be violated. It is not surprising that the pro-abortion forces are attempting to make the most of their legal victories to date.

An extravagant but not untypical statement of what the reformers expect from the courts is that of Dr. Jerome M. Kummer, a psychiatrist at UCLA, long active in the abortion lobby, who rhapsodized over Judge Gerhard Gesell's decision in voiding the District of Columbia law: "Events in abortion reform have progressed at a logarithmic rate. We are on the eve of a 'home run with the bases loaded' when the U.S. Supreme Court hears *United States vs. Vuitch* . . . If my expectations are realized, the court will strike down *all* abortion statutes on grounds that such laws are unconstitutional, violating the woman's (and her physician's) rights."[2]

The Supreme Court, of course, did not even rule on the question of "rights" at all, in reversing Judge Gesell's decision in the *Vuitch* case. We saw earlier that his decision had been rendered primarily because the D.C. law supposedly lacked a proper definition of health and hence was "unconstitutionally vague." Having first ruled that it even had jurisdiction in the case, the Supreme Court then confined its judgment to the narrow issue of health and concluded that "health" in the statute meant the normally accepted definition of that word; its meaning was not in the least vague. Mr. Justice Black, delivering the majority opinion of the court, wrote that "Webster's dictionary . . . properly defines health as 'the state of being sound in body or mind.' Viewed in this light, the term 'health' presents no problem of vagueness. Indeed, whether a particular operation is necessary for a patient's physical or mental health is a judgment that physicians are obviously called upon to make routinely whenever surgery is considered."[3] Thus, the Supreme Court disagreed with Judge Gesell, and, by implication, with the other decisions which have held that abortion laws are "unconstitutionally vague"; at the same time, the court affirmed the idea that "mental health" is to be included in the general definition of "health."

This proposition seems reasonable enough in isolation. It is only when we recall that "mental health" is today used to justify abortion for whatever distress a woman who doesn't want to have a child may feel that we see the anti-life potentiality in this Supreme Court decision. The Supreme Court, in effect, agreed that a child's right to life may be sacrificed for something less than the mother's life; and it affirmed that it is the doctor who "routinely" makes the judgment as to what constitutes a "health" reason for "surgery."

Mr. Justice White, in a concurring opinion, said that it "should . . . be absolutely clear that a doctor is not free to perform abortions on request without considering whether the patient's health requires it."[3] But in the absence of any more concrete specification in the statute as to what constitutes a true health reason which would justify an abortion, we are still left with a highly fluid and open-ended situation. A physician-abortionist such as Washington, D.C.'s Dr. Milan Vuitch can conceivably continue performing abortions for anybody who wants one and *call* it a "medical" judgment in each case. Who is to question his medical judgment, and on what basis? He's the doctor. And the Supreme Court has also said in this decision that the burden of proof rests on the prosecution in showing that any abortion performed has *not* been performed for true health reasons. If Mr. Justice White does not think the end result of this decision could be something close to abortion-on-request where the law allows health grounds, Mr. Justice Stewart quite explicitly believes that it could. The opinion of Justice Stewart, which we quoted earlier, was to the effect that "health" was whatever a doctor decided. Since Justice Stewart dissented from the court, his opinion has no force in law. But it is clear that the activities of the mass-production abortion clinics in the District of Columbia since the Supreme Court upheld the law reflect an actual situation much closer to Justice Stewart's view than to that of Justice White, who voted with the court.

This Supreme Court decision is thus a victory for life, as it was hailed from a number of quarters, only in the highly qualified sense that *one* favorite legal argument of the pro-abortionists, the argument of vagueness, has been struck down. But unless the Supreme Court rules on the right of the child to life and spells out under what circumstances a child might be legally sacrificed, if at all, we could be left, on the basis of a decision such as this, with an abortion law situation where only the activities of the non-physician abortionist are declared illegal, and outlawed. Physicians operating in hospitals would be relatively immune from prosecution. Abortion-on-demand statutes claim to accomplish no more than this!

These considerations point to a conclusion which we have already reached in considering abortion legislation, namely, that abortion laws which allow the procedure on undefined "health" grounds do not afford guarantees for the unborn child's *right* to life.

In December, 1971, the Supreme Court heard arguments in two further appeals connected with abortion laws: in the cases of the Texas law, a traditional statute, and of the Georgia law, an ALI-type statute. Potentially these cases pose the question of the child's right to life versus the woman's alleged "right" not to carry an unwanted child to term.[4] However, the Supreme Court could decide the issue on general "health" grounds, leaving the situation pretty much as it is; or on procedural grounds. No clear affirmation of the child's right to life would emerge in either case.

In the absence of a clear and decisive affirmation of the child's legal and constitutional right to life, it seems unlikely that the laudable efforts now being made in the courts by pro-life forces will get very far. A number of such efforts are being made on what would seem the fairly obvious grounds that relaxed abortion laws, especially of the abortion-on-demand variety, violate the unborn child's right to due process and the equal protection of the laws.

However, in February, 1972, in precisely such a case, a New York state appeals court failed to be convinced by the legal arguments advanced. This court tranquilly ruled that an unborn child *cannot* be considered a "legal" person with the right to life guaranteed under the Constitution! This remarkable ruling came in a suit instituted by Fordham law professor Robert M. Byrn, challenging the state's abortion-on-demand statute on behalf of the unborn children scheduled to be aborted in New York City municipal hospitals. The case was a particulary hopeful one since Professor Byrn had managed to secure standing as a court-appointed guardian of the "class" of unborn children on whose behalf he had filed suit. He had also managed to secure both a preliminary injunction against the performance of abortions by city hospitals and a lower court ruling that an unborn child was indeed a living human being entitled to the protection of the law.

It was particularly disappointing, therefore, when the appeals court ruled against him. "The medical affidavits submitted by the guardian have not been factually disputed," the appeals court said, and added that "New York courts have already acknowledged that, in the contemporary medical view, the child begins a separate life from the moment of conception." Nevertheless this appeals court upheld, in effect, the right of the New York State

Legislature to allow this "separate life" of the child to be taken at will and with impunity. This decision was one more uncomfortable reminder of the tenet of the new morality that we are now entitled to kill certain kinds or classes of human beings without denying f>r a minute that they are human beings.[5] The decision will be appealed, and undoubtedly similar cases will be pursued, but such court decisions are discouraging.

Nevertheless, not all the courts have yet been won over to the anti-life view of the new morality.

Of potentially great significance is the decision handed down in December, 1970, by a three-judge federal court sitting in Toledo which upheld the constitutionality of the Ohio law which permits abortion only to save the life of the mother. This federal court decision is an elegant and convincing piece of analysis, and an effective response to a suit on behalf of still another "Mary Doe" for whom an abortion was sought; it deals with the constitutional issue directly, and in the process it provides answers to a good many of the legal arguments which the pro-abortion forces have been regularly using in their efforts to achieve abortion reform or repeal through the courts.

As to the charge of "vagueness" of the Ohio law, the court replied that it had resulted from the plaintiffs' own "strained construction of the language used."[6] "The words of the Ohio statute," the court went on, "taken in their ordinary meaning have over a long period of years proved entirely adequate to inform the public . . . of what is forbidden. The problem of the plaintiffs is not that they do not understand but that basically they do not accept its proscription."

Dealing with a woman's supposed "right" not to bear a child she has conceived, the court found that "rights, the provision of which is only implied or deduced, must inevitably fall in conflict with the express provisions of the

Fifth and Fourteenth Amendments that no person shall be deprived of life without due process of law." Or again: "Once human life has commenced, the constitutional protections found in the Fifth and Fourteenth Amendments impose upon the state the duty of safeguarding it."

To the familiar argument that an "unwanted child" might become a "battered child," the court rejoined, with startling common sense (in this day), that those who do not want their children can always put them up for adoption.

This federal court decision upholding the Ohio abortion law represents a clear note of sanity in an otherwise depressing abortion situation in America today. Nor is it the only court action which reaffirms the rights of the unborn. Three-judge federal courts have also upheld the traditional Louisiana law (August, 1970) and the Kentucky law (May, 1972). Similar decisions upholding traditional laws have also been handed down in the past two years by the state Supreme Courts of Iowa, Louisiana, and Vermont. Trial courts in Massachusetts and Minnesota and an appeals court in Texas have also refused to accept the stock arguments for legalized abortion.[1] In Michigan, in July, 1971, the State Supreme Court in a suit in which the estate of a stillborn child sued for damages, ruled that the unborn child is a person.

This ruling, written by Justice Thomas E. Brennan, declared: "The phenomenon of birth is not the beginning of life; it is merely a change in the form of life . . . The phenomenon of birth is an arbitrary point from which to measure life. True, we reckon age by counting birthdays. The Chinese count from New Years; the choice is arbitrary.

"A fetus having died within its mother's womb is dead; it will not come alive when separated from her. A fetus living within the mother's womb is a living creature; it will not die when separated from her unless the manner, the time or the circumstance of separation constitute a fatal trauma," he said adding: "The fact of life is not to be denied. Neither is the wisdom of the public policy which regards unborn persons as being entitled to the protection of the law."[7]

Nevertheless, even in cases far removed from the issue of abortion, not all courts seem to be showing the same civilized enlightenment as the Michigan Supreme Court. In two cases involving injury to the unborn in automobile accidents, the Supreme Courts of Iowa and Ohio ruled in November, 1971, in a sense exactly opposite to the Michigan ruling, holding that a child must be born alive to qualify as a legal person; three months later the Massachusetts Supreme Court enunciated the same principle in a case where the parents had alleged that deficient prenatal care was responsible for the stillbirth of their baby daughter.[8] All these cases serve to show that the legal status of the personhood of the unborn child, though it has ancient and honorable legal foundations and antecedents, as we saw in the previous chapter, is far from being firmly established in the minds of some of our judges. It is not clear, in cases like these, how far the courts are being influenced by the diminished respect for the sanctity of life which the Abortion Imperative has generally brought in its train. What is clear is that the courts have not upheld the rights of the unborn in anything like the degree we might have expected merely from considering the general principles on which our legal system is based.

Moreover, even if the court decisions affecting the unborn were more generally favorable than they have been, it is hard to see how mere court rulings could restore the restrictions on abortion which have already been removed in Alaska, Hawaii, New York, and Washington; or how the upholding in the courts of state laws which allow abortion only when the mother's life is in danger will affect the fourteen other states where the laws have already been liberalized in one degree or another and where, in some cases, abortion is already available virtually on demand under a broad interpretation of mental health clauses in the law. The courts cannot legislate and establish new laws protecting the unborn where the prevailing laws no longer provide that protection.

Furthermore, apart from a clear consensus in the courts affirming the child's right to life, there does not seem to be anything to prevent state legislatures from reforming or repealing traditional laws, however "constitutional" they may have been declared by the courts. The New York appeals court in the Byrn suit on behalf of the unborn children scheduled to be aborted in New York City municipal hospitals declared that "in our opinion, the extent to which fetal life should be protected is a value judgment not commited to the discretion of judges but reposing instead in the representative branch of government."[5] The federal court which upheld the Ohio abortion law expressly included the comment that "the controversial problems of the plaintiffs should be addressed to the state legislature and not to the courts for solution." [6] Defeats in the courts, such as in the Ohio case, will undoubtedly prompt the abortion lobby to redouble its efforts in the state legislatures—where its record has been remarkably impressive. On the other hand, victories in the courts will not necessarily reinstate the unborn child's right to life where the legislature has abrogated it. It seems likely, therefore, that the legislatures of the 50 states, and not the courts, will remain the principal and decisive battleground in the fight for life against abortion law repeal.

Nevertheless, the battle in the courts themselves is far from over, as shown by the already numerous instances where the traditional restrictions against abortion have been declared to be unconstitutional; and by the permis-

sive attitudes of some courts towards existing laws. The
Abortion Imperative has had an impact on the judicial
branch of the American government as it has on other
areas of American life. In February, 1972, the American
Bar Association approved by "an overwhelming voice vote
a resolution calling on all 50 states to adopt unrestricted
abortion up to the 20th week of pregnancy."[9] Vigorous dissenting opinions disputing the judgments were filed in
both the pro-life judgments which upheld the traditional
Ohio and Louisiana abortion laws, and more judicial decisions favoring abortion could be in the offing. Even the
Supreme Court of the United States, in the matter of por-
nography, has shown itself capable of ruling primarily on
the basis of "contemporary community standards." We
have already seen what some "contemporary community
standards" seem to be with regard to abortion.

It is therefore imperative that we examine the line of
reasoning by which some American courts are managing
to deny any inherent rights to the unborn. In an era when
so many judges and lawyers have shown themselves capable of disregarding these rights, the law has obviously become much too important to leave to the lawyers; for if the
rights of any can be successfully denied, the rights of all
are in danger.

In *Babbitz vs. McCann*,[10] a three-judge federal court
held that the Wisconsin statute making it a criminal
offense to perform an abortion except when necessary to
save the life of a mother was an unconstitutional invasion
of a woman's "right to refuse to carry an 'unquickened
embryo.' "

Studying and pondering the text of this decision at
length, we are left trying to understand how the judges
could presume to decide a case at law on the basis of a
"right" nowhere mentioned in the Constitution nor
remotely implied in it (the alleged right of a woman to

destroy an "unquickened embryo") while at the same time passing over a right that *is* specifically mentioned in the Constitution: the right of all persons to the equal protection of the laws.

It is all the more puzzling in this particular case since the Wisconsin statute explicitly recognizes the unborn child as a person. In the words of the statute, " 'unborn child' means a *human being from the time of conception until it is born alive.*" (W.S.A. 940.04; emphasis added.) Wisconsin case law dealing with property and inheritance also indicates that the state will protect the fetus from the moment of conception.[11] It is, moreover, puzzling how the old Common Law notion of "quickening," which disappeared from the English law as early as 1803,[12] ever got back into circulation as a valid legal or scientific concept.

The reasoning and legal citations by which three federal judges in Wisconsin arrived at their judgment can only be described as remarkable. In their decision, they speak of the "right to privacy in home, sex, and marriage," and here we can only applaud. They proceed to stress "the concept of private rights, with which the state may not interfere in the absence of a compelling state interest," and here again we can scarcely disagree. We are, however, bound to have some reservations about invoking this line of thought as a possible justification of abortion when we remember that Oregon Senator Robert Packwood, whom we have encountered as the sponsor of a national abortion-on-demand bill, has also introduced federal legislation, widely supported by people favoring liberalized abortion, which holds in effect that the state *does* have a "compelling interest" in seeing that parents limit their families to two children. If legislation such as this were ever to pass, the supposed interference with "privacy in home, sex, and marriage" represented by the Wisconsin abortion statute would seem mild indeed!

It is only for a moment, however, that we can think Wisconsin's three federal judges have opted for privacy. For we can only rub our eyes in disbelief when the realization is finally borne in upon us that they think their discussion of privacy *applies* to abortion!

True, they cite another court case about the "right of every individual to the possession and control of his own person"; but in the case of abortion we are automatically dealing not only with a woman's control and possession of her own body but also with *another* person, the child. They quote the Supreme Court on the private right to "marry, establish a home, and bring up children," yet seem unconscious of the irony inherent in their construction of this right as license to *destroy,* not bring up, the children. They cite an interpretation of the Fourteenth Amendment to the effect that a person has the freedom to marry or not to marry, and seem oblivious that this indeed points squarely to the fact that a woman's right to bear, or not to bear, a child is a right that is necessarily and in the nature of the case exercised *before,* not after, she is playing host to another human being inside her body.

Spouses have responsibilities to each other, as well as to any children they may have; these responsibilities, spelled out in a vast and complex body of law, are not nullified because the spouse had a *prior* freedom to marry or not to marry. Once they *have* married, this freedom no longer obtains; once she *has* conceived, the woman no longer has a right not to bear a child.

When our judges finally do manage to advert, almost as an afterthought, to any possible rights possessed by the child, they casually dismiss the whole issue with a single remark, "We hold that the mother's right transcends that of such an embryo." We must really remind ourselves that these are United States federal judges speaking. For—to take one convenient modern example—a true Aryan's rights were similarly held in Germany under Hitler to "transcend" the rights of allegedly lesser peoples, just as in certain parts of the world today the rights of the "proletariat" are held to transcend the rights of those who belong by definition to the "exploiting classes." But what possible warrant is there in the Constitution or laws of the United States that the rights of some "transcend" the rights of others?

Whatever warrant there may be, the judges carefully refrain from citing it. They produce a thicket of legal citations and references for a number of the relatively trivial issues touched upon in their decision, but dismiss the central question of whether the unborn child has any legal rights or not with a frivolous remark totally unsupported by reason, legal precedent, or constitutionality.

A Constitution which could cloak the wilful destruction of living human beings behind the veil of so-called "privacy" is not the Constitution we learned about in school. The vast majority of law-abiding Americans are disposed to respect the dicta of the federal courts, but a travesty such as this simply brings discredit upon both the courts and the law. In the long run, justice itself will be the principal casualty if court decisions of this type are not overturned.

Those who would justify abortion by appealing to rights of "privacy" and "control of one's own body" may think they have fashioned a gaudy new wardrobe for the emperor; an examination of *Babbit vs. McCann* reveals all too glaringly that, in fact, the emperor has on no clothes.

V

The Arguments for Abortion "Reform"

THOSE who hold that abortion is, morally, a species of murder can scarcely be heartened by the train of events that has seen the laws "reformed" to allow increasing resort to the practice in state after state, while, in some states, it has simply been declared legal. Even those who do not agree that abortion is murder probably agree that murder is *serious*; it is not possible for those who do consider it murder to view its legalization with equanimity.

While it is clear that the drive for legalization stems from a lessened respect for human life (which in turn stems from a weakened understanding and acceptance of a moral law independent of human will and desires), it is not clear to what extent the American people as a whole have abandoned the moral law as a guide in a matter of life and death such as abortion. The evidence from polls and public opinion studies on this point is conflicting. A Gallup Poll published in November, 1969, for example, found forty per cent of its respondents agreeing that a woman should be permitted to terminate a pregnancy on request any time within the first three months.[1]

Time magazine, in June, 1969, cited a Louis Harris Poll which found sixty-four per cent of respondents holding that abortion should not be a matter of law but should be left to prospective parents and their physician. A survey conducted for the U.S. Commission on Population Growth and the American Future found in a 1971 poll that one half of Americans favored the removal of all legal restrictions on abortion (38 per cent believed the government should help make abortion available to all who wanted it).[2] The results of the referendum in Washington State where voters approved abortion-on-demand by roughly 5 to 4 would seem to confirm the melancholy testimony of such opinion polls as these.

Nevertheless, it is not clear that the question of abortion has really been posed to the American people in all its dimensions. In one sense, the battle against abortion has scarcely begun. Until very recently, the opponents of abortion have hardly been opposing abortion in the same degree that its proponents have been proposing it. The evil and ugliness of abortion, and what its acceptance by our society will mean for women, children, families, the medical profession, human rights, and our legal and constitutional structures have hardly been favorite topics in the mass media; nor are they in the forefront of the popular American consciousness. For many Americans, abortion may be not much more than a word. It is being talked about; many people want it—how can a democratic form of government deny what large numbers of people seem to want?

More sophisticated studies than the polls cited above, however, indicate that public acceptance of abortion in America actually varies a great deal depending upon the reasons advanced in favor of it. This public acceptance declines sharply as justifications depart from the kinds of medical, eugenic, and criminal "indications" embodied in laws patterned on the American Law Institute's model abortion law. Thus 71 per cent of respondents in one study favored allowing abortion if a woman's health was "seriously endangered"; 56 per cent if the pregnancy resulted from rape; 55 per cent if there was a "strong chance" of a defective child; 21 per cent if the family had a low income; 18 per cent if the woman was unmarried; and only 15 per cent if the woman was married but did not want another child.[3] Another study in *The Milbank Memorial Fund Quarterly* found only 37 per cent of Jews, 25 per cent of non-believers, 8 per cent of Protestants and 5 per cent of Catholics *favoring* abortion-on-demand—which is what we have noted the pro-abortion movement wants to get established as the law of the land in every state in the union,[3] regardless of true public opinion on the matter.

In early 1971, one of America's best known demographers, Dr. Judith Blake of the University of California in Berkeley, published a study which indicated that the range of American attitudes towards the phenomenon of abortion was both broad and complex; this study, based on a number of public opinion polls and surveys over an entire decade, has to be considered of major importance. It demonstrates conclusively that, in spite of increased propaganda for abortion over the same decade studied, American acceptance of abortion still depends upon the supposed validity of the "indications" justifying it. Although Dr. Blake herself evidently favors permissive abortion for population control reasons, and thinks our traditional state laws restricting abortion "constitute some of the more repressive of our pronatalist policies,"[4] she is obliged to conclude from her data that 80 per cent of the American people *disapprove* of simple abortion-on-demand. Only 13 percent disapprove of abortion if the woman's health is endangered by the pregnancy, according to her calculations. About twice that many—but still only 25 per cent of the population—disapprove if the child might be born defective. Dr. Blake's study makes it clear that Americans assume and expect that there is some valid reason for abortion, medical or otherwise, when they go on record as favoring it. Even then, it is true that these permissive American attitudes reflect what seems to be a decline in our national respect for the sanctity of life; nevertheless they are far from reflecting the convictions of those who have succeeded in making abortion-on-demand the focus of both the legal and the legislative battle in America.

As might be expected, Catholics as a group oppose abortion much more strongly than Americans as a whole, according to Dr. Blake's study, but not as strongly as the Church's absolute condemnation of any direct, intended abortion might suggest. Dr. Blake's study also demonstrates that abortion is less favored by women and the disadvantaged, whom abortion-on-demand is especially supposed to benefit, than it is favored by men and by the educated and affluent. Thus her study explodes one of the favorite myths about abortion.

Dr. Blake is forced to conclude from her study that, if the question of the legalization of abortion depended only upon public opinion, we would probably not have seen the degree of legalization that we have already seen. She believes abortion-on-demand must ultimately come as a result of an élite working through the courts.

All these public opinion studies, especially Dr. Blake's, suggest that American public opinion can be influenced against abortion to the degree that medical and other reasons cited in favor of it can be shown to be invalid or at least questionable. Opponents of abortion must continue to demand that the questions of rape, mental health, and the like be discussed. Even if the pro-abortion movement has moved on to abortion-on-demand, for any reason or for no reason, the American people have not moved on to this as yet; when abortion is discussed, the average person may well *think* that abortion for some good reason is involved if he has not yet been personally caught up by the Abortion Imperative.

We must now, therefore, examine the case for the "reform" of abortion laws on the basis of specific indications for abortions accepted by the ALI-type laws. The experience of the United States in the past few years suggests that abortion "reform" of the ALI type may be no more than a stage on the road towards abortion-on-demand. Nevertheless opponents of abortion must insist that the abortion debate continue to examine the actual validity of the arguments advanced for abortions in the situations permitted by these ALI-type laws. For these arguments can be shown to be weak, indeed practically non-existent. To the degree that American public opinion can be convinced of this weakness, it may turn against the legalization of abortion.

The "arguments" for a degree of abortion "reform," of course, are implicit in the situations where ALI-type laws allow legal abortions. We may recall that these "indications" are: 1) *Medical*: to preserve the life or physical health of a woman; 2) *Psychiatric*: to preserve her "mental health"; 3) *Eugenic*: to prevent the birth of deformed or defective children; 4) *Criminal*: to destroy children conceived as a result of rape or incest.

Medical Indications for Abortion

The laws of a majority of American states still permit abortion legally only to preserve the life of the mother. Ironically enough, just as the drive to "reform" or repeal these laws is getting into high gear, the progress of modern medicine is eliminating most, if not all, of the very medical indications once considered valid reasons for terminating a pregnancy. Conditions such as tuberculosis, cardiac disease, nephritis, uncontrolled vomiting, and the like, formerly believed to call for abortion in some cases, are no longer viewed in the same light by many medical practitioners today. New techniques and experience have demonstrated that such conditions can be successfully managed through the entire duration of a pregnancy.

It is not surprising, therefore, that respected members of the medical profession have strongly questioned the relevance of the usual medical indications for abortion. As far back as 1951, Dr. Roy J. Heffernan of Tufts, addressing a meeting of the American College of Surgeons, gave his opinion that "anyone who performs a therapeutic abortion is either ignorant of modern medical methods or unwilling to take the time and effort to apply them."[5]

Dr. David C. Wilson, writing in the book *Abortion in America,* which has long been one of the handbooks of the pro-abortion movement, flatly states that "the present trend, as expressed in the literature, indicates that proper management will permit a successful termination of pregnancy regardless of the physical and mental diseases of the patient."[6]

Dr. Alan F. Guttmacher, President of Planned Parenthood-World Population, whom we have already encountered as one of America's most influential advocates of abortion, actually authored a medical paper back in the 1950's which he titled "The Shrinking Indications for Therapeutic Abortion."[7] The indications for them may be shrinking, according to Dr. Guttmacher, but this does not seem to him to constitute a reason for cutting down on the abortions themselves. On the contrary, a book he recently edited bears the title: *The Case for Legalized Abortion*

Now! In this book he candidly says, "Today it is possible for almost any patient to be brought through pregnancy alive, unless she suffers from a fatal illness such as cancer or leukemia, and, if so, abortion would be unlikely to prolong, much less save life." Dr. Robert E. Hall, President of the Association for the Study of Abortion, and another one of the principal leaders in the pro-abortion movement, has dramatically cast doubt on whether "medical" reasons enter into the abortion picture at all today, when he declares that doctors "should not be asked to determine which women qualify for abortions. We are no more qualified to do so than accountants or street cleaners."[8]

Daniel Callahan, who has made perhaps the most comprehensive review of the medical literature on abortion to date, remarks that he "was able to discover in the current abortion literature only one sustained argument that medical indications for abortion, strictly taken, still constitute a major occasion for abortion." Professor Germain Grisez summarizes the medical situation as follows: "There appear to be only the following types of cases concerning which there is general agreement:

"1) Some cases, including hydatidiform mole, in which the fetus is dead or has been reabsorbed. Such cases, though technically involving an interruption of pregnancy, present no ethical question.

"2) Some types of cancer and other tumors require removal of the uterus during pregnancy. We shall see in considering the ethical question that these cases present no problem; there is general agreement that removal of the uterus is allowable.

"3) Ectopic pregnancies—i.e., those which involve implantation outside the uterus, usually in the tubes, but occasionally in the abdominal cavity—require removal. In most cases ectopic pregnancy presents no ethical problem . . .

"4) Heart and kidney diseases which are complicated by progressively diminishing or failing heart and/or kidney functions, especially during the first three months of pregnancy. These cases present an important ethical question, because there does exist a very broad medical consensus that there are legitimate grounds for therapeutic abortion in such cases, while an absolute prohibition of abortion seems to exclude the procedure."[9]

This summary of the current medical situation indicates that, in the first three types of cases where modern medical opinion believes that an induced interruption of pregnancy is called for, there is no moral problem. These cases would not require true "abortions" in the sense in which we are using the term in this essay. Only in the cases in the fourth category would abortion be forbidden by Catholic teaching, regardless of the medical consensus. Even then, it is important to remember that abortion in these cases would be *legal* under the most restrictive laws in America; hence the question of whether they are legitimate medical indications need not enter at all into the debate on the relaxation of abortion *laws.* The laws have never forbidden abortions in such cases.

As for other medical indications for abortions, however, there are serious doubts whether therapeutic abortion— abortion on true medical grounds in the interests of the mother's life or health—any longer constitutes a real medical problem. Yet it is precisely at the moment of modern medicine's triumph over the diseases formerly believed to justify abortion that the drive to legalize abortions has intensified! Here we see the Abortion Imperative at work in its purest form. As real medical reasons for the procedure disappear, and the chief medical consideration becomes the possible *harm* the doctor might do to the woman in the course of aborting her pregnancy, we see the demand for abortions rising!

Moreover, medical doctors, in performing abortions, are
no longer performing a medical, healing function at all,
properly speaking; their role is reduced to one of a purely
technical nature; they wield the curette or operate the suction device. As Dr. E. W. Overstreet has pointed out, patients do not normally demand a specific therapy from a
doctor; they present a specific problem to him and he se-
lects the therapy.[10] With abortion, however, the doctor me-
chanically carries out the woman's request; no strictly
medical judgment is involved. The acceptance of abortion-on-demand will thus involve a revolutionary transformation of the nature of the medical profession itself. A
class of doctors will be created performing no healing
function and making no medical judgment, but merely
functioning as skilled technicians of death.

Dr. Robert E. Hall, quoted above, disputes the significance of this change for the medical profession. Speaking
of those doctors who have objected that abortion turns
them into mere technicians, he comments: "They don't
consider that when a patient comes to them and says, 'I
want you to deliver my baby' that this is 'obstetrics on
demand.'"[11] Yet Dr. Hall's use of language here suggests
that even he discerns a rather basic difference between
obstetrics and abortion. It is, in fact, the difference between helping the woman to carry and deliver her child—
a life-preserving, positive function—and helping her to
"terminate" her pregnancy—a brutal, death-dealing function in the literal sense of the word. The medical profession, since the beginning of human civilization, has en-
deavored to perform a function aimed at the preservation
of life and health. Even those doctors who in the past performed therapeutic abortions still sincerely believed they
were thereby preserving the mother's life or health. New
concepts of abortion, especially abortion-on-demand,
however, are the pure negation of everything the medical

profession has ever stood for. The doctors who perform abortions today are not preserving anything; they are involved in killing unborn children, nothing else. We have what Patrick Cardinal O'Boyle has aptly styled "exterminative medicine."[12]

Those who argue that abortion should be strictly a matter between a woman and her doctor do not seem to see that they are thereby eliminating the doctor *as* a doctor. This is only one of the contradictions inherent in the Abortion Imperative.

Psychiatric Indications for Abortion

As the medical reasons for abortion "shrink," the "mental health" of the mother comes to be used as justification for a correspondingly greater number of abortions. In Oregon, where the number of abortions increased by a factor of fifteen under an ALI-type law, 96 per cent of the abortions carried out initially were done on psychiatric grounds; in Maryland, under a similar law, the same figure has been recorded, 96 per cent, consistently, over a much longer period.[13] The California figure has been eighty-eight per cent, the Colorado figure eighty-nine per cent, while in Virginia (where abortions soared sevenfold after the passage of an ALI-type law) a figure of eighty-six per cent has been reported. A study of hospital abortions in ten states with ALI-type laws revealed an average of 95 per cent of all abortions performed for so-called "mental health."[14] We may immediately wonder whether such a remarkable incidence of mental cases serious enough to require abortion is reflected in the mental health statistics of these states. It would seem that mental cases are filling the obstetrical wards faster than they are filling the psychiatric wards!

In fact, of course, this remarkable incidence of alleged mental illness is simply another instance where the Abortion Imperative has introduced its characteristic kind of corruption into a profession, in this case that of psychiatry. These "mental cases," though often certified by psychiatrists, are mostly fraudulent; the mental health indication is widely used to allow any woman who wants one to get an abortion. Once abortion-on-demand is made legal, these mental cases in the obstetrical wards disappear as suddenly as they appeared when it became legal to get abortions on mental health grounds. Dr. Bernard J. Pisani, Director of the Department of Obstetrics and Gynecology at Saint Vincent's Hospital in New York City, reviewing available figures on the first six months of experience with abortion-on-demand, found that only 0.5—one half of one per cent!—of all abortions performed were done on psychiatric grounds (in only 1.3 per cent of all cases were any *medical* reasons claimed). Dr. Pisani comments: "It is my deduction that 98% of the procedures are performed for social, economic, or population control reasons."[15]

In Alaska, 90 per cent of the women who had abortions under the new law had them because "they did not want to be pregnant." Only some 6 per cent cited any medical pretext.[16]

It is not surprising that abortions on psychiatric grounds virtually disappear once abortion is legalized. For the necessity to claim mental illness as a subterfuge is eliminated. In actual fact, the psychiatric literature seems to cast more doubt on the legitimacy of abortion for mental illness than does the medical literature for physical illnesses. Indeed there seems to be considerable evidence that abortion may do consistently more harm to a woman than carrying a pregnancy to term. As the well-known psychiatrist, Dr. Frank J. Ayd, Jr., has remarked, "You can scrape the baby out of the womb, but you cannot scrape the baby out of the mind."[17]

In the following extract, for example, it is perfectly clear that the authors, two doctors, while clearly not opposed to the performance of abortions as such, nevertheless fail to find much warrant for performing them on mental health grounds: "There does not seem to be any one [mental] condition which absolutely indicates interruption of pregnancy. The mental state is seldom justification for induction of abortion. Abortion per se is unquestionably a shock. It may be conceivably more detrimental than continuation of the pregnancy. If it could be shown that conception might lead to permanent psychosis in certain definite cases, then the termination of pregnancy would clearly be in the best interests of the patient . . . but the contrary appears to be the rule. The psychosis initiated by pregnancy rarely persists but tends to recover after an apparently short period . . . Women who show permanent impairment of mentality following childbirth belong to the class of potential psychotics for whom pregnancy is merely a subsidiary factor . . . Upon the mentality of such women a therapeutic abortion cannot be curative and it may exert a deleterious effect that is more harmful than the continuation of the pregnancy."[18]

Dr. David C. Wilson, whose contribution to the decidedly pro-abortion anthology, *Abortion in America*, has already been quoted, cites a review of the medical literature to the effect that "severe emotional changes follow abortion in a large percentage of cases."[19] More importantly, other studies indicate that it is among truly mentally ill women with the most serious psychiatric conditions to begin with that the psychiatrically adverse effects from abortion are likely to be the greatest.

A recent study reviewing thirty years of experience in

Sweden with legal abortion comments: "All researchers are agreed that those who have developed a state of mental insufficiency after an abortion have usually had such symptoms earlier. Thus, we have a situation where the stronger the psychiatric indications are for a legal abortion, the greater will be the risk of unfavourable mental sequelae after the operation. In such situations we are faced with a practically insoluble problem, and the chances of an unfavourable result are high, whatever is done."[20]

What is both ironic and tragic is that psychiatry's very concept of what constitutes true mental illness and mental therapy comes to be affected by how psychiatry is being used to justify abortion. Thus, in a 1971 study in the *Journal of the American Medical Association,* we find psychiatrist authors solemnly assuming that what they call "the acute psychological distress associated with pregnancy" is itself a form of mental illness sufficient to justify abortion. In other words, the pregnancy itself is admitted to be the *cause* of the "psychological distress" which justifies the performance of the abortion; thus it seems hardly worthy of a professional journal to dignify by publication the further "finding" that the symptoms of distress disappear when the pregnancy is interrupted! This is comparable to saying that a toe no longer feels pinched when a tight shoe is removed! Nevertheless it provides the theoretical justification for thousands and thousands of abortions.

In cases of real mental illness, however, this same JAMA study admits that "the more serious the psychiatric diagnosis, the less beneficial . . . the abortion." Then comes the sort of conclusion that should be read by every state legislator who ever voted for a "mental health" clause in an abortion statute, or, for that matter, by the justices of the U.S. Supreme Court who have, in effect, found "mental health" a valid extension of the "health" indication for abortion: "The finding that the more seriously ill women do less well emotionally after abortion than the more 'normal' ones seems to us of special significance. Traditionally patients with a serious neurosis or psychosis were those whom therapeutic abortion committees would choose to abort. The assumption was that the patient's illness would be made worse by continuation of the pregnancy. By contrast, the more normal women would be denied abortion on the grounds that they could tolerate the pregnancy reasonably well. Our findings, instead, suggest that the more 'normal' women are the ones who benefit most obviously from abortion, whereas patients with a well-established neurosis or psychosis continue in their course without usually much change either for better or worse. In fact, there is some evidence that the more severely disturbed patients incorporate the abortion into their illness. For example, patients who initially present with a severe depression are likely, after the abortion, to attach their guilt to the procedure. Schizophrenic patients may involve the abortion into their delusional preoccupations . . ."[21]

A study such as this turns on its head the commonly accepted reasons for performimg an abortion on "mental health" grounds. Yet this is somehow not perceived as a reason for stopping or curtailing abortions on these grounds, even though the psychiatric evidence against them becomes more and more striking with each study done!

Dr. Julius Fogel is a physican who may have a unique kind of testimony to offer on the subject of psychiatric abortions, since he is not only a practicing obstetrician-gynecologist but also a practicing psychiatrist. Dr. Fogel has, according to a press account, "been advocating and performing therapeutic abortions for years." Yet he is convinced that harmful psychological consequences can follow abortion. "We are only beginning to learn something of the effects on the women involved," Dr. Fogel believes. "I think every woman—whatever her age, background or sexuality—has a trauma at destroying a pregnancy. A level of humanness is touched. This is a part of her own life. She destroys a pregnancy, she is destroying herself. There is no way it can be innocuous. One is dealing with the life force . . ."

Dr. Fogel does not claim that mental illness automatically follows an abortion. "Often," he remarks, "the trauma may sink into the unconscious and never surface in the woman's lifetime. But it is not as harmless and casual an event as many in the pro-abortion crowd insist. A psychological price is paid. I can't say exactly what. It may be alienation, it may be a pushing away from human warmth, perhaps a hardening of the maternal instinct. Something happens on the deeper levels of a woman's consciousness when she destroys a pregnancy. I know that as a psychiatrist."[22]

The Group for the Advancement of Psychiatry, a professional association, recently conducted a study to determine the effect of the increasing demand for acceptance of abortions on the psychiatric profession. This study was believed imperative since psychiatrists are the ones most often called upon to certify that an abortion is "necessary." The study accepts, with only minor qualifications, the statement of a British psychiatrist to the effect that "there are no psychiatric grounds for termination of pregnancy"; and the only slightly less categorical statement of an American psychiatrist that "there are no unequivocal psychiatric indications for therapeutic abortions." But if this is so, psychiatrists are evidently not in a position to recommend abortions. The Group for the Advancement of Psychiatry sees this clearly, and says, "We believe it essential that psychiatrists, through their professional organizations, begin to recognize their own limitations and back

away from the invitation to accept responsibility for making decisions [about abortions]."[23]

Similarly, the Executive Council of the American Psychoanalytic Association, after a two-year study, concluded
it could find "no consensus or basis" for general prediction
of the psychological results of abortions; at the same time,
one of the highest ranking doctors in the U.S. Government,
Dr. Louis H. Hellman, an Assistant Secretary in the Department of Health, Education, and Welfare, has called
the practice of mental tests for women desiring abortions
a "gross sham."[24]

Once again, however, the Abortion Imperative super-
venes and blunts the purely professional judgments that
psychiatry has to offer: 1) that there are no valid psychiatric grounds for abortion; and 2) that considerable evidence exists that abortion can actually cause mental disor-
der or contribute to it. Even as they admit both
propositions, however, psychiatrists are found to favor
abortion. Dr. Fogel, as we have seen, has been "advocating
and performing therapeutic abortions for years," in spite
of his professional judgment that they are harmful to his
patients. Both the Group for the Advancement of Psychiatry and the American Psychoanalytic Association,
having washed their hands of the attempt to find any psychiatric justification for it, nevertheless go on to recommend abortion as a woman's "right"! Dr. Louis M. Hellman, for his part, wants elective abortion as an
"emergency procedure" until better means of birth control
are perfected—unless the U.S. Government switches to a
population control policy. In that case, Dr. Hellman believes, "we'll have to use all available methods, including
abortion."

We may legitimately wonder how the practice of psychiatry or psychoanalysis affords any special insight into
what are, and what are not, human *rights*. The public at

large surely has as much expertise here as any of the experts. It is an *abuse* of expertise to attempt to recommend as a "right" what cannot be justified on scientific or professional grounds—when, indeed, these grounds are frankly admitted to be a "gross sham."

Eugenic Indications for Abortion

The prospect of deformed or Cetarded children commonly evokes popular sympathy, as the plight of "thalidomide babies" brought out a few years back. Yet once again it is amazing how the drive to justify abortions on eugenic grounds intensifies just as modern medical science becomes more and more proficient in treating the problems of defective children. Here, again, we see the Abortion Imperative at work. The new vaccine for rubella, or German measles, for example, should soon make the characteristic defects of some children whose mothers had the disease during the first few months of pregnancy as rare as pock marks have become since the development of inoculations for smallpox.

Often it is the parents of "defective" children who are most strongly opposed to abortion on so-called eugenic grounds. The Nobel-prize-winning writer, Pearl S. Buck, the mother of a child retarded from phenylketonuria, has said, "Could it have been possible for me to have had foreknowledge of her thwarted life, would I have wanted abortion? Now, with full knowledge of anguish and despair, the answer is no, I would not. Even with full knowledge I would have chosen life . . . I fear the power of choice over life and death at human hands. I see no human being whom I could ever trust with such power—not myself, not any other. Human wisdom, human integrity are not great enough . . .

". . . My child's life has not been meaningless," Mrs. Buck

goes on. "She has indeed brought comfort and practical help to many people who are parents of retarded children or are themselves handicapped. True, she has done it through me, yet without her I would not have had the means of learning how to accept the inevitable sorrow, and how to make that acceptance useful to others."[25]

Which of us does not have to learn to accept sorrow? The world scorns the old belief that this world is a "vale of tears," but if the elimination of what Mrs. Buck calls "inevitable sorrow" can only be managed by taking life, then it is about time this old belief should be revived in our society. It does not require much real experience of life to understand that there are many things that we simply must put up with. This point has rarely been made in the abortion debate; but if we admitted that society were somehow obliged to solve everybody's problems, we would thereby open the door for drastic solutions such as abortions in those situations where—as is manifestly the case with certain "natural" defects—society *cannot* do anything about them.

One point Mrs. Buck does not make about retarded or defective children—which is known to anybody who has worked with such children—is the unique contribution they themselves make to the quality and diversity of human life. What a different and unimaginable world it would be if all of us enjoyed perfect health and a uniformly high I.Q.! All of us are inspired by people who persevere in spite of handicaps; the world is a distinctly better place for a Helen Keller who succeeds in overcoming seemingly insuperable obstacles. Even retarded children have their contribution to make; these children often have a sweetness and a capacity for love and trust which can only put the rest of us to shame.

In his book, *Life, Death, and the Doctor,* Dr. Louis Lasagna shows himself capable of writing about abortion as if the child really *were* nothing but a tonsil or an appendix. His clinical detachment seems complete until he gets on the subject of defective children. It turns out he is himself the father of a child retarded from "Mongolism." The whole tone of his narrative suddenly changes. "For mother and father," he writes, "there is the warm satisfaction to be derived from a parent-child relationship that works. Mongoloids are often extremely lovable children, sweet and affectionate. There is an added measure of emotion when a head resting gently and trustingly on your shoulder belongs to a child in special need of love and help. The excitement and pleasure of watching a youngster achieve certain goals is, if anything, greater when the child's rate of development is much slower than that of a normal child."

Dr. Lasagna goes on: "For the other children in the family the presence in the home of a retarded child can be an extraordinarily meaningful and beneficial experience. The normal siblings have an opportunity to develop real understanding for the handicapped and a feeling for the broad spectrum of individual differences and genetic endowment. A tolerance for the physiologically underprivileged is a valued acquisition at any age, and the younger it can be achieved, the better."[26]

Even if we were to admit, notwithstanding all this, that we were entitled to destroy the lives of the defective before they are born, the strictly practical problem would still remain of determining which children, in fact, should be considered defective. Statistics indicate that about 10 per cent of all children born are defective in some degree; as many as 3 to 5 per cent of all children born may suffer from a serious defect of a possibly crippling nature.[27] Though modern medicine has made progress in diagnosing cases of probable defects before birth (as it has made progress in *treating* defects of all kinds!), defects such as congenital heart disease cannot be detected before birth. The likelihood always remains great that we would destroy large numbers of perfectly normal children in order to eliminate those who would truly be defective.

Specifically, the likelihood of a child's being born defective even if his mother *does* contract rubella during the first three months of pregnancy, for example, can vary anywhere from 15 to 20 per cent overall, with a 40 to 60 per cent chance of a defective child only if the mother contracts the infection during the first month of pregnancy. Put another way, up to 85 per cent of all babies whose mothers have had rubella during the pregnancy will *not* be defective but normal in every respect![28]

Another study by Dr. Theodore Friedmann, a professor of pediatrics at the University of California at San Diego, points out some of the inherent difficulties in the prenatal diagnosis of genetically caused diseases. About 40 of the more than 1600 human diseases known to be caused by genetic defects can now be diagnosed by inserting a sterile needle into the amniotic sac which surrounds the child in the uterus, removing some of the amniotic fluid, and examining the fetal cells which the fluid contains. The process is called amniocentesis, and it is not a simple one. Care must be taken not to puncture the placenta or the child. The possibility of damage to both the mother and child is admittedly real, and "one may expect traumatic complications to increase temporarily as less experienced physicians with insufficient specialized training begin to perform amniocentesis." Medically speaking, it should not be done before the 16th week of gestation when an *abortion*, if the child proved to have a genetic defect, would be a "life-threatening operation" for the *mother,* as we saw in Chapter I.

In any case, there is no way to determine when to employ the technique, unless a woman has already borne a child with one of the genetically caused defects that can be diagnosed. If the defect is carried by a recessive gene, as most of them are, the probability of correctly identifying which children are going to be defective is not very great. "We can expect to find only a small number of new cases," Dr. Friedmann writes, "since the initial cases are missed [!] and subsequent pregnancies carry only a 25 per cent probability of producing an affected child."[29]

If these are some of the medical difficulties involved in determining which children might be borne defective, it would seem logical to defer the killing of the child until after birth to insure the liquidation only of those children who were defective. After delivery the baby could be examined; if he had congenital heart disease, cataracts, deafness, malformation, or something of the sort, painless ways of putting him out of his misery would not be beyond the ingenuity of modern science. A Nobel-prize-winning biologist in England, Dr. Francis Crick, has seriously advocated a law which would declare that a child not be considered legally alive until two days old and certified as healthy by a medical examination—this, apparently, in the interests of human "quality control" and sanctioned by what Dr. Crick calls a "new ethical system based on modern science."[30] (Dr. Crick also advocates compulsory death at age 80.)

The flagrant amorality of such a crude suggestion is certainly breathtaking. But what can we say about the morality of a law which allows the killing of unborn children merely if there is a "risk" that they *might* be born defective? As of the spring of 1972, the law allows this in sixteen American states, not counting those states or districts where court decisions have ushered in permissive abortion.

Abortion in Cases of Rape

When a child is conceived as a result of rape, the mother finds herself in a truly tragic situation; she is genuinely a victim herself, unlike the mother who simply does not want to bear the child, for whatever reason. It is perhaps understandable that a woman who has been raped, like the woman who may bear a defective child, evokes sympathy—and not always merely of a sentimental kind. Even some theologians have tried to justify abortion in cases of rape as a legitimate form of self-defense against the fetus considered as a continuation of the rapist-aggressor-father.

Yet the innocence of the child cannot be gainsaid; he is no more responsible for his conception than the rest of us were responsible for ours. If an unborn child is human and has a right to life, it would seem hard to deny that right to him merely because he was not lawfully conceived in wedlock. It is a tragic situation for the mother; but it is a *temporary* one. It will endure approximately nine months, and the child can be put up for adoption. But the child's very existence is at stake. A consistent respect for the right to life will not, therefore, admit the principle that the child's life may be taken if conceived as a result of rape.

Statistically, only a miniscule percentage of abortions are performed for reasons of rape; it is far from certain whether we are really talking about rape in the true sense of the word in all these cases. "Rape" can easily be blamed for embarrassing or inconvenient pregnancies. Only 1.2 per cent of the therapeutic abortions performed in Oregon under a liberalized law were done on grounds of "felonious intercourse" (which includes incest as well as rape).[31] One study holds that there are no more than 750 conceptions annually in the United States as a result of rape[32]—

there are around 3.5 *million* children born in the United States every year. There is evidence that the shock of rape tends to suppress ovulation, making conception impossible. A Minnesota study of 3,500 cases of rape revealed no resulting pregnancies.[33] The Chicago prosecuting attorney's office could recall no pregnancies in nine years of prosecuting rape cases in one of America's largest cities.[34]

Dr. Denis Cavanaugh comments pertinently on the whole question of abortion on grounds of rape: "In Czechoslovakia, in 1966, only 22 of 86,258 abortions were performed for rape. In Colorado, in the first year of experience with the new law, 46 of 407 abortions were done for rape. This suggests that the chance of rape is over 400 times more likely in the center of the United States than it is in Czechoslovakia."[35]

All these considerations are, of course, cold comfort for the woman who has in fact been raped and is carrying the child of her aggressor. But even if we could accept the premise that a child conceived as a result of rape should be aborted, the actual incidence of such cases would hardly be of the magnitude to justify drastic changes in the law. A society which is *just* as well as compassionate will consider more severe criminal penalties for the rapist rather than allowing the innocent child conceived as a result of rape to be killed automatically for something someone else did.

Abortions in Case of Incest

Father David Granfield has probably said the last word on the subject of incest: "Incest is a monstrous kind of justification for the taking of the life of another human being because the parents of the child were partners in the crime that resulted in his conception. The child's mother, herself a felon, pleads her own misdeed as a justification for killing the fruit of the very crime that is pleaded as a justification."[36]

All in all, the case for abortion on the indications generally allowed by laws following the pattern of the American Law Institute's model statute ranges from very weak to non-existent. This conclusion emerges without taking the morality of abortion into consideration at all: there simply are no valid medical, psychiatric, eugenical, or criminal indications for abortion to weigh in the balance not merely against the taking of an existing human life, but against the dangers and inconveniences of the operation itself. Perhaps the very flimsiness of the case for abortion "reform" has helped push the reformers on to abortion-on-demand, abortion as an alleged woman's "right."

But if the public opinion studies cited at the beginning of this chapter mean anything, they mean that the American people have not yet accepted the logic of the Abortion Imperative. The American people are not committed to the relaxation of our abortion laws, regardless of the reasons for abortions or the lack of them. The American people, where they seem to approve of abortion, generally approve of it on the assumption that there *is* some reason or "necessity" for it. This attitude may betray a lamentable utilitarianism and a failure to understand the importance of maintaining principles in the moral and legal spheres; but it also suggests that the American people can be influenced away from abortion if they can be shown how really weak the case for abortion is on the basis of the indications usually allowed in liberalized ALI-type abortion laws. We have seen here how weak that case is. An indispensable educational task for those who oppose abortion is to get across to the American public how weak it is. In the practical sphere this will mean never allowing the pro-abortionists to debate the question merely on the level of whether a woman should be allowed to get an abortion or not; but in every case insisting on a discussion of the reasons why abortions are alleged to be necessary. If these reasons can be openly debated, and the facts brought out, the pro-abortionists are going to have a much harder time of it trying to convince the American people of the plausibility of their position.

VI

The Arguments for Abortion-on-Demand

THOUGH opponents of relaxed abortion laws must continue to demand the *reasons* why the laws should allegedly be relaxed, we have now seen that there are *no* valid medical, psychiatric, eugenic, or criminal reasons for relaxing them. The point in demanding the alleged reasons for abortion is to destroy the abortionists' case in the eyes of the American people. At the same time we must recognize that the organized pro-abortion movement has already moved beyond the need for any "reasons" for the practice. We have called this attitude the Abortion Imperative.

A Protestant observer, Professor Ralph B. Potter, Jr., of the Harvard Divinity School, in a knowledgeable survey of the abortion debate,[1] has ably summarized the arguments most often brought forward by the proponents of abortion to prove that abortion-on-demand has become "necessary." In this chapter, we shall make use of Professor Potter's summary as a convenient starting point for a brief

113

discussion of each of these arguments. The argument he lists derived from the so-called "population explosion" we shall consider in a separate chapter.

To Protect the Life and Health of Women by Making Medically Safe Abortions Available to Those Who Cannot Be Deterred by Rigid Laws or High Risks.

This, of course, has always been the most widely advanced argument for any degree of relaxation of the abortion laws. Some women are going to seek abortions whether they are legal or not, it is argued. The least we can do to save these women from being butchered by back-alley abortionists is to make abortion legal and have it done in hospitals. This appears to be a compelling argument for many.

We can only wonder how compelling it seems when we transfer exactly the same argument to another situation: some men are going to commit armed robbery regardless of what the law says. The least we can do to save these men from being killed or maimed in the process is to remove the legal penalties from armed robbery.

This kind of argument ignores the question of how often a woman who is tempted to have an abortion may be deterred from such a tragic decision because it is illegal. Surely the law must save as many lives, including fetal lives, as it can. If it is replied that abortion laws obviously do not deter all women seeking abortions, we can reply that neither do the laws deter all men from committing armed robbery. In fact, 1,513,000 cases of grand larceny were recorded in the United States in 1969;[2] yet no rich and powerful lobby exists to argue that the laws against larceny should not exist because they have failed to prevent the crime they are framed to counter. If the laws against any crimes are removed from the books, we may naturally expect more people to commit those particular crimes than commit them now. It is quite true that almost anything "illegal" can be completely eliminated by the simple expedient of declaring it henceforth "legal." But the substantive question still remains whether it is practical, prudent, or, most especially, *right,* to do so.

One thing we do know is that non-hospital abortions by unqualified practitioners have not been eliminated in countries where abortion has been legalized. Nor is it true that legalizing abortion removes all danger to the mother —as is shown by the rate of maternal deaths and complications registered in New York since abortion-on-demand went into effect.

Denmark, Norway, Sweden, Finland, East Germany, the Soviet Union, Hungary, Poland, Czechoslovakia, and Bulgaria have all liberalized their abortion laws to allow very permissive abortions. In Hungary, legal abortions actually exceed live births! Yet, as Daniel Callahan's exhaustive study on the subject testifies, "in all the [se] countries there remains some incidence of illegal abortions."[3] Both women and practitioners apparently dislike working through the official abortion boards; or are seeking abortions beyond the stated time limit; or simply prefer to keep their abortions secret even though they are legal. The result is that clandestine operations continue even where abortions are virtually legalized.

In Japan, where abortion is practiced on a scale to be found nowhere else in the world, one study has estimated that around 2.3 million abortions were performed in the year 1953; only around half of these, however, or 1.2 million,[4] were "legal" abortions, reported in accordance with the law. Yet there is no real obstacle at all to obtaining a legal abortion in Japan. Nevertheless, whether because women wished to conceal their abortions—a desire which is said to be surprisingly common for a country where abortion seems to be widely accepted and practiced[5]—or because doctors wished to conceal the number they had actually performed for income tax or other reasons, the legalization of abortion has failed to eliminate clandestine operations in Japan.

The *British Medical Journal* reports the same phenomenon in Britain in the wake of an extremely permissive abortion law: "The original protagonists for abortion law reform often argued that a large proportion of cases of spontaneous abortion hitherto treated in hospitals, and nearly all the associated deaths, were the result of criminal interference. Legalization of abortion would, they postulated, eliminate these. They brushed aside contrary arguments . . . . [New] figures . . . are therefore of some importance, indicating as they do that, despite a sharp rise in the number of notified therapeutic abortions from 1968 to 1969, there was not unfortunately any significant change in the number of cases of spontaneous abortion requiring admission to the hospital. Moreover, figures published by the Department of Health indicate that the number of fatalities associated with all types of abortion in England and Wales in 1968 was similar to that in previous years . . ." A more recent report actually speaks of a "boom" in illegal abortions in England owing to a shortage of abortion clinics licenced by the Ministry of Health.[6]

What happens when abortion is legalized is: a greater total number of abortions, legal and illegal. People become more abortion-minded when the practice is legal. Women who might formerly have been deterred by a restrictive law join those determined to get an abortion at any risk or cost, law or no law; if the practice is legal, it becomes acceptable and right and even desirable in the eyes of many. This is the message of the posters and advertisements which proclaim (in case there is anybody left who hasn't got the message): "Abortions Are Now Legal In New York State . . ."

Since the total number of abortions is greater when the practice is legalized, the total number of maternal deaths and complications from abortion is also greater. In Northern Europe, for example, there is a maternal death rate of around 40 per 100,000 legal abortions performed; in England, the rate is 36 per 100,000 legal abortions (in National Health Service hospitals).[7] When we compare this with a maternal death rate of 28 per 100,000 deliveries in the United States for all causes related to pregnancy and delivery in 1967,[8] it becomes clear that even legal abortion in hospitals is not by any means as safe as child-birth, as is so often alleged in pro-abortion propaganda.

It is true that the reported maternal death rate is much lower in some of the Communist countries of Eastern Europe, since abortions in these countries are generally prohibited beyond the twelfth week of pregnancy, with strict criminal penalties in force for abortions performed beyond the legal time limit. Thus, though they allow abortions permissively in some cases, Communist governments have not abandoned a rigid control of the practice. The lower maternal death rate in Eastern Europe from legal abortion is thus scarcely an argument for removing abortion from the province of the criminal law entirely, as is being advocated in America.

Illegal abortion, with consequent deaths and injuries, is asserted to be a massive problem in the United States. It is still often claimed that between 1 million and 1.2 million illegal abortions are performed in the United States each year. During 1970, *Life, Newsweek, Pageant, The New York Times Magazine,* and *Ramparts* were among the national magazines which ran articles citing one of these two figures as established fact. Former United States Senator Joseph D. Tydings prefers the 1.2 million figure in his

book *Born To Starve,* but fails to include any documentation for it. Neither do any of the national magazines cite
their sources for the figures they use.[9] Yet a citation of the
figure from *Life* has been used to justify invalidating restrictive laws against abortion in at least two recent court
cases.[10]

An entirely typical statement of the problem is as follows: "Although the covert character of such surgical
procedures renders reliable statistical estimates difficult,
there seems to be little doubt that criminal abortions in
this country approach a figure of close to 1,000,000 annually."[11] We may be tempted to wonder at the absence of any
doubt as to the accuracy of this one-million figure, when
it is expressly stated that "reliable statistical estimates"
are unavailable!

The maternal death rate from criminal abortions is implied to be correspondingly high in the books and articles
which accept the one-million figure; a figure of 8 to 10
thousand maternal deaths annually is often encountered.
One supposedly serious student of the problem flatly states
that "criminal abortion currently accounts for thousands
of deaths annually in the United States."[12]

Yet there is no factual basis whatsoever either for the
claims about the number of illegal abortions performed or
the number of maternal deaths which allegedly result
from illegal abortions. Abortion is not even mentioned in
the latest *Statistical Abstract of the United States.* If we
look into any convenient almanac or fact-book on the
shelves of the public library, we will find no statistics at all
on illegal abortions. If we check with our state Health
Department or with the U.S. Department of Health, Education, and Welfare, we will similarly uncover no figures
for the simple reason that such figures are nonexistent.

The figure of "one million illegal abortions each year"
has long since been exploded as a myth. Dr. André E.

Hellegers of Georgetown University has noted that the estimate is based on a 1934 study which drew its data from case histories given by 10,000 women who attended the Margaret Sanger Birth Control clinic in New York between 1925 and 1929. "I leave to your imagination," Dr. Hellegers has commented, "how representative that group must have been of the United States in 1925."[13]

As for maternal deaths, there are solid figures on them in the regular statistics (unless the back-alley abortionists are managing to conceal the dead bodies of their victims on a truly gigantic scale). In 1967, according to the latest *Statistical Abstract of the United States,* exactly 987 women died as a result of all causes connected with pregnancy and delivery.[14] How many of these deaths could have been due to criminal abortions? Even if all of them were—a manifestly ludicrous assumption— we would still have a maternal death figure only around one-tenth of what the abortion lobby has claimed.

It is true that some maternal deaths might be attributed to infection or some other cause, and hence not show up in these particular statistics. But as Dr. Christopher Tietze, Director of the Bio-medical Division of the Population Council and an acknowledged expert on this subject, has pointed out, only some 45,000 women of child-bearing age die each year in this country from all causes. "It is inconceivable," Dr. Tietze has noted, "that of 45,000 deaths so large a number as 5,000 are from one source." He thinks that no more than 500 could possibly be due to abortions.[15] Another careful study suggests that the true number may be no more than around 225, and perhaps even as low as 60.[16]

On maternal injury from criminal abortions, the same kind of exaggerations abound as we have encountered in the case of maternal deaths. One Chicago radio station, for example, editorialized in May, 1970, about the 20,000 women who had supposedly been carried bleeding into Cook County Hospital with injuries inflicted upon them by criminal abortionists. The next day the station was obliged to admit that the correct figure was 102 women.[17]

Speakers for such causes as "Women's Liberation" continue to speak of "all those women who have died of botched abortions" over the years,[18] but a more informed public will be more concerned at the more than 50,000 Americans who are verifiably killed each year in automobile accidents than about the fantasies of the pro-abortionists. Indeed the number of *fetal* deaths in New York City since abortion-on-demand is a demonstrably greater social problem than anything the pro-abortionists have managed to come up with. In the light of the true facts, it is incredible that our courts and our legislatures should be taken up with the legalization of abortion to the degree that they are.

The Commission on Population Growth and the American Future, in its report *Population and the American Future,* delivered to the world in March, 1972, similarly endorsed wildly exaggerated figures which have also become a part of mythology when it spoke of estimates ranging "from 200,000 to 1,200,000 illegal abortions per year in the United States." Merely the range indicated here reveals how little foundation in fact can be claimed for either figure—or any other figure. This particular range actually came out of an abortion conference sponsored back in the fifties by Planned Parenthood; as little was known then about actual statistics on the true number of illegal abortions as is known today. Nevertheless the 200,-000 to 1,200,000 range is often cited as perhaps more scientific or more credible than the straight 1 million or 1.2 million figures for illegal abortions.

In truth, however, even the more honest and sophis-

ticated among the ranks of the abortion lobby are aware
of the facts about criminal abortions, and about the maternal mortality and morbidity truly resulting from abortions.[19] Perhaps, as we have already suggested, that is why
they have shifted their arguments from the dangers of
criminal abortions to the alleged "right" of a woman to
control her reproductive life even if it means killing a
child she has conceived. The Abortion Imperative is not to
be denied merely because there is no evidence for the
principal contention with which the whole pro-abortion
movement began: the impossibility of "medically safe"
abortions for those women determined to have abortions
regardless of the law. The philosopher George Santayana
once defined a fanatic as one who redoubles his effort after
he has forgotten his aim; in a true sense, the votaries of the
Abortion Imperative are surely fanatics.

To Preserve the Autonomy of the Medical Profession.

This argument for abortion-on-demand begs the question of whether any profession can operate completely un-
regulated by law. If doctors came to believe that their
autonomy or independence somehow counted more than
the preservation of human life, they would thereby be denying their vocation as society's first-line preserver and
protector of human life. Such an attitude would vitiate the
high standards of the noble profession of medicine which
generations of practitioners have built. Doctors must risk
the law's normal penalties for malpractice, every bit as
much as bankers or lawyers must risk it if, say, they divert
funds in their trust to their own use. What profession is
autonomous? Nothing compels a doctor to perform an
abortion, as the abortion lobby itself tirelessly repeats. If

he is afraid that the law will second-guess him on an abortion and prosecute him, he doesn't have to perform it,
especially, it would seem, when the medical literature itself casts doubt on whether the operation is ever necessary
from a strictly medical point of view. In the rare case of
extreme danger to the mother's survival, the doctor believ-
ing abortion medically indicated, would be on the firmest
possible legal ground in performing an abortion under the
most restrictive abortion laws now in force. Why should
any doctor wish more than this from the law?

As we have already seen, acceptance of abortion-on-
demand will radically change the whole nature of the
medical profession and the doctor-patient relationship;
the doctor will be nothing more than the executor of the
woman's decision and the executioner of her child. Moreover, as the Protestant theologian Paul Ramsey has
pointed out, "once abortion is placed solely in the hands of
the patient and her licensed doctor, once it is simply regulated like any other procedure of standard medical practice, doctors can successfully be sued for medical malpractice if they refuse an abortion. A doctor is legally guilty of
malpractice if he does not extend medical care and skill
up to the standard that is customary among physicians in
the community of which he is a part. In such suits heretofore, the doctor's protection has been our present laws,
plus the fact that because of the pedagogy of these laws
abortion is not yet 'standard medical practice' in all the
many cases in which the operation will be demanded in
the future."[20]

Thus abortion-on-demand will not preserve the autonomy of the medical profession; it will destroy it! The
argument for abortion-on-demand to preserve the autonomy of the medical profession turns out to be still one
more example of the kind of doublethink we can expect

from the Abortion Imperative. We can only marvel at the number of physicians who have been willing to undermine the basis of their own profession by embracing abortion-on-demand.

It is even more remarkable when we remember that the Hippocratic oath, which physicians were once obliged to take, includes the pledge: "I will not give a woman an abortive remedy." It has not been from any specifically religious tenet that the medical profession has traditionally upheld the sanctity of unborn life. But today, it seems, the Hippocratic oath, which has been around longer than Christianity, must be increasingly suspended or swept aside (like, *inter alia,* the Holy Bible, the Declaration of Independence, and the Constitution of the United States) whenever it comes into conflict with the Abortion Imperative. In 1940, as the world was falling into the universal conflagration of World War II, Dr. Joseph DeLee wrote in *The Yearbook of Obstetrics and Gynecology:* "At the present time, when rivers of blood and tears of innocent men, women and children are flowing in most parts of the world, it seems silly to be contending over the right to live of an unknowable atom of human flesh in the uterus of a woman. No, it is not silly. On the contrary, it is of transcendent importance that there be in this chaotic world one high spot, however small, which is against the deluge of immorality that is sweeping over us. That we, the medical profession, hold to the principle of the sacredness of human life and of the right of the individual even though unborn is proof that humanity is not yet lost and that we may ultimately obtain salvation."[21] *This* is the attitude that will truly preserve the autonomy of the medical profession.

To Insure That Only Wanted Children Will Be Born.

In the novel, modern concept of the "unwanted child," we encounter one of the most glaring instances in which the Abortion Imperative simply overturns the basic principles upon which our law, morality, and civilization have been based. Rights are apparently no longer inherent in persons; nor is anyone morally obliged to respect what were formerly understood to be rights. For the proposition that we may legitimately destroy an unborn person because he is unwanted really asserts two things: 1) that the rights of human persons derive from others (whether or not others "want" a particular human person); 2) and that there exists no prohibition independent of desire or expediency (e.g., "Thou Shalt not Kill!") which might forbid infringing upon the right to life of a particular "unwanted" human person. This is the "new morality" which we have already encountered in Chapter II.

If the two assumptions of the new morality are granted, it is hard to see how we can continue to have any law, morality or civilization at all. A while back *Time* magazine ran a cover story on the aged, characterizing *them* as the "unwanted generation."[22] Indeed, why should they, anymore than unborn children, have the right to live, if nobody wants them and there exists no moral prohibition against killing them?

We should carefully note that the "unwanted child" argument does not deny the humanity of the fetus. The humanity of the fetus is assumed; the existence of a human child is, in fact, the main point; it is just that he is unwanted. Some have even carried this idea to the point of asserting that the child has a "right" not to be born, if he is unwanted. Surely no "right" can be assigned to persons who do not exist!

Dr. Sophia J. Kleegman of the New York University College of Medicine argues that "the rights of the fetus should . . . include the right to be born with sufficient physical, mental and emotional endowment to have the minimum potential for living."[23] What she means is that if the child does not, or rather *may* not, have such an "endowment," then he can simply be killed in accordance with the strictly expedient human judgment of another. It is a strange kind of "right" which can only be exercised on the unborn's behalf by somebody else. As Daniel Callahan has commented, "You have a right to die; your living will trouble me; hence, I will exercise for you your right to die."[24]

Of course, we are not talking about a right to die only, but about an asserted right to kill and be killed, which is self-contradictory, and evacuates the very concept of a right of any meaning. Indeed, if society alone confers rights, society can with equal facility withhold them. This is exactly what we find with abortion-on-demand. The unborn child's right to life is annulled. Meanwhile he acquires a strictly meaningless new "right": "to be born with sufficient physical, mental and emotional endowment." The latter "right" is an empty sort of consolation if he is not allowed to be born at all; in any case, society obviously cannot guarantee with what "endowment" a person might be born.

Society cannot *admit* the principle that only the "wanted" have the right to life. Society does not confer that right. A woman and her doctor can no more alienate that right than the state legislature can alienate it. The fact that a pregnancy is unwanted or inconvenient cannot even be a consideration. Are not many pregnancies unwanted or inconvenient when they first occur? Are they always considered in the same light after the child is born? "A woman who is in travail hath sorrow because her hour is come; but as soon as she is delivered of her child she remembereth no more the anguish, for joy that a man is born into the world." (*John* 16:21) The difficulties and sacrifices inherent in carrying and giving birth to children have been a part of humanity's lot from the beginning. None of us would be here if our mothers had not endured suffering on our behalf. It is amazing that the difficulties and sacrifices which mothers have always had to endure should suddenly come to seem unbearable precisely at the moment when medical and social assistance for the woman in her travail is available to a greater extent than ever before in history.

Though many women today apparently find themselves in the unhappy situation of not "wanting" the children they have conceived, society has no business encouraging them in this attitude. Society has the obligation, first, to try to save them from themselves by restrictive laws against abortion, and secondly, to establish positive programs to assist them with the very real difficulties which in so many cases they do have. The Birthright programs which have been springing up in a number of cities represent a kind of "referral agency" committed to other solutions than abortions for "unwanted pregnancies." Originating in Toronto, Birthright programs have rapidly spread to some 40 other cities.[25] Such programs would seem essential to help restore the respect due unborn life even when the mother's circumstances are difficult.

Other positive programs would hardly strain either the ingenuity or the resources of the richest and most highly developed society in human history—a society which, as we have verified, has been recently directing a dismaying and terrifying amount of its social energy towards the problems of getting more abortions done. If, as a society, we continue to sanction the appalling thesis that a woman has the right not to want the child she has conceived, we will only have *more* unwanted babies, and still more abortions.

To Guarantee That Each Child Will Receive Careful Nurture Within a Family Able to Expend Adequate Amounts of Time, Money, and Loving Care Upon It.

Just as society cannot guarantee with what endowment a person may be born, so society cannot guarantee that each child will receive careful nurture within a family able to expend adequate amounts of time, money, and loving care upon it. That abortion is the recommendation for those children who may not enjoy all these benefits is an implicit admission that, indeed, society cannot make any such guarantee. The votaries of this argument are looking at the failure of society to maintain the poor in the manner to which *we* have become accustomed, and they are concluding that the poor would be better off if they weren't around to disturb the conscience of the rich and affluent. We will never understand the Abortion Imperative until we realize how disturbed the pro-abortionists are that the *wrong people* are getting all the abortions. White, middle-class women can easily get their "safe" hospital abortions here or abroad. The problem is that "undesirable" people keep on breeding. This is not a racial question, incidentally, but a *class* consideration.

Welfare costs are already approaching some kind of upper limit, yet the problems of the poor and disadvantaged seem as great as ever. It doesn't seem possible to educate all of them, since education costs are sky-rocketing too. Nothing is rendered any easier by the fact that an automated society, increasingly, *creates* its welfare cases among the uneducated and unskilled. As long as all these people are around, the liberal conscience still dictates that something should be done for them—yet nothing seems to work. Anyone who has worked in the practical sphere of attempting to influence state legislators realizes how pathetically—even touchingly—eager some of them are to believe that maybe after all, abortion is the answer; perfectly respectable members of the medical profession are pushing it; it must be all right. *Something* has to be done, after all. Maryland State Senator Margaret C. Schweinhaut was right on the mark about some of her colleagues when she described the true aim of an abortion-on-demand measure being debated in Annapolis as an authorization to eliminate the unborn babies of ghetto women "so they won't become wards of people like us."[26] Better dead than in the red.

The New York *Times,* on February 18, 1972, protesting a court decision curbing Medicaid payments for nonmedical abortions, editorialized that "it costs the taxpayers many times more for poor women to have children and add them to the welfare rolls than to have elective abortions which might enable the women to enter or remain in the job market."

Though it is laudable that state legislators and the New York *Times* sincerely wish to find solutions to the problems of our society, it is not possible to exempt them from the responsibility of considering the morality of various solutions proposed. Though we must always strive to eliminate social evils, we have no guarantee written into the nature of things that we will always succeed—and certainly no right to start eliminating people because our efforts to eliminate their problems seem to be failing. Indeed we may be sure that each child born will be more likely to receive careful nurture and loving care to the degree that society demands moral solutions to problems of all kinds. In endorsing abortion-on-demand, however, a society has in effect abandoned any pretense of a commitment to objective morality; and this abandonment of morality will have social effects which reach far beyond the sphere of abortion. Henceforth, anything will go.

To Enable Women to Attain Equal Status Through Escape from the Risk of Unwanted Children.

No woman is ever "forced" to bear a child except in the sense that we are all obliged (by nature) to face the possible consequences of acts we undertake. There are certain conditions under which, if we choose to indulge a passion for sunbathing, we will surely end up with a sunburn. And so it is with pregnancy. There is only one way to become pregnant, and, except in the single (and tragic) case of rape, the woman necessarily consents to the act by which she may become pregnant. Her "right" to decide whether to bear a child or not is superseded as soon as she is carrying another human being inside her body. Similarly, a father's "right" to spend all his earnings on his own amusement is forfeited upon his acceptance of the obligations inherent in the marriage contract. To assert otherwise would be to assert the principle that people are *not* responsible for the consequences of acts they undertake, and this would constitute an invitation to anarchy.

By "equal status" seems to be meant that women should no more have to carry and deliver children than men should. Dr. Barbara Roberts of the Woman's National Abortion Action Coalition explicitly adopted this stance in a radio debate. "Men don't have to bear children as do women," she remarked. "It's not fair."[27] This idea unfortunately ignores a rather elementary fact of biology, namely, that women do conceive and bear children, and men do not. Changing the abortion laws will not change anything about this basic biological fact. Attempting to change the biological fact by resorting to abortion really amounts to revolting against the human condition—an enterprise that has been attempted countless times in the course of human history beginning with the first attempt in the Garden of Eden. Indeed, much of the moral evil that has been done by men through history has been done in the course of these futile attempts to revolt against their own human condition.

Actually, this so-called new right of women to have an abortion is another instance of one of the oldest forms of the exploitation of women. A woman does not conceive a child by herself. For that a man is required, and the male proclivity to consider sexual activity as an end in itself, apart from procreation (or love or marriage) is well known; it is proved by the long and melancholy history of prostitution, among other things.

On a social level, the institution of marriage is a means of imposing upon the man a greater degree of sexual responsibility; in marriage he is obliged to support not only the child he has fathered but also the mother of the child. If he has fathered a child out of wedlock, strong social pressures have hitherto dictated that he should at least "marry the girl." The social utility of these marriage arrangements is obvious even before we consider the moral demands which religion enjoins upon us in the matter of marriage and of the relationship between the sexes. But regardless of social or moral considerations, a man could hitherto be legally obliged to support a child he has fathered out of wedlock.

With abortion-on-demand, however, none of this will any longer apply. Why should the man be obliged to support the child when he no longer has any say about whether the child can even be born or not? His *responsibilities* for the child disappear along with his parental rights over the child. If in fact he doesn't want the child, he can simply tell the woman to get an abortion; she has no claim on him to help her bear and raise the child. Some of the claimants for women's rights seem to be demanding for women the same possibility of sexual irresponsibility that, from a purely biological standpoint, men naturally enjoy; but the fact remains that women are still the ones who get pregnant. Women are still the ones who have to have the abortions. As an admirable black militant lady has succinctly expressed it, "There isn't a man around who will ever have to have one."[28]

Thus the woman's new right to have an abortion is nothing more than the legal opportunity to risk *her* life and health in the process of destroying a child she has conceived in company with a man; he doesn't have to undergo anything. Adolescent fantasies of sex without responsibility, such as we find in *Playboy* magazine or the James Bond spy novels, can be achieved under abortion-on-demand beyond a male's wildest dreams: if there are any slip-ups, the woman can always be aborted. It is astonishing that even one single woman has ever been found to applaud this state of affairs wherein women will be the very ones who will suffer most! Once abortion-on-demand has become the accepted thing, we may imagine that pressures upon the pregnant woman to destroy her inconvenient child will come not only from men but from parents, physicians, and social workers. We may also imagine situations where even a woman who wants her child will find it hard to resist the pressures for abortion. These pressures exist already. In Virginia, a husband has actually gone to court in an effort to force his wife, a mental patient, to undergo an abortion.[29]

Women, especially, should be desirous of maintaining the real rights of human beings rather than seeking an illusory "equality" with men. They are profoundly superior to men in so many ways, but, like the unborn, they are vulnerable and easily exploitable; both history and experience attest that there are all too many men around willing to exploit them.

To Avoid Discrimination by Race and Social Class Through Making Abortion Equally Available to All at Low Expense.

The French writer Anatole France long ago commented on the "majesty of the law" which granted to the rich and poor alike the right to sleep out at night beneath the bridges of Paris. All laws discriminate against the poor in the sense that almost any kind of wrong-doing is facilitated if one happens to have money; but this particular kind of "discrimination," once again, lies in the nature of things, and can hardly be repealed by a majority vote of one of our state legislatures.

We could only wish that the solicitude of those who want to see cheap and easy abortions for the poor could be extended instead to the problems the poor have in getting regular medical care. What we have seen, however, is that public funds for abortions seem to be all too readily available, while public funds for the cardiac or arthritic pains of the poor are in chronically short supply.

In any case, there is no "equal right" to have an abortion for the simple reason that there is no "right" to take the life of another human being at all. It is unfortunately true that the well-to-do are often able to buy abortions by making use of a liberal interpretation of existing abortion laws. But the proper answer to abuse of the abortion laws by the rich should not be to make abortions easier for the poor; it should be to make them harder for the rich. Enforcement of legal restrictions on abortion should indeed be impartial between the rich and the poor. The reason some are able to take advantage of the abortion laws as they exist is not that these laws favor the rich in any way; it is rather that the abortion laws are not being effectively enforced.

To Realize the Promise of Full Civil Liberties by According Women Unquestioned Control over the Use of Their Bodies, and Guarantee Couples Unchallenged Rights of Privacy.

If, as we have seen in considering the question of the "unwanted child," society alone allegedly confers whatever rights individuals possess, what happens to the woman's "right" to control her own body? Evidently, society can deny this right to her (on the premise of the abortionists), on the same basis that it denies the unborn child the right to life!

This is no mere debating point, without practical significance. Judging from changes in abortion laws in Communist countries since 1920, this is the precise situation which obtains in totalitarian countries where the state does decide what rights people may or may not have.

In 1920, women in the Soviet Union were granted the right to have abortions. By 1936, alarmed at the number of abortions and the increasing indifference to family responsibilities in the U.S.S.R., the Soviet state tightened up its abortion laws and decreed that women no longer possessed their supposed right to abort. In 1955, this "woman's right" suddenly reappeared, compliments of the state. The same phenomenon has occurred in Romania.[30] When human rights are conferred by the state, a funny thing happens: now we see them, now we don't.

In America, things have not yet reached this point, but legalization of abortion is a long step in that direction. If it truly has the power to create rights at will, society can

equally decree the *duty* to have abortions as certain population planners in America are already vociferously advocating.

The moral and intellectual bankruptcy of all this leaps
to the eye. We cannot pick and choose among human
rights. The child either has inherent rights, or he hasn't.
If he hasn't, the woman hasn't any inherent rights either,
and she has no business demanding abortion as a "right."

Dr. David C. Wilson, in a medical paper on the "Abortion
Problem in the General Hospital,"[31] makes a significant
remark: "It is difficult to understand the shock a woman
may feel when she realizes that another being is living
inside her body." Dr. Wilson may consider this still one
more argument in favor of abortion, since his paper appears in a book highly favorable to the pro-abortion cause;
but the remark actually destroys at one stroke any possibility of an argument for abortions based on the woman's
alleged right to control "her own body." Obviously, somebody else is involved, according to Dr. Wilson, "living inside her body." The child is involved. Nor can any conceivable rationalization extend the right to "privacy" to
include private killing. Most murders, stabbings, mug-
gings, and the like are carried out by private persons. The
law does not refuse to take cognizance of them for all of
that; no more can it refuse to take cognizance of abortion.

The argument for abortion-on-demand from the alleged
right of a woman to control her own body is a transparent
sophistry.

In his recent comprehensive book on all aspects of the
abortion question, Professor Germain Grisez of Georgetown University quotes Dr. Robert E. Hall to the effect that
poorer, ward patients are "less aware of their need to be
aborted."[32] Perhaps we should recast the Beatitude:
Blessed are the poor who don't know that they "need"

abortions! It cannot be a comfortable thought for an élitist such as Dr. Hall to realize that, under abortion-on-demand which he, for one, has worked so hard to achieve, it is not the poor who are getting all the abortions after all, but affluent white girls!

VII

Is There a Population Explosion?

ALTHOUGH it is impossible to do justice here to what is called the population explosion, we must nevertheless consider several salient points about it. "Overpopulation" is increasingly cited as one of the principal reasons why unrestricted abortion has now become "necessary." We may note in passing that the same alleged need for *Lebensraum,* or living space, was brought forward to justify the extermination programs of the Nazis in Germany. Just as many people acquiesced in the programs of the Nazis because of the supposed overriding needs of the German Fatherland, so today many people, frightened by the horror stories told by the population Cassandras in our midst, seem to have been persuaded that abortion is necessary as a population control measure . . . Japan, for example, has dramatically reduced its population growth rate by allowing abortions virtually on demand.

It is quite true that killing does reduce the population, if that is indeed the only consideration. In point of fact, how-

136

ever, we do not have to take at face value all the hysteria about the so-called population explosion.

1) *The catastrophic predictions of many scientists and demographers are based on a number of "if's" which are far from inevitable.*

The first of these "if's" concerns the actual present population of the world. We are told that it is around 3.5 billion, having increased by 2.5 billion in a little more than a century; it is calculated that it will double in about 35 years.[1] But—one of the experts candidly admits—"the statistics are not exact, of course. There is no way of registering the daily births and deaths for much of Asia, Africa, and South America. But the experts are in close agreement about the figures."[2] This must inevitably remind us of the "one million illegal abortions per year in the United States," for which, however, there are no reliable statistics . . .

Whatever the accuracy of the figures, it is perfectly true and demonstrable that world population has grown phenomenally. We *do* have the figures for North America, Europe, and some other parts of the world, and we know that population growth in the past century has been unprecedented. If—and this is the second big "if"—departing from our present large population base, we project indefinitely the same *rate* of growth we have witnessed in the past hundred years, we will be able to calculate a given date when the sheer weight of human bodies will equal the weight of the earth itself; or a date when there will be more than one person for every square foot of the earth's surface. In fact, such projections are regularly being made by some of the more frantic scientists.[3] (One of the interesting things about the population alarmists is that the most extreme among them almost invariably turn out to be biologists; real demographers tend to be a good deal more cautious in their projections.)

These apocalyptic projections, however, are the purest science fiction. They depend on an indefinite or a very long-term extension of the present growth and doubling rates of the world's admittedly large present population. But the present growth and doubling rates of the population *cannot* continue indefinitely, and not merely because we will all die of starvation or disease or nuclear war long before the earth's available living space is all used up. The current growth and doubling rates cannot continue for quite another reason; the rapid rise in population growth we have seen in modern times is due, as one economist puts it, "not to rising birth rates, but to a recession of the death rate . . . And every sensible person should realize that death rates cannot go on receding indefinitely."[4]

Since, eventually, everybody is going to die, death rates simply cannot keep going down indefinitely; they have to come into equilibrium with birth rates, as they were before modern medicine brought about dramatically increased life expectancies the world over, thereby triggering the modern "population explosion." Not only must the recession of the death rate eventually cease, there are indications that it *has* ceased. In October, 1970, the World Health Organization announced that the steady decline in death rates observed over the past 150 years (coinciding precisely with the "population explosion") appears now to be coming to a halt; mortality rates are fast approaching, or have reached, an irreducible minimum.

"The findings have important implications for the problem of the population explosion," a news story disclosing WHO's conclusions stated. "One of the causes of net population increase . . . has been medical advances reducing infant mortality and combatting once-fatal diseases in later life. If those advances have about reached their limit —and if sooner or later the same phenomenon will be duplicated in presently underdeveloped countries whose standards are rising—then at least one of the factors in the population increase will become stabilized."[5]

As for continuing high birth rates, the economist we have just quoted above makes a further point: "All demographers know that birth rates, even in the overpopulated countries, are not up. They have been stabilized for years, and in the prosperous countries are actually down in some cases sharply. *The United States at present has the lowest birth rate in its history."* [6] (Italics added) The U.S. birth rate, in fact, has declined every year from a high of 25.3 per 1000 in 1957 to a low of 17.4 in 1971; a report by the Washington Center for Metropolitan Studies indicates that there were 15.5 per cent fewer children under 5 years of age in 1970 than in 1960—this decrease of children coincides with the greatest increase in the number of people of child-bearing age. This decrease of births has been accelerating over an entire decade; it would seem that the increased availability of abortions occurred too late in the decade to have substantially affected the figures.[7]

As if to underline the hazards of trying to predict merely by projecting existing trends, the U.S. Census Bureau announced, in August, 1970, "a major downward revision in population projections for the next 30 years . . . It is possible, the Bureau said, that there will be nearly 100 million fewer Americans in the year 2000 than had been forecast in one maximum projection made just three years ago."[8]

Subsequent studies have continued to confirm this new trend. In its issue of November 5, 1971, for example, the New York *Times* reported on three different new studies —the 1970 National Fertility Study, a survey by the U.S. Census Bureau, and a compilation by the National Center for Health Statistics. All of these studies not only confirmed marked reductions in actual births; they confirmed a sharp and rapid drop in the number of children women *intended* to have. Birth expectations are gen-

erally regarded as highly accurate overall indicators of
future births, and these three reports all confirmed a
"half-a-child" drop in such expectations. Informed
demographers are now talking about a "birth dearth" or
"baby bust" more than they are talking about a "population explosion."

Of course, the new forecasts may be just as faulty as the
old. Nevertheless, an "expert" population projection
which is three years later found to be off by 100 million,
for example, can hardly be considered exact science. We
may be pardoned for demurring when, to counter an alleged overpopulation which cannot be demonstrated, we
are asked to accept policies such as abortion-on-demand
which overturn the most basic legal and moral principles
by which American society has always governed itself.
The evidence for this future overpopulation clearly remains of the most speculative sort.

The other big "if" of the prophets of population disaster
concerns the capacity of the world to feed itself—not only
its present large population, but the much larger population it will certainly have when birth and death rates
reach a new equilibrium. "This problem has been dealt
with most capably by British economist Colin Clark who
enjoys international repute as an expert in the area of
economic development and demography," Professor Rupert Ederer writes. "Using accepted statistical techniques
and reliable data on world land resources, Clark has calculated that presently available land on this earth suitable
for agriculture . . . could feed—using the best agriculture
techniques presently available—47 billion people at maximum, i.e., at American standards of diet. Accepting that
Americans eat more than they need to, Clark further estimates that for people living at Japanese standards of food
consumption and timber requirements, the world's poten-

tial agricultural and forest land could supply the needs of 157 billion people."[9]

Dr. Jean Mayer, Professor of Nutrition at Harvard and another renowned authority on the subject, has reached conclusions similar to Colin Clark's. "Considering the world as a whole," he writes, "there is no evidence that the food situation is worsening and there is at least a likelihood that food may at some time (20 or 30 years from now) be removed altogether as a limiting factor to population." Noting that since 1850 the increase in food production has been still more rapid than the phenomenal increase in population, and that since the early 1950's especially, the average rate of increase for world food production has been 3 per cent per year while the population has increased on the average only 1.7 per cent, Professor Mayer underlines the further spectacular increases in food production which can result from the application of what is already known about scientific agriculture, especially from the economical harnassing of photosynthesis in plants, and adds, "all this is no longer science fiction. It is as much a reality as the Federal Income Tax."[10]

Nor does all this represent an argument, unresolvable by laymen, among experts—some experts holding that the world can support any foreseeable population, while other experts cry "overpopulation" as the contemporary version of the "yellow peril." We can attest that, whatever our future perils may be, food and other basic resources seem reasonably in balance both now and for the future.

It is well known to everybody, for example, that the United States and some other advanced countries such as Argentina, Australia, Canada, France, and New Zealand have been, in some cases for decades, paying their farmers to *curtail* food production. The United States Government currently rents some 20 million acres from American farmers so that they will not grow food on them; one study recommends that another 62½ million acres of land should similarly be retired from production.[11] Canada is actually trying to turn some of its wheat surpluses into building materials![12]

And now, in the underdeveloped world, we have the so-called "green revolution," based on new high-yielding varieties of wheat and rice. "In three years, Pakistan has been transformed from an aid-receiving grain importer to a country with enough wheat for itself and a surplus of rice. Record rice harvests have been reported also in Ceylon and the Philippines and the new grains are producing improved crops in Africa and Latin America as well."[13] Another agricultural expert, Lester R. Brown, has testified: "This 'green revolution' may affect the well-being of more people in a shorter period of time than any technological advance in history."[14]

2) *The problems of pollution, congestion and under-nourishment in the world today are not necessarily, or even principally, the result of overpopulation.*

By the standards of its available technology, a sparse band of Indians in a South American rain forest is surely suffering from the effects of "overpopulation." "Before the invention of agriculture," Lester R. Brown has noted, "the plants and animals supported by photosynthesis on the total land area [of the earth] could support a human population of only about 10 million."[15] The reason for this was that the resources of the earth had not been organized for the production of food. With every development of agricultural technology, however, the number of people who can be supported increases phenomenally. Today, the most densely populated country in the world, the Netherlands, with 375 persons per square kilometer,[16] given today's available agricultural technology, is one of the most prosperous countries in the world.

"The Dutch [agricultural] productivity figures are the

most remarkable in the world," Colin Clark writes. "Only about 70% of the country is farmed. The rest consists of urban and industrial sites, or of dunes and heaths which could only be fertilized at great expense, and which are preserved for forestry and recreation. Dutch agriculture produced 1,070 tons of grain equivalent per square kilometer of farm land . . . the requirements (at Dutch standards of consumption) for 365 persons."[17] In other words, although it is the most densely populated country in the world, the Netherlands can produce on its own land adequate food to feed its own population at a high standard of living.

Scientists Paul Ehrlich and John P. Holdren have disputed the relevance of population density figures in general and the Dutch example in particular to the determination of what constitutes overpopulation. They speak of a "Netherlands fallacy," and point out that "the Netherlands actually requires large chunks of the earth's resources and vast areas of land not within its borders to maintain itself. For example, it is the second largest per capita importer of protein in the world . . ."[18] What this argument fails to take into account, of course, is what the Netherlands *exports,* and from which other countries trading with the Netherlands benefit.

Both prosperity and the high Dutch rate of production result not from a small population but from its possession of advanced technology. The same applies to other countries. Hong Kong, for example, which houses 3.1 million people on 398 square miles (12,700 per square mile) has been able to double its output of goods and services in ten years.[19]

Yet poverty and underdevelopment are held to be the result of "overpopulation" in countries with vastly smaller population densities than Holland or Hong Kong. England's population density, for example, is four times greater than that of China, with its "teeming millions." India, with 156 persons per square kilometer—less than half the density of the Netherlands—and China, with only 75 per square kilometer, continue to be cited as frightening examples of "overpopulation." In actual fact, the conditions in which most of the people in both these countries live probably differ little, if any, from the conditions in which their ancestors lived centuries ago when the total population was smaller by millions and millions; hence their poverty and underdeveloment can hardly be ascribed to population growth. The population density of the United States is only 10 per square kilometer—compared to 69 for Asia and 92 for Europe.[20]

It is often said that "half the world is going to bed hungry every night." Colin Clark has also shown how grossly inaccurate this statement is. The myth began with an assertion by the first Director General of the U.N. Food and Agriculture Organization (FAO) that two-thirds of mankind was suffering from hunger. Later the figure was reduced to one half of mankind, but the second figure was hardly more accurate than the first. The basis for it was a definition that considered malnourished anyone who, in Colin Clark's words, "did not eat as well as the inhabitants of France or Britain, i.e., deriving 20 per cent or more of their calorie intake from animal products, fruits and vegetables, and fats and oils. No medical evidence whatsoever was produced to support the assertion that this constituted the borderline of malnutrition. In fact, when one looks at the medical records of France and Britain, it appears that a good many of the inhabitants are suffering from overnutrition . . ."[21]

In short, it did not require the FAO to inform us that a good part of the world does not eat as well as prosperous, industrialized Britain and France; we already knew that. But it is a far cry from that fact to the assertion that half or two-thirds of the world is "going to bed hungry." The true fact of the matter is that the world is feeding itself better than it ever has. If some do not eat as well as others, we are no doubt confronted with a challenge to do better to ease the lot of the less fortunate. But the nutrition situation of the world as a whole today has to be compared with the kinds of famine and hunger from which mankind has periodically suffered throughout most of its existence on earth, prior to the industrial revolution and the rise of modern agricultural technology.

For mankind has almost always been on the edge of misery and starvation. Our prospects on the food front are in many ways more hopeful than they could ever have been for our ancestors. The Paul Ehrlichs *threaten* us with famine, and use this threat as a plea for abortion-on-demand, but in England alone during the 13th Century, famine and hunger struck in 1203, 1209, 1224, 1235, 1239, 1243, 1257, 1258, 1271, 1286, 1289, 1294, 1295, 1298.[22] (It is interesting that it was during precisely this period that the English Common Law began to throw the mantle of its protection over the child "quick" in his mother's womb.)[23] One of the most heartening events of the past few years is that, in spite of threats of famine, phenomena such as the Irish or Bengali famines have *not* recurred—because of better communications and the availability in many countries of surpluses which could be shipped to famine-threatened peoples. The widespread recent starvation in Nigeria is no exception since it was due to war, not to the inability of the world, or even of Nigeria alone, to feed the starving; the same is true of the Bengali refugees who fled to India following military action by the Pakistani army in East Bengal.

If we suggest, however, that the answer to "overpopulation" may lie in a more rational economic development and organization, as Pope Paul VI suggested in his 1965 address to the United Nations, we usually meet with two objections:

a) Rapid population growth makes economic development impossible since the extra mouths to feed eat up any gains made. This explanation seems deceptively simple, especially since Europe and the United States developed during periods of rapid, unprecedented population growth; and France, which led Europe in most material and cultural respects in the Eighteenth Century, fell behind in the Nineteenth, when her population growth rate also began to decline.

b) Economic development solves nothing since the congestion, environmental pollution and the mountains of garbage we see rising around us in urban America today are in fact nothing else than that ole' Devil "population explosion" again, this time in its developed version. This argument assumes, of course, that our present American economic system of what we may call "programmed waste" is the only possible kind of "developed" economy, and nothing could be further from the truth than that! As one observer has commented about our present economic arrangements, ". . . most of what we produce . . . simply replaces garbage: new cars, for example, to replace junk cars . . . If we produced half as many automobiles lasting twice as long, nothing would change except the size of the junk yards. We produce some five million electric refrigerators each year, but the number of families that own electric refrigerators goes up by only one million. Of 4.4 million clothes washers manufactured annually, nearly 70 per cent are bought by people who replace their old ones. (And then, of course, there are the electric slicing knives, toothbrushes, can openers, and hundreds of other marginal consumer gadgets . . .)."[24]

In glancing at these two objections to economic development as the answer to rapid population growth, then, we are struck by the curious consistency which, whether we are rich or poor, developed or undeveloped, identifies population as the constant villain: the underdeveloped countries must control population in order to be able to develop, we must control it because we *are* developed!

We cannot here argue in detail that congestion and pollution are not the result of population growth as such. We shall simply let an acknowledged friend of population control programs argue it briefly. Mr. William P. Bundy, former Assistant Secretary of State for East Asian Affairs and now a visiting professor at M.I.T., recently wrote: "Mr. Nixon's new 'national goals research staff' told us the obvious the other day: that the problem in the United States is not food, total space, or even energy supply, but rather the ever-growing choice of a few congested areas in which to live."[25] As our metropolitan areas become more unmanageable, and their air unbreathable, many of our rural areas are in fact declining. For example, about half the counties in the United States actually *lost* population during the 1960's, and at the present time some 70 per cent of all Americans live on only 2 per cent of the land.[26]

". . . In a vast section stretching from the Canadian border south to Texas, a slow but steady depopulation is continuing," a feature story in the Washington *Post* recently reported; this newspaper is favorable both to population control and abortion-on-demand. "Most counties have been losing people for decades," according to the *Post.* "Some in Kansas peaked in population in 1890. Greenwood County's decline has been under way since 1900, with a steady population drop interrupted only by a temporary oil boom in the 1920's. The 1970 census records the latest ebb: Greenwood County slipped from a population of 11,253 to 9,141 during the past decade, a loss of nearly 19 per cent."[27]

The same phenomenon is observable in other parts of the world where rural dwellers flock into metropolitan areas, often to live in crowded, unsanitary, ramshackle slums. The living conditions are no doubt deplorable in these slums, but the fact remains that their inhabitants came to them for the most part voluntarily, no doubt in search of the better life supposedly available in or around the cities. This points to a problem not of "overpopulation" as such but of social organization and of the distribution of goods, jobs, and economic activity. Japan, which has spectacularly reduced its population growth by means of easy abortions, nevertheless has a congestion and pollution problem which equals that of any other industrialized country: *under*populated Australia also has an industrial pollution problem in spite of the fact that only 12 million people live in an area 80 per cent as big as the United States.

On the other hand, one of India's leading ecologists, Professor R. Misra of Benares Hindu University, has observed that the pollution problem in India "is not so bad on account of the dispersion of 80 per cent of the population over villages." "Urbanization and industrialization are creating difficult situations," he added.[28]

Mr. William P. Bundy's conclusion seems irrefutable: "Population growth is not really the major factor in the physical pollution of the environment; growth per person in living standards, and thus in raw materials consumed and waste produced, is far more important."[29]

In the context of our present discussion of abortion, let us transpose this last statement into a question: Can the three cars per family, the multitudes of plastic containers and metal beer cans, and the all-pervasive air-conditioning our economy seems determined to produce, and so many people seem to want, really be used as excuses for scraping live babies out of their mothers' wombs? In affluent America today, where the principal nutrition problem remains obesity not malnourishment, this is about what the argument for abortion-on-demand from the "population explosion" amounts to. Once again, the Abortion Imperative seems to override any of the pertinent facts about population.

The pertinent facts about population suggest that we may soon be grappling with widespread dislocations stemming from a too rapid *decline* in our population growth rate. We have spoken of that decline above. Dr. Ansley J. Coale, Director of the Office of Population Research at Princeton, believes that "a zero rate of increase in the United States starting immediately is not feasible and I believe not desirable. The reason is the age composition of the population that our past history of birth and death rates has left to us. We have an especially young population now because of the postwar baby boom. One consequence is that our death rate is much lower than it would be in a population that had long had low fertility. That is, because our population is young, a high proportion of it is concentrated in ages where the risk of mortality is small. Therefore, if we were to attain a zero growth rate immediately, it would be necessary to cut the birth rate about in half. For the next 15 or 20 years, women would have to bear children at a rate that would produce only a little over one child per completed family. At the end of that time we would have a very peculiar age distribution with a great shortage of young people. The attendant social and economic disruptions represent too large a cost to pay for the advantages that we might derive from reducing growth to zero right away . . ."[30]

Dr. Arthur S. Fleming, a Secretary of Health, Education and Welfare in the Eisenhower administration, told the White House Conference on Aging, in November, 1971, that the problem of raising the income of the elderly was the most serious problem before the conference. One quarter of all persons over 65 in the United States live on incomes below the poverty level. We can imagine how this problem will be magnified as the percentage of elderly in the population increases, while the number of tax-payers in their productive years decreases proportionately.[31] We can imagine too in a population with a disproportionate number of old people that the cry for "mercy killing" will become as insistent as the cry for easy abortion today.

Other industrialized countries have already been affected by the problems of too-rapid population decline. Japan is already importing Korean labor, while the Netherlands—which we have already cited as the most densely populated country in the world—is importing as laborers young Spaniards, Italians, Croats, Serbs and even Turks![32] Demographers at a recent European population conference in Strasbourg, France, have expressed grave concern at the dislocations being caused by a shortage of young people even as non-productive, retired people continue to increase proportionately to the population at large.[33]

Before Zero Population Growth can get its campaign fully underway, the entire terms of the population problem may have changed, and we will be occupied with the consequences of declining population growth rates!

If these are the true facts about the so-called "population explosion," then, what can we think of an official Commission which deliberately by-passes the significance of all the available data and uses its official status instead to advance the cause of abortion-on-demand? This is exactly the situation of the U.S. Commission on Population Growth and the American Future, chaired by John D. Rockefeller III. Established by Congress in 1970, the Commission delivered its report in March, 1972, and called not only for abortion-on-demand, not only for government-financed abortions, but for many other frankly anti-familial measures such as contraceptive services for minors, teaching the contraceptive and abortion mentality in the schools, under the title of so-called "sex education," making sterilization more widely available, and "comprehensive" institutional day care for all children. Those children who escape abortion and get born, in the new society envisaged by this Rockefeller Commission, can apparently look forward to a regimented institutionalized upbringing.[34]

It is not as if all the data we have discussed had not been available to the Commission with its large budget and professional staff. Indeed its report confirmed every major point covered above when it said that "the United States today is characterized by low population density, considerable open space, a declining birthrate, movement out of the central cities."[35] How then could the Commission arrive at such drastic recommendations? The answer seems to lie in the Commission's admission that "one of the basic themes underlying our analysis and policy recommendations is the substitution of *quality* for *quantity;* that is, we should concern ourselves with improving the quality of life for all Americans rather than merely adding more Americans." (Emphasis added)

Prescinding for a moment from what sort of quality we would *really* have in a society where killing-on-demand had become the conscious *policy* of the government, let us translate the Commission's admission into plainer English, as follows: "Since we cannot justify abortion-on-demand and the other anti-life measures we are after on the basis of the 'population explosion' which it was our mandate to study—unfortunately it turns out that there isn't any 'population explosion'—we will have to justify our anti-life recommendations on some other basis than sheer numbers of people; hence we must shift our concern over to the 'quality of life.' "

Ridiculous as it seems, this is exactly where the Commission on Population Growth and the American Future finds itself. We initially defined the Abortion Imperative as the belief that, whatever other considerations might obtain, we must at any rate get on with abortions and ever more abortions. Mr. Rockefeller's Commission could not have provided a more striking example of the mentality which has been created by the Abortion Imperative!

3) *Whatever the problems which stem from accomplished or expected population growth, we cannot abandon moral means in seeking solutions.*

Any reasonable view of the real facts about population, congestion, and pollution will preclude the desperate measures which are being urged upon us by population controllers. We must constantly remind ourselves of the strong element of selfish interest in the spectacle of the rich, educated, and affluent calling so loudly for population control—they mean population control especially for those they consider "undesirable" or "uneducated." ". . . Just as the once invisible under classes tried to get theirs," Peter Shrag has written, "those who already had it announced the environment was being destroyed."[24] The spectacle of a *Rockefeller* heading the Commission seemingly determined to do in the "once invisible under classes" will surely not be lost on the rest of the world!

But even if our situation were really as bad as the population Cassandras say, we would still not be justified in resorting to immoral means in solving our problems. Dr. Ehrlich thinks we are all doomed if we don't get our population under control, but in the sense he is talking about we are all doomed anyway. Not a single one of us but will die, if not in one of Dr. Ehrlich's famines, then at the very least of old age. In the meantime, we must strive to live our lives in accordance with the moral law which mankind has often transgressed, but rarely denied in principle; we must maintain respect and reverence for human life, especially the lives of others, whatever misfortunes might befall us. These are not merely Christian imperatives: it was Socrates who said that it was better to suffer evil than to inflict it.

The idea that we may destroy some of our unborn brethren in order to maintain our affluence, comfort, convenience, or standard of living—in a fearful yet wholly exact sense—is the morality of shipwrecked survivors who would kill and eat one of their number in order to survive. None of us is going to survive forever. How can we justify doing evil for whatever imagined temporary gain?

VIII

The Inroads of the
New Morality in America Today

WE have now examined the phenomenon of abortion from the social, legal, medical, psychiatric, eugenic, criminal, and demographic standpoints, and we have been unable to find any validity in the arguments usually advanced for legalized abortion. Instead we have found that to admit the legitimacy of abortion undermines the foundation on which our society, our laws, our institutions and our professions have traditionally been based. The arguments for abortion ultimately reduce themselves to one: many people want abortions. The slogan "abortion-on-demand" perfectly reflects this situation, and, reduced to its essential meaning, doesn't require any arguments or justifications beyond what people want.

The logic of abortion-on-demand will not confine itself to the accommodation only of those who want abortions. As we have seen, many are determined to impose abortion

154

no matter what. To alter the old Latin adage, *fiat abortio ruat caelum:* let abortion be done though the sky fall! We have called this contemporary attitude the Abortion Imperative.

Initially, of course, nobody argued for abortion reform on the naked grounds that, well, we simply must have abortions. Only recently has the logic of the abortion-on-demand mentality become clear. Even now, in seeking further public acceptance for its cause, the abortion lobby continues to dwell on as many pathetic cases as its fevered imagination can devise. As a writer in the *Lutheran Standard* has remarked, "To hear some proponents tell it, one would think every tenth woman is raped, every fourth fifteen-year-old is made pregnant by her father, that mass funerals should be held for the victims of illegal abortions, and that it is no longer safe to walk on sidewalks near tall buildings because pregnant women are jumping out of the thirteenth floor."[1]

Nevertheless, both the logic and the actual progression of abortion reform have moved beyond provision for these pathetic cases towards simple abortion-on-demand. Nor do the pro-abortion forces appear to have given themselves to second thoughts or regrets at the death-dealing frenzy which has followed the enactment of the laws they have promoted. For example, after the first ghastly results of the New York experience began to become manifest, the New York City Board of Health moved to prohibit abortions outside hospitals—that is, to prohibit them in doctors' offices or in clinics without equipment to deal with various kinds of complications. Instead of favoring this Board of Health regulation as an obvious safeguard for the health of women which they have so long professed to champion, the more strident voices within the abortion lobby were instead outraged. "They're cutting the law in half!" cried Mr. Lawrence Lader of the National Association for the Repeal of Abortion Laws (NARAL). A tireless advocate of the abortion cause, Mr. Lader declared that what he called the "medical establishment" was "flouting the will of the people and of the legislature."[2] He threatened to take the issue to the courts if the clear "intent" of the law were not carried out. Once again the main consideration seemed to be to get abortions done at all costs and under whatever circumstances, while the true health and medical considerations which had once figured in the arguments for abortion were summarily laid aside.

We might wonder what further claim upon society's serious attention might remain to an organization which has revealed its true aims and motives to the extent that NARAL has; yet both NARAL and Mr. Lader are treated with the utmost seriousness. The *New York Times* actually provided Mr. Lader the hospitality of its editorial page to allow him to plead for the retention of the New York abortion-on-demand law in a special signed editorial, even though the gross excesses stemming from the law were rapidly becoming obvious to just about everybody else except NARAL and the *Times*.[3]

The new courses being charted by organizations such as NARAL (now that the abortion-on-demand balloon has gone up, and, astonishingly, has not been shot down), are worth meditating upon by any who may still be tempted to consider that abortion should perhaps, after all, be left to the woman's choice. At a national conference held in the fall of 1970 in Boulder, Colorado, NARAL considered the following workshop suggestions, as reported by Mr. Frank Morriss, a correspondent who covered the conference:

—"Abortions anywhere the medical profession recommends—doctors' offices, clinics, or presumably any place where a table can be set up and which has electricity for

the 'aspirators' that suck out the child like so much garbage;

—"Abortion by 'para-medical' personnel, that is, by non-
doctors, 'birth-control'-type technicians who presumably
have some training for the more simple cases, leaving
'serious' matters to real physicians;

—"Removal of all conscience clauses that protect doctors and hospital personnel from penalties for refusing to
perform abortions;

—"Legislation allowing suits against doctors who refuse
to honor a woman's 'right' to have an abortion;

—"Lifting of all grants, tax exemptions, and other gov-
ernmental aid of any kind from Catholic hospitals which
refuse to allow abortions."[4]

Lest it should be thought that such proposals are peculiar to a "far-out" organization such as NARAL, we should
notice that similar proposals are coming from many other
sources; once again, they follow *logically* from the premise of abortion-on-demand; unfortunately, many people
still fail to grasp that this logic is going to work itself out
in practice unless the whole abortion mentality is resisted
more vigorously than it has been up to now.

For example, no less a personage than the Chairman of
the Department of Obstetrics and Gynecology of the Harvard Medical School, Dr. Duncan Reid, has proposed a
nationwide system of special abortion centers. Under his
plan, trained paramedical personnel would perform the
abortions under a doctor's supervision; most women would
be able to leave the facility a few hours after their abortion. Each facility would be located near a regular hospital, and hospitalization would be limited to those cases
where there was medical risk or complications. (Naturally, under Dr. Reid's plan, a federal public health agency
would support and manage this network of abortion centers, and the abortions would be free!) Dr. Reid believes

this network of free abortion centers is required by the general welfare because of the problems created by over-population.[5] We can only wonder how his training in obstetrics has qualified him to consider problems of demography, but, as we have observed already, lack of training in demography (or, apparently, even in simple arithmetic) has not prevented myriads of biologists from holding forth authoritatively on "overpopulation."

Another obstetrician-gynecologist, Dr. Michael J. Halberstam, writing for a professional audience in *OB-GYN News* and a popular audience in *Redbook* magazine, repeats essentially the same theme when he insists that liberal abortion laws have failed and "will continue to fail unless we recognize two basic facts—that what most supporters of 'liberalized' abortion want today is abortion-on-demand, and abortion is not necessarily a task for doctors." He pleads for special abortion centers staffed by para-medical technicians not only because hospitals and the regular medical profession will be overwhelmed by the volume of abortions, but also because medicine is a healing, life-saving profession and shouldn't be involved with the destruction of life through abortions![6] This physician's concern for the integrity of his profession of medicine is no doubt laudable; but his irresponsible encouragement of abortions by non-doctors shows little concern for human life *or* human health. Here, finally, we see the practical results of the argument, advanced before dozens of legislative committees, that abortion should be a matter between a woman and her doctor.

Some of the other "far-out" proposals of NARAL are already being acted upon, notably in New York. " 'There will be lots of lawsuits,' said Dr. Robert E. Hall shortly before he filed one of the first, against Presbyterian Hospital for refusing to let him perform an abortion on 18-year-old 'Sally Poe' without the consent of her parents. The

Association for the Study of Abortion, of which Dr. Hall is President, has funds to support important test cases."[7]

Los Angeles psychiatrist Dr. Jerome M. Kummer, writing in a medical journal, has even proposed the following novel doctrine: ". . . it seems appropriate to question the propriety of Catholic hospitals forbidding therapeutic abortions, primary sterilization, and related procedures. Physicians and patients whose personal religious views differ from Catholic doctrines should be (must be!) permitted to follow the dictates of their consciences. Catholic hospitals, by virtue of their tax-exempt status and support by the community at large, in certain respects are public institutions and must respect the rights and beliefs of patients and physicians of differing views. A Protestant or Jewish hospital would not think of imposing its views on Catholic patients . . . For Catholic hospitals to permit . . . procedures forbidden by Catholic doctrine would not constitute endorsement or sanction but, rather, a measure of respect for the conscience and rights of others in the fullest spirit of our American traditions and of the ecumenical movement."[8]

(We can only speculate whether Dr. Kummer would accept the further logic of his own position that, out of ecumenical respect for the *Catholic* conscience, non-Catholic hospitals or physicians should *refrain* from allowing abortions . . .)

It is fair to state, however, that some of the shrewder leaders of the pro-abortion movement have not gone along with all of the more extravagant demands being made. Dr. Robert E. Hall, for example, is holding out for hospital abortions only; no para-medical technicians operating in special sidewalk clinics for him. "I've fought for repeal for seven years," he declared after the New York law passed. "And I don't want to see it jeopardized by our experience . . . if deaths or complications result, the whole effort to liberalize the abortion laws in this country will be set back."⁹

Dr. Alan F. Guttmacher thinks abortion-on-demand should be available only within the first twelve weeks of pregnancy.¹⁰ This position, like Dr. Hall's, seems apt merely to divert the gaze of society from the scandal of completely untrammeled abortion—from the dead and injured mothers, the babies aborted alive, the rebelling nurses, and all the rest—and thus secure the *principle* of abortion on demand all the more firmly as the new norm of our society. Of the legal abortionist, no less than of the illegal, could it then be said that "in secret places doth he murder the innocent." (*Psalms* 10:3)

Behind all the well-financed activities of the pro-abortion lobby there is an intense *moral* passion and zeal. The people who are promoting and performing abortions think they are doing *good*. This is one of the reasons why protests about the flagrant immorality of abortion tend to fall on deaf ears; the immorality is interpreted as a new kind of morality. The lawyers who fight the test cases for the Mary Does and the Sally Poes, the judges who rule that a woman's right to privacy means she can destroy the child she has conceived, the legislators who vote for abortion-on-demand and the lobbies and voters who support them, the "concerned clergymen counselors" who direct women to abortionists, the social workers who gently but firmly advise them for their own good, the psychiatrists who compassionately sign the papers certifying falsely that a woman's "mental health" is jeopardized by carrying a pregnancy to term, the physicians who perform the abortions, the public officials who find funds in their chronically starved budgets to finance the operations, the female assistants "who have all had abortions themselves" and who reassure the tragically misguided women—all of these people consider that they are involved in a humanitarian and highly moral enterprise. They are idealists. They are good Samaritans, one and all. They are "helping" women with "problem pregnancies." They may have abandoned not merely the Judeo-Christian ethic but the American system in the process; but no matter—society is a more enlightened and humane community as a result of what they are doing. They are only giving women what they want—something wise parents stop doing for their children when they are at about age one so that they won't be spoiled rotten. In the era of the Abortion Imperative, however, giving women what they want becomes a new and higher type of morality. As one abortion referral service in New York advertises: "Our service is compassionate. Our main concern is the welfare of the woman, before and after her abortion."[11]

Once a Dr. Robert E. Hall has made the moral decision that he can legitimately, as he describes it, "interrupt the growth of a potential human being in order to preserve the well being of a living woman and her family,"[12] it is not enough that he merely do the "good" he has decided upon; it is necessary that society ratify his moral decision. Once abortion has come to be held not only acceptable but desirable, it is intolerable that anybody should still demur and talk of "murder." Society must sanction abortions once it has left off condemning them. The law must allow them; hospitals must perform them; our taxes must support them. Society cannot be neutral; the argument that it should be is a temporary tactic. Abortion must henceforth be *right*; society must declare it so. Otherwise the magic spell might be broken, and the vast and growing complicity of all who have been involved in promoting, performing or undergoing abortions might stand exposed for what it is: a complicity of evil and horror that spreads like an oil slick and pollutes whatever it touches: constitutional guarantees and equal justice under law; scientific and intellectual integrity; the honor of the medical and nursing professions; public honesty and the political process; the family; human rights; morality in the true sense.

Once abortion is accepted as morally good, people enter a magic circle where real moral values are exactly reversed by the purest Orwellian doublethink. Evil becomes good, killing becomes helping, death supposedly enhances the quality of life. This is the new morality; it is the fuel in the powerful engines of the Abortion Imperative. We have already encountered it in considering the testimony of men of science and learning who call for abortion even though they know perfectly well that the unborn child is a human being, and say so. What we observed in the case of these men was an assertion of human *control* over human life, unhampered by any fixed, transcendent moral prohibitions. Henceforth we will make up our morality as we go along. Morality is the product of the human will. With the drive for abortion on demand, this new morality comes into its own in society at large, and we suddenly find many people prepared to admit that because of pollution, overpopulation, unwanted pregnancies, or whatever, *we can kill if we see fit.*

A recent editorial in *California Medicine,* the official journal of the California Medical Association, is unusually frank in spelling out exactly what the new morality means: "There are certain new facts and social realities which are becoming recognized, are widely discussed in Western society, and seem certain to undermine and transform [its] traditional ethic. They have come into being and into focus as the social by-products of unprecedented technologic progress and achievement. Of particular importance are, first, the demographic data of human population expansion which tends to proceed uncontrolled and at a geometric rate of progression; second, an ever growing disparity between the numbers of people and the resources available to support these numbers in the manner to which they are or would like to become accustomed; and third, and perhaps most important, a quite new social emphasis on something which is beginning to be called the quality of life, a something which becomes possible for the first time in human history because of scientific and technologic development. These are now being seen by a growing segment of the public as realities which are within the power of humans to control and there is quite evidently an increasing determination to do this.

"What is not yet so clearly perceived is that in order to bring this about choices will have to be made with respect to what is to be preserved and strengthened and what is not, and that this will of necessity violate and ultimately destroy the traditional Western ethic with all that this portends. It will become necessary and acceptable to place relative rather than absolute values on such things as human lives, the use of scarce resources and the various elements which are to make up the quality of life or of living which is to be sought. This is quite distinctly at variance with the Judeo-Christian ethic and carries serious philosophical, social, economic, and political implications for Western society and perhaps for world society.

"The process of eroding the old ethic and substituting the new has already begun. It may be seen most clearly in changing attitudes toward human abortion. In defiance of the long held Western ethic of intrinsic and equal value for every human life regardless of its stage, condition or status, abortion is becoming accepted by society as moral, right, and even necessary. It is worth noting that this shift in public attitude has affected the churches, the laws and public policy rather than the reverse. Since the old ethic has not yet been fully displaced it has been necessary to separate the idea of abortion from the idea of killing, which continues to be socially abhorrent. The result has been a curious avoidance of the scientific fact, which everyone really knows, that human life begins at conception and is continuous whether intra- or extra-uterine until death. The very considerable semantic gymnastics which are required to rationalize abortion as anything but taking a human life would be ludicrous if they were not often put forth under socially impeccable auspices. It is suggested that this schizophrenic sort of subterfuge is necessary because while a new ethic is being accepted the old one has not yet been rejected."

Thus *California Medicine* on the new morality: we might wish the proponents of abortions generally could be as honest. Nor does the journal think the new morality can be applied only in the case of abortion, without affecting other areas of human life and society. "Medicine's role with respect to changing attitudes towards abortion may well be a prototype of what is to occur," the *California Medicine* editorial continues. "Another precedent may be found in the part physicians have played in evaluating who is and who is not to be given costly long-term renal dialysis. Certainly this has required placing relative values on human lives and the impact of the physician on this decision has been considerable. One may anticipate further development of these roles as the problems of birth control and birth selection are extended inevitably to death selection and death control whether by the individual or by society, and further public and professional determinations of when and when not to use scarce resources."[13]

Our first reaction to an editorial such as this might be to wonder at the conceit of doctors busily planning a world in which *they* will decide who shall live and who shall die. Do they imagine that people will keep on going to such doctors as they? Or that a medical profession thus transformed into society's official executioner will enjoy the same kind of respect the medical profession now enjoys? Can the new concept of medicine envisaged in *California Medicine* really be considered anything but an aberration, we ask, wholly untypical of the average physician in America today?

Unfortunately, something close to the contrary appears to be the case. Judging from the highly visible and often enthusiastic support for abortion-on-demand, doctors in America are embracing the new morality on a truly massive scale. Their professional associations such as the American Medical Association, the American College of Obstetricians and Gynecologists, the American Psychiatric Association, the American Psychoanalytic Association, the American Public Health Association, and others have all endorsed one degree or another of extremely permissive abortion.[14] This trend is remarkable in a profession as conservative as the medical profession. A few years back, in one of the first of the court cases seeking to have a restrictive statute declared unconstitutional, no less than 178 deans and professors of medicine across the country put their names to a brief filed in the California Supreme Court seeking to overturn the California law; one of the co-signers of this brief was Dr. Roger O. Egeberg, then dean of the UCLA Medical School but not long afterward named the nation's highest ranking medical officer—Assistant Secretary for Health in the U.S. Department of Health, Education, and Welfare.[15] In May, 1970, Dr. Egeberg told an American Medical Association Conference that, in his opinion, abortions should be strictly a matter between a "patient" and her doctor.[16]

Dr. Egeberg is not the only high-ranking physician in government who has been active in promoting abortion on demand. Indeed the roster of physicians in government reads like a roll of prominent pro-abortion physicians. Dr.

Egeberg's colleague in the Department of Health, Education, and Welfare, Dr. Louis M. Hellman, Assistant Secretary for Population Affairs, was one of four doctors in New York, along with the ubiquitous Dr. Robert E. Hall, who filed a suit to overturn the state's traditonal law (before the legislature repealed the law);[17] as we saw in Chapter IV, Dr. Hellman continues to use his official position to promote abortion-on-demand even though Congress specifically excluded abortion as a method of family planning in the programs Dr. Hellman administers. Dr. R. T. Ravenholt, Director of the Office of Population for the U.S. A.I.D. program, has pioneered in promoting U.S. Government financing of research to develop abortifacients.[18] So has Dr. Phillip A. Corfman, Director of Population Research for the National Institute of Child Health and Human Development[19]—only in the era of the Abortion Imperative, perhaps, could the development of abortion-inducing agents be deemed a proper function of an agency supposedly devoted to "child health" and "human development"! Dr. Bertram Brown, Director of the National Institute of Mental Health, has publicly said that he would approve an abortion for his own wife if she did not want the child.[20]

We have already discussed the permissive abortion policy instituted in military medical facilities by Dr. Louis M. Rousselot, Assistant Secretary of Defense for Health and Environment, a policy only reversed by the personal intervention of President Nixon himself, declaring that abortion was "unacceptable" and contrary to his belief in "the sanctity of life."[21] While it is heartening that the President himself has not been caught up in the demands of the Abortion Imperative, it is not reassuring to realize that physicians in public service seem to be busily promoting abortion in spite of the views of the Chief Executive.

It is hard to understand how physicians, of all people,

can be among the first-line promoters of abortion. They are in a better position than most of us to confirm what *California Medicine* thinks "everybody really knows," namely, that every abortion kills a human being. The act of carrying out the execution can scarcely be regarded as pleasant under any circumstances. Nevertheless we still find obstetrician-gynecologists such as Dr. Julius Fogel "freely" admitting that he has "aborted hundreds of fetuses whose arms, legs, faces, heads and bodies were partially formed" and yet finding nothing particularly wrong with the whole business. "This is common and I have long been used to the sight," Dr. Fogel says. The article describing Dr. Fogel's activities goes on: "As with many specialists in this field, he knows of many cases where aborted fetuses intended for death have declined the invitation; stubborn, they were left on a table, where they finally succumbed."[22]

A European doctor, after having been involved in the performance of 12,000 abortions, has written dispassionately: "In my country, Yugoslavia, as in other countries where abortion has been legalized, [the] need for the best possible technique is dramatized by the vast number of hospital abortions being done. We think the answer lies in suction curettage . . . Some curettes are made of metal; transparent ones made of plexiglass, plastic, or glass are preferred since they permit visualization of the tissue passing through the tube."[23]

Such attitudes towards the clinical destruction of human beings are not merely the result of the fact that doctors are accustomed to and inured to the sight of gore. They represent a special *moral* attitude towards human life: yes, it's a human being, all right, but then we *control* human beings. We're in charge of life. Physicians are ineluctably involved in the act of abortion, at least until we finally get the assembly-line clinics operated by "technicians" now being called for. But today's moral claim to control human life is hardly restricted to doctors. It is also found pre-eminently among scientists and other learned men, as we have already discovered.

If there has ever been a debate within the American scientific community about the rightness and desirability of abortion and other anti-life practices, it seems to have been resolved; there is no longer any such debate. In the medical profession, at least, there were some signs of protest against the new morality; we have read of doctors attempting to change the permissive abortion policies of their hospitals or medical associations or resigning in protest at such policies. But the articles, editorials, and letters regularly printed in such scientific journals as *Science* and *Bioscience* over the past several years simply assume the inevitability and desirability of abortion, and the only question remaining to be debated seems to be whether or when abortion will have to be made compulsory. Scientific experimentation with human embryos has, in the past few years, become accepted as both normal and necessary.[24]

In his presidential address to the annual convention of the American Association for the Advancement of Science held in Chicago in December, 1970, Dr. H. Bentley Glass, a geneticist, remarked: "Human power is advancing with extraordinary rapidity in this realm of control over the genetic characteristics of the unborn. Perhaps . . . our race, far from having any aversion from power, will welcome this power . . . will seek it, and grasp it tenaciously. Unlimited access to state-regulated abortions will combine with the now perfected techniques of determining chromosome abnormalities in the developing fetus to rid us of all births that today represent uncontrollable defects such as mongolism (Down's syndrome) and sex deviants such as the XYY type. Genetic clinics will be constructed in which, before long, as many as 100 different recessive heredity defects can be detected in the carriers, who may have to be warned against or *prohibited* from having offspring."[25] (Italics added.)

These are the words of the outgoing president of America's most important scientific association addressing hundreds of the members of that association assembled in convention. It is not recorded that any voices from within the American scientific community represented at the AAAS Convention raised any objections whatsoever to Dr. Glass's extraordinary doctrine of life control, although the convention was practically disrupted by scientists objecting to scientific cooperation with the military. Dissident scientists actually prevented incoming AAAS President Glenn T. Seaborg, Chairman of the Atomic Energy Commission, from addressing the convention. The scientist-protesters had intended to "indict" Dr. Seaborg for the "crime" of using "science against the people."[26]

But among the scientists there were no protesters to be found, apparently, to "indict" Dr. Glass' explicit blueprint for fashioning new human beings in the image and likeness which *he* thinks is desirable. When we come to think about it, the idea of trying to remake human beings in the laboratory is one which might even give Dr. Strangelove pause. Yet the American scientific community as a whole does not appear to be very upset by the idea. That what Dr. Glass is advocating at their convention is quite frankly totalitarian does not seem to be either perceived or considered important. American scientists in general seem already won over to the new morality. They no longer have any ground to stand on in opposing totalitarianism, were they ever to become aware that totalitarianism—for them too—is what is involved in the ideas of Dr. H. Bentley Glass.

"The once sacred rights of man must alter in many ways," Dr. Glass told the AAAS convention. "Thus, in an overpopulated world it can no longer be affirmed that the right of the man and woman to reproduce as they see fit is inviolate . . . No parents will in . . . future time have a right to burden society with a malformed or mentally incompetent child . . ."[27] (In the meantime, what will keep the right to conduct scientific investigations "inviolate," or who will guarantee the right of scientists to burden society with "malformed" or "mentally incompetent" ideas?)

Lest it should seem that we are exaggerating the degree to which American scientific thinking simply assumes the validity of the new morality, we should add to the voice of Dr. Glass that of Dr. Philip Handler, President of the prestigious and quasi-governmental National Academy of Sciences. In 1970, Dr. Handler thought that "fairly soon, we must surely take the minimal step of aborting homozygotic fetuses bearing serious genetic disease detectable by routine safe procedures." A year later he was asserting that "we've already decided that abortion is an acceptable way to keep down the population" and that "it may be that some people are dispensable."[28]

Thus, it is quite clear that the heads of both the National Academy of Sciences and of the American Association for the Advancement of Science have associated themselves with the maximum demands of the Abortion Imperative. And behind the scientific community, of course, is all the power and prestige of the "establishment." Scientific research of all kinds in America has been increasingly financed by the federal government, i.e., by the American taxpayer. At the same time we cannot neglect the vital role which the great tax-exempt, non-profit foundations have played in fostering "technical" solutions to social problems without regard to the morality still generally held by the average American. Organizations such as Planned Parenthood-World Population, the Population Council, the Association for the Study of Abortion, and the Sex In-

formation and Education Council of the United States—
which seem to have interlocking directorates of the same
anti-life crusaders, and which have been so instrumental
in propagating the new morality and so contributing to the
rise of the new morality's Abortion Imperative—could
never have flourished to the extent that they have without
support from the tax-exempt foundations. Increasingly, of
course, these organizations are obtaining direct support in
the form of grants from the federal government, but a
pro-abortion source estimates that the Ford and Rockefeller Foundations alone have invested more than $100,000,-
000 in population control activities.[30]

A figure such as John D. Rockefeller III perhaps typifies
the new anti-life alliance between private wealth and
power and the resources and power of the federal government. While the philanthropies of his family have long
fostered and supported anti-life research and activities,
Mr. Rockefeller himself has served first as Co-Chairman
of President Lyndon B. Johnson's Committee on Population and Family Planning and subsequently was named
Chairman by President Richard M. Nixon of the U.S. Commission on Population Growth and the American Future,
where we encountered him earlier in these pages. By his
selfless and civic-minded service on committees such as
these, Mr. Rockefeller has helped to insure the expenditure of *our* money on his own favorite causes. If only *his*
money were all that was involved. (It was Nelson Rockefeller, the Governor of New York, who ostentatiously made
a special trip to Albany to sign into law the abortion-on-
demand statute enacted by the New York Legislature, and
who two years later vetoed an attempt by the same legislature to reinstate the old law.)

The basic moral attitude which John D. Rockefeller III
brings to his public activities concerned with health,
population and the environment is perhaps illustrated by

some of the comments he made in addressing an international conference on abortion convened by Dr. Robert E.
Hall's Association for the Study of Abortion: "[A] limited
view of the moral issue [of abortion] has resulted in restrictive abortion laws. But there are times in the affairs of
men when the attempt to legislate morality creates greater
problems than it solves. The inescapable fact is that present abortion laws cause greater tragedies than the
tragedy of abortion itself. Something is terribly out of balance here."

"We must concern ourselves with the most fundamental
rights of children," Mr. Rockefeller told the conference,
and he took care to enumerate what he thought the fundamental rights of children were: "to be wanted, loved, and
given a reasonable start in this world." As is usual with the
particular school of thought he appears to represent, he
passed over any right the child might have to *live*—without which all of his solicitude is meaningless, so many
crocodile tears. He simply asserted, predictably, that abortion-on-demand would "inevitably be the long-range answer."[31] (Incidentally, those who continually invoke
"necessity" or "inevitability" as the justification for killing
the unborn have failed to grasp the elementary moral
truth that necessity, morally speaking, is something that
we must *suffer;* it can *never* be an excuse for inflicting
harm on others—but then, as we have abundantly seen,
the excuses brought forward in the name of the Abortion
Imperative do not in any sense represent "necessity" anyway.)

If these are the moral views of the man believed fit by
both a Democratic and Republican administration to head
presidential groups concerned with population and family
planning and the quality of the environment, we may
wonder why a tax-supported commission was necessary to
provide a national forum and a rubber stamp for his

views; but we perhaps need not wonder that similar attitudes are encountered among others working in these particular fields. In point of fact, those who believe that more
extensive and organized and government-financed fami-
ly-planning programs are somehow the *answer* to the
Abortion Imperative have not yet faced up to the remarkable fact that *all* the groups and organizations engaged in
family planning, so-called, are *also* engaged in promoting
abortion as a method of family planning ... Indeed, where
the "necessity" of government-sponsored family planning
is accepted as the priority objective, and the new morality
is accepted, it does not appear likely that abortion will long
be rejected simply because it involves killing an already
living child. Acceptance of the new morality *means* acceptance of the proposition that man, not God, decides
what measures are necessary and licit to achieve his,
man's, priority objectives. The rest follows:man proceeds
to carry out the measures necessary to his priority objectives without regard to what used to be understood as
moral restraints.

The only "answer" to the Abortion Imperative is a different moral outlook on life than the one which currently
prevails in our society. But where are the men to be found
who will dare to speak out and challenge the new morality
of expediency? Expediency takes into account, again in
Mr. John D. Rockefeller III's phrase, only "the way that
many human beings actually behave."[32] It does not concern itself with how they *ought* to behave. Could it perhaps finally be the theologians, men by definition concerned with the claims of the Creator upon "the way that
many human beings actually behave," who will make
clear what is really at issue in the abortion debate? We
may always hope so, but, in truth, many theologians today,
with perhaps a good deal less excuse than either physicians or scientists, have themselves been increasingly dis-

respectful of whatever claims God might have upon man. This has unfortunately been true even of some Catholic theologians; we shall examine some representative cases in the next chapter. Here we may conclude our discussion of the new morality by seeing how it is understood by one prominent Protestant theologian.

The Reverend Joseph Fletcher has been a teacher of pastoral theology and Christian ethics at the Episcopal Theological School in Cambridge, Massachusetts, and is one theologian who is not afraid to follow the dictates of the new morality to their logical conclusion. Well known as the author of *Situation Ethics*, Rev. Fletcher holds that Christian ethics rejects all "norms or laws but the one command—to love God in the neighbor." (Sic!) Since there are apparently not even any "norms or laws" defining who the neighbor might be, however, Rev. Fletcher has felt free to cite abortion as just one more instance of "love."

"When," he wrote in *Situation Ethics*, "a lady in Arizona learned, a few years ago, that she *might* bear a defective baby because she had taken thalidomide, how was she to decide? She asked the court to back her doctor and his hospital in terminating the pregnancy, and it refused, to the judge's chagrin, since the law prohibits nonmedically indicated abortions without exception. Her husband took her to Sweden, where love has more control of law, and there she was aborted. God be thanked, since the embryo was hideously deformed. But nobody could have known for sure. It was a brave and responsible and right decision, even if the embryo had been all right."[33]

The average person, unaffected by Dr. Fletcher's breathless view of "love," might find his view of it indistinguishable from what is commonly understood as "ruthlessness." The new morality is nothing else but that. Long an apologist for abortion, Dr. Fletcher has, with perfect consistency, gone on to ask also, in effect, "Why stop with the unborn?" "The only difference between the infant and the fetus," he has informed the readers of *The Atlantic Monthly*, "is that the infant breathes with its lungs . . . Now, then, if through ignorance or neglect or sheer chance (like the forty-seventh chromosome*) the damage has not been ended prenatally, why should it not be ended neonatally?"[34] What Dr. Fletcher means is: Why should not the defective baby be killed *after it is born?* Why not, indeed?

---

*The "forty-seventh chromosome" causes "Mongolism" in infants; normal infants have forty six chromosomes, twenty-three from each parent.

IX

Can We Impose
Our Morality on Others?

"THE blight on society has come, to a considerable extent," wrote one pro-abortion physician, "through the interposition of one church between women and their physicians. Insofar as they are based on its religious dogma, anti-abortion laws impose on all American women the view held by a minority."[1] A Manhattan lawyer has asked herself in all seriousness: "Why *do* the abortion laws stay on the books?" She reached the same conclusion as the doctor: because of the influence of "one church." "By 1968," she observes, "all the major religious groups except the Roman Catholic Church were on record in favor of abortion reform or repeal."[2]

On March 19, 1972, the Washington *Post* printed a full-page paid advertisement placed by Women for the Unborn of Merrick, N.Y., which compared abortion with slavery; on March 27, the *Post* printed a letter from some members

176

of the Women's National Abortion Action Coalition in which, without any evidence being offered, Women for the Unborn was described as nothing but a "front" organization for the Catholic Church. On the basis of this unsupported declaration both the WONAAC ladies and the *Post* evidently then saw nothing amiss in an attack on the Church as "long a bastion of women's oppression ... making frantic efforts to maintain the slavery of women to their biology."

All these observers are wrong on all counts, of course. It is not true that all opponents of abortion are "fronting" for the Catholic Church. It is not true that American statutes on abortion are based on Catholic moral teaching or "dogma." All the relaxed statutes have gone on the books since 1966 as a result of the influence of the abortion reformers themselves; it is unaccountable how all their defects were not mentioned while they were being proposed. The traditional laws which still remain in a majority of states were passed in the last century, for the most part, when Catholics constituted only a tiny minority of the American population. (Catholics were excluded entirely from the British Parliament which, in the early 1800s, enacted the law upon which much of the subsequent abortion legislation in America was based.)

Nor does any American abortion law reflect a specifically Catholic morality. Traditionally these laws have all allowed abortion at least to save the life of the mother, and, in some cases, to preserve her health as well. But Catholic morality forbids any direct abortion at all. Catholic morality allows the medical sacrifice of fetal life only if it is the indirect result of some other operation which is itself intended to save the mother's life and which cannot be delayed.[3]

It is not, as so often alleged, that the Church "favors" the child's life over the mother's; the Church merely forbids the direct killing of the child, for any reason. The Church also forbids the direct killing of the mother, for any reason, even, say, to save the *child's* life. In earlier days, mothers sometimes were actually sacrificed to save the child. Fr. John R. Connery, S.J., has cited a fellow Jesuit theologian of the Seventeenth Century who attacked as "butchers" those doctors who held it was permissible to do a section on a mother to save the life of the child (or provide for his baptism); this Seventeenth-Century theologian flatly charged such doctors with "killing an innocent person."[4]

It is also untrue that only Catholics are opposed to abortion—else how can we account for restrictive abortion laws in traditionally Protestant countries such as the United States? Even in very recent times, many Protestants have been outspoken in opposing abortion . The Rt. Rev. Richard S. Emrich, the Episcopal Bishop of Michigan, has recently written, "Abortion is, for me, and for millions of others, the killing of innocent human life. It is not like eating fish on Friday, or going to church on Sunday, or, like the Mormons, refusing to drink coffee. It is a completely central, fundamental, basic moral question involving the value of human life and I simply cannot say, 'Let's be tolerant. You kill and I won't kill.' If the law permits abortions for any reason up to 90 days, I am compelled to say that what is wicked then would be legal. I will not be quiet for the sake of 'peace' or 'tolerance' any more than I would be quiet before gas chambers. In some ways, we are a pluralistic society but if we cannot agree on the value of human life, then I say we are a corrupt society."[5]

Professor Ralph B. Potter of the Harvard Divinity School summarized the characteristic Protestant position on abortion when he wrote that "abortion has been viewed as the annulment of God's special providence, the ungrateful despising of His miraculous gift, and the rejection of His summons to the vocation of parenthood."[6] Karl Barth, considered a giant among modern Protestant theologians, emphasized that "the unborn child is from the very first a child . . . He who destroys germinating life kills a man and thus ventures the monstrous thing of decreeing concerning the life and death of a fellow-man whose life is given by God and therefore, like his own, belongs to Him."[7]

It seems clear that those Protestant denominations which have accepted or endorsed some degree of permissive abortion are turning away from the usual Protestant emphasis on the moral sovereignty of God over human life and death. Paul Ramsey, Professor of Christian Ethics at Princeton University and a powerful contemporary Protestant voice against abortion, made the following comment upon a recommendation by the Methodist Board of Social Concerns that the regulation of abortion be removed from the criminal code: "There is no Protestant theologian who has given prolonged attention to the morality of abortion, and brought to bear on that question the whole idea of God and man as we Christians know it, who could believe his eyes upon reading the statement on responsible parenthood now issued in the name of one denomination of Christ's people."[8] Paul Ramsey has also called for more "exactitude" in describing the act of abortion; instead of saying "interruption of pregnancy," we should say, "killing the fetus in order to terminate the pregnancy."[9] In this way we will always bear in mind what abortion really is.

Traditional Jewish morality also holds that abortion is "strictly forbidden unless directly affecting the life of the mother."[10] The Union of Orthodox Rabbis of the United States and Canada has unequivocally condemned the practice. Rabbi Meyer Cohen, the group's Executive Director, has termed abortion "doubly sinful and repugnant" because the unborn child is innocent and defenseless.[11] In

Jerusalem, seven hundred rabbis recently called into assembly by Chief Rabbis Isaac Missim and Yehuda Unterman voted unanimously to condemn abortion "as a transgression against religion and humanity."[12] The well-known Jewish philosopher and writer, Will Herberg, has bluntly dismissed the idea that the new morality can somehow make the killing of the unborn acceptable: "I do not know what an 'old morality' is or what a 'new morality' would be like. What I detect is not a 'new morality' opposed to the 'old' but the erosion of moral standards through a pervasive hedonistically self-serving moral obtuseness that is reaching epidemic proportions."[13]

Thus, although it may be an effective political tactic to assert that only Catholics are opposed to abortion, this assertion, like so many of the claims made by the proponents of abortion, has no basis in fact. The truth is that Catholics in America have always co-existed with abortion laws which have *not* embodied the Catholic teaching on abortion. If there is a single instance in American history when Catholics have mounted a serious effort to have the Catholic morality on abortion (or contraception, or sterilization, or divorce) made the law of the land, the burden of proof lies on others to show when it occurred. In opposing the relaxation of abortion laws or the outright legalization of abortion today, Catholics are obviously defending the existing laws, whatever they are, as a "lesser evil"—not as reflecting Catholic morality. It is true that this Catholic stance can become downright ludicrous when Catholics are found defending permissive laws of the ALI type which are completely unacceptable to the Catholic conscience; but in comparison with the removal of all legal restrictions on abortions, liberal ALI-type laws *are* a lesser evil.

Given the actual situation, then, we must wonder whence comes the allegation that Catholics or the Catho-

lic Church are trying to "impose" their morality on anybody. As we have seen, it is the Abortion Imperative which
calls for the imposing upon America of a new morality of
utilitarianism, expediency and instant satisfaction of
whatever desires people might take it into their heads to
have, e.g., the desire not to be pregnant after one *is* pregnant. This new morality is profoundly alien not merely to
Catholic teaching but to the American tradition. Once this
is understood, the question becomes: how can we, as Catholics, *not* fight the scourge of abortion, even if, in doing so,
we risk further criticism of ourselves and the Church?
Simply to acquiesce in the demands of the Abortion Imperative may create the illusion that we are abiding by the
rules of pluralism and not providing any pretexts for anti-
Catholicism; but the situation created by the Abortion Imperative is one in which the words of the Gospel apply:
"Woe unto you when men speak *well* of you!" (*Luke* 6:26)

Strangely enough, however, it is precisely at the moment when America most needs a constant and powerful
Catholic voice in favor of life that we discern among some
American Catholics a decline in the will and conviction to
oppose abortion in the political arena. There is still no
question about where the Catholic Church herself stands
on the moral issue of abortion. The Catholic bishops of
America have regularly reiterated the Church's teaching.
Most strongly, at their meeting in November, 1970, the
bishops flatly characterized abortion as "murder." "The
child in the womb is human," the bishops stated. "Abortion is an unjust destruction of a human life and morally
that is murder. Society has no right to destroy this life.
Even the expectant mother has no such right. The law
must establish every possible protection for the child
before and after birth."[14]

In spite of the unambiguous voice of the Catholic bishops of America, and in spite of the fact that any opposition

to abortion which develops is almost automatically labeled "Catholic," the fact is that Catholic opinion on abortion is today divided as perhaps never before in the
Church's history. The Abortion Imperative has not been
without its effect even on Catholics. Catholics of some
prominence have come forward to hold that the Church's
unequivocal condemnation of abortion is not so absolute
as generally believed; others have simply abandoned the
Church's teaching though they are still identified in the
public mind as "Catholics." Still others, while perhaps
conceding that abortion is morally a form of murder, oppose fighting the legalization of abortion in the political
arena since, in a democratic, pluralistic society, what is
immoral need not necessarily be illegal. It is worth looking
at characteristic representatives of these schools of
thought, since each of them has had some influence on the
present state of Catholic opinion on the abortion issue.

Fr. Charles E. Curran, for example, is a professional
moral theologian who claims to find in the modern development of Catholic theology a less than absolute condemnation of abortion.[15] Fr. Curran criticizes traditional Catholic moral theology because, according to him, it has
"tended to define the moral action in terms of the physical
structure of the act considered in itself apart from the
person placing the act and the community of persons
within which he lives. A certain action defined in terms of
its physical structure or consequences (for example, euthanasia as the positive interference in the life of the person; masturbation as the ejaculation of semen) is considered to be always wrong." Fr. Curran believes that thus
defining moral actions in terms of their "physical structure or consequences" results in moral solutions which are
too "facile" and which any "Christian ethicist" ought to be
"suspicious" of.

In the case of abortion, Fr. Curran postulates a situation

where "the best available medical knowledge indicates that the woman cannot bring a living child to term." He doesn't specify what medical situations he has in mind but thinks, apparently as a general principle, that "if the doctor can abort the fetus now, he can avert very probable physical and psychological harm to the mother from the pregnancy which cannot eventually come to term." We note that Fr. Curran does not lay it down as a requirement that the pregnancy cannot be brought to term, but only that "the best available medical knowledge" indicates that it cannot. In such a "conflict situation," as he styles it, though it is not clear what the "conflict" is, Fr. Curran thinks the moral problem should be solved on the analogy of defense against unjust aggression, where killing is morally permitted not only to save life but also to protect other goods of comparable value. The analogy of unjust aggression seems preferable to Fr. Curran to defining abortion in terms of what he calls the "physical structure and consequences of the act."

Although such an abortion would, of course, destroy the entire *person* of the child, and thus could not by any stretch of the imagination be considered merely a "physical action" considered in itself, "apart from the person placing the act and the community of persons within which he lives"; and although the child, completely innocent, is in no way involved in any sort of aggression, unjust or otherwise, Fr. Curran nevertheless seems to think he has adequately made his point. He goes on to ask rhetorically: "Why should the doctor sit back and wait for nature to take its course when by interfering now he can avoid great harm to the mother?"

It is difficult to understand why Fr. Curran thinks "defining" actions in "physical" terms alters their moral significance in any way. There is no way to define stabbing except in the "physical" sense of plunging a knife into

somebody's flesh. Should we ever deliberately stab someone, the *moral* wrong we would do would be no less "personal" for all that the action would have to be defined in
physical terms. The action would still be no less "personal" because carried out by a person against another
person; it would be wrong because it is contrary to what we
apprehend as right moral order. There is nothing "facile,"
nor is there anything we should be "suspicious" of, in condemning stabbing on moral grounds, even though stabbing is manifestly a "physical" action.

Furthermore, Fr. Curran's suggestion that we could
morally "assist nature" by performing an abortion is actually a denial both of morality and of personhood. As persons, we fulfill the demands of the moral law by freely
deciding to do those acts which the practical judgment of
our conscience determines to be good and by freely deciding to eschew those acts which are evil. To place the free,
voluntary acts of the moral beings which we are on the
same level as the things which "nature" causes—in the
present case, to induce the abortion which nature might
bring—is simply to evacuate human acts of moral significance. No distinction is made between what just happens
and what we, as persons, do. Just because a man might, in
the course of nature, drown in a tidal wave does not provide us with any moral warrant whatsoever for pushing
him in. Yet this is precisely what Fr. Curran is claiming:
because a pregnancy might not be naturally brought to
term, we are justified, according to him, in seeing to it that
the pregnancy will not be brought to term by assaulting a
nascent human being.

Fr. Curran postulates the avoidance of "great harm" to
the mother as the reason for taking the choice of life and
death into our own human hands. We might easily think
of situations where pushing certain individuals into the
tidal wave would equally avoid "great harm" to someone.

The principle remains the same. We cannot, in St. Paul's words, "do evil that good may come of it." (*Rom.* 3:8) This principle is basic to the moral life of human beings. It is not merely a Christian imperative, but, as we have noted, a Socratic one as well ("it is better to suffer evil than to inflict it"). Although there exists a vast sphere within which human beings can and must strive to alleviate human suffering, there are limits to what we can do to avoid evil which happens to us; and one of the most obvious of these limits is that we must not ourselves *do* something that is itself evil. The well-known maxim that the end does not justify the means is another way of expressing this same moral truth.

That a professional theologian should so cavalierly abandon this principle, as Fr. Curran does, almost in passing, must inevitably strike us as surprising. But it is not as surprising as it would have been before we had encountered scientists who come out for abortion at the very moment when science has proved the humanity of the fetus from the moment of conception; doctors who justify it at the very moment when the progress of medicine has eliminated the classical "indications" for it; social planners who see it as necessary to eliminate poverty at the very moment when technology makes the elimination of human want technically feasible for the first time in human history; lawyers and judges who pass over guarantees enshrined in the Constitution in order to speak in favor of it on the basis of rights nowhere to be found in the Constitution; women who claim a "right" to control their own bodies by denying the child's right to live . . . And so on. A moral theologian who starts out by denying the very basis of the moral life may disconcert us momentarily, but we cannot long consider him strange in company such as this. Of all such company, but especially of the moral theologians who have joined it, the prayer of Jesus to the Father applies: "I give thee praise that thou hast hidden all this from the wise and the prudent, and revealed it to little children." (*Luke* 10:21)

The really puzzling thing is why Fr. Curran thinks Catholic theology, which has held out for the right to life of the fetus through all the centuries of crude, unsterile surgery, should suddenly today make a concession on abortion to avoid "great harm" to the mother. Today's abortionists might well retort: "Who *needs* your concession? We've already moved beyond considerations of the mother's health. We demand abortions for anybody who wants them." But Fr. Curran is not the only Catholic prepared to make disastrous concessions, whether needed or not.

Dr. Daniel Callahan is a prominent representative of the school of thought among modern Catholics which simply abandons the Catholic teaching on abortion out of hand. In an exhaustive study entitled *Abortion: Law, Choice, and Morality,* Dr. Callahan, a former editor of *Commonweal* magazine, has developed his own position on abortion which bears no resemblance to anything remotely describable as "Catholic," though Dr. Callahan continues to be identified in the public mind as a "prominent Catholic layman." After almost 500 pages of statistic-laden argumentation and discussion, he arrives at the conclusion that the "decision" about abortion should be primarily in the hands of the women. In a pluralistic society, each woman, Dr. Callahan thinks, will rely upon her own ethical tradition, whatever it is, in making abortion decisions. Judging from the statistics in his own state of New York since the law which places the decision in the woman's hands became effective, we may guess that the women getting abortions there are relying about as much on any ethical tradition whatever as Dr. Callahan relies on "his" Catholic tradition. He has certainly set a characteristic modern example of simply rejecting any "tradition" and insisting upon working out entirely for himself what his view of abortion is to be. We should not be surprised if modern women insist on making "abortion decisions" in the same fashion.

There would be no need to consider Dr. Callahan's views in a Catholic context at all except that the publication of a book such as his by someone identified as a Catholic does create the impression in the minds of many that it is now perfectly proper for Catholics to hold whatever views they please on moral questions such as abortion. There is also the impression that he only reluctantly abandoned the Catholic position as a result of his careful examination of the "data" on abortion; in actual fact, as his treatment of the subject reveals, he doesn't completely understand what the Catholic position is even now, and apparently never held it, so that he could abandon it.

In fairness to him, he makes no claim to be setting forth any kind of Catholic view; that claim is made for him by others. For his part, he severely criticizes the Church's teaching as "one-dimensional." His aim is to formulate what he calls a workable "abortion policy" for a pluralistic society; he writes not as a Catholic in a pluralistic society, but, rather, as a *pluralist* in a pluralistic society! His study aims to take into account both the empirical data on abortion and those moral principles which he believes are accepted by society generally. Basically, his appeal is the empiricist's appeal to human experience, although he admits that, by itself, experience does not "deliver principles."[16]

Nevertheless he finds the ultimate justification even for moral principles in human experience. Principles, according to him, "must show themselves to be coherent with our entire reading of the nature of things . . . They must seem to be borne out in our lived experience producing what we would count as moral progress, sensitivity, and order."[17] We can only wonder whether he thinks his principle of leaving the abortion decision in the hands of the woman has been borne out by the "lived experience" of New York since July 1, 1970.

Values, too, he thinks are "attached" by human beings to things and even to other human beings. He does not appear to recognize that human beings possess value in themselves. "When we speak of the 'sanctity of life,' " he says, "we are, then, speaking of the value we attach to human life."[18] If the value of a human life is merely something we attach to it, however, we can quite evidently *detach* value from life as readily as we originally attached it; this is already demonstrated by the regular practice of the abortionists.

Dr. Callahan is apparently not disposed to forbid or restrict the detaching of value from life in given instances by invoking against such a proceeding any strictly *moral* rule or principle, e.g., "Thou shalt not kill." He thinks abortion "ought to be approached as a problem involving a multiplicity of values."[19] Among the values he sees as pertinent to the making of abortion decisions are 1) the survival and integrity of the human species; 2) the integrity of family lineages; 3) the integrity of bodily life; 4) the integrity of personal choice and self-determination; and 5) the integrity of personal body individuality.[20]

At first sight it might seem that taking into account a multiplicity of values would do greater justice to the moral problem of abortion; but this would be true only if complexity and simplicity were somehow equivalent to right and wrong. Dr. Callahan actually appears to believe that this is the case. "Abortion is a serious moral problem," he writes, "and any solution which tries to dissolve its *complexity* is for me unacceptable."[21] (Italics added) But does it make sense to make the morality of an action dependent upon the degree of its complexity? Trying to determine *whether* an action is moral or immoral can be devilishly complex in many situations as, for example, in the case of the Vietnam war; once all the facts about the situation have been truly ascertained and weighed, however, the moral principles to be applied are simple. The complexity lies in determining whether a particular moral principle applies, or does not apply, to the situation being considered; simple actions can be immoral and complex actions can be immoral but the morality of either kind of action is not proportioned to its simplicity or complexity, as Dr. Callahan seems to believe.

Moreover, if values are mere human constructs which we "attach" to things, there is really no reason why Dr. Callahan's particular set of values rather than some other values should govern abortion decisions. We might with equal validity posit or construct other values to be taken into account in deciding about abortion. Dr. Callahan's criteria are perfectly arbitrary; they are no more than his own—or society's—preferences in the matter. Furthermore, there would be no criterion in deciding *between* these values even if we could all agree that they were the ones to be taken into account.

Finally, if we accept that moral decisions in other areas can be made on the basis of the very same multiplicity of values which Dr. Callahan posits for abortion decisions, we can all too easily conjure up situations where (say) slavery, racial discrimination or even genocide could be justified as easily as Dr. Callahan ends up justifying abortion as long as the choice is the woman's. Why shouldn't the choice equally be the slaveholders' or the dominant race's? Slavery too was a "complex" moral issue, especially after it got established *in principle* in society. Abortion is not yet socially established to the same degree, but we can be sure that, when it is, the "complexity" of the moral problem of abortion will only be increased!

None of these remarks is intended to suggest that Dr. Callahan himself would find slavery, racial discrimination or genocide anything but abhorrent. The fact remains that he has provided no moral grounds for excluding them from the system he has constructed, any more than he has provided any moral grounds for excluding abortions for simply any reason or for no reason at all—a state of affairs which even he appears to boggle at, though he manages to keep his distaste well under control in the process of seeing to it that women are generally to be allowed their "choice."

Given his basic premises and preferences, we may guess that Dr. Callahan would find criticisms such as these, even if he accepted the logic of them, beside the point. He is attempting to formulate a broad abortion policy for society, not a general moral policy for society. He does not appear to perceive that any society requires a moral policy which is prior to its social policy on abortion or on anything else; or that policies adopted by a society in one sphere may affect those adopted by society in other spheres. He rejects the "domino theory" applied to anti-life practices, i.e., that acceptance of abortion will lead to mercy killing or infanticide, and does not admit that abortion represents any basic attack on Western values,[22] as the journal *California Medicine* so clearly perceives; nor does he believe that the widespread practice of abortion "poses a clear and present danger to the common good."[23]

We can only wonder what his conception of the common good might be; it would certainly seem to exclude the unborn. In this respect, and in spite of the careful nuances of his position, it is hard to see where he differs in any basic way from Garrett Hardin and the National Association for Repeal of Abortion Laws (except perhaps in his greater "sensitivity"—which, however, like "complexity" is not a function of morality as such). For him there would pre-

sumably be no connection between the medical euthanasia permitted and practiced early in Nazi Germany[24]
and the later mass-murder camps such as Auschwitz and
Buchenwald; nor would he seem to see anything but co-
incidence in the fact that the mass deportation of human
beings in cattle cars to Siberian slave-labor camps was
decreed and carried out by the same Soviet state which
had legalized abortion-on-demand almost as soon as it
came to power.

(It is perhaps of some interest that Dr. Callahan regularly and uncritically accepts the claims of Communist
governments at face value; he betrays not the slightest
hint of understanding what his own data in fact establish,
namely, that even if there were no other objections to the
Communist form of government, the abortion policies and
practices of Communist countries would suffice to condemn these regimes. Almost uniformly, Communist governments have proved unable to provide either adequate
housing for families or sufficient income for bread-win-
ners, thus "liberating" women for work outside the home
with a vengeance; having thus systematically helped create the "need" for abortions, the Communist governments
have then generally conceded women the "right" to have
them. Nor should it be forgotten that the invention of the
suction curettage machine is one of the few "firsts" that
Soviet industry really can boast of![25])

But it is not only the general role of a society's "moral
policy" that Dr. Callahan fails to understand; like Fr. Curran, he misconceives the real basis of the individual's
moral life and of human conscience. Although he perceives that even from a Christian standpoint "man has
been given some proximate control over human life," he
fails to see the moral limits of this control and erroneously
thinks that man's "proximate control . . . places upon human shoulders the burden of deciding under what condi-

tions man has the right to such control."[26] He explicitly rejects the idea that God might have laid down these conditions by delivering a specific moral law to mankind. Dr. Callahan thinks it a "falsification of consciousness" and a "weakness" to "act as if God has *disclosed* [his emphasis] or imposed upon man a set of inflexible moral rules which man has only to discern and obey."[27]

Supposing it is "weak," what if it is true? Not merely the Catholic Church, not merely Christian Churches generally, but the other world religions have consistently taught that there is a transcendent moral law beyond the "decisions" of man himself. The claims of this moral law upon mankind are not eliminated by equating it with what Dr. Callahan has decided to call "a set of inflexible rules." Nor are they eliminated by the next step he takes, which is to discard the "inflexible rules" on the grounds that they admit of exceptions. It is necessary to quote his own words at some length in order to take in all the breath-taking illogic of his position:

"The fact that in practice rigid codes very often admit of many exceptions and extenuating circumstances testifies to the meliorating impact of experience and the need to resolve conflicts among basic values. 'Thou shalt not kill' —unless one kills in self-defense, in a legitimate war, in imposing capital punishment, and so on. The first is the rigid rule, the second is the traditionally accepted understanding of that rule. The falsification of consciousness arises when, despite the conceded exceptions, the rules are still treated as 'God given,' through either reason or revelation. That even rigid codes have been forced to admit exceptions and complexities should actually make clear that *all moral rules are human artifacts.*"[28] (Emphasis added)

It would not in the least follow that moral rules were "human artifacts" merely because exceptions to them were generally recognized. We need think only of the bit of popular wisdom which finds that the exception *proves* the rule. But Dr. Callahan's misconception here goes deeper than reaching a conclusion which does not in fact follow. The exceptions he cites to the commandment "Thou shalt not kill" are not exceptions at all in the sense that he takes them to be. They are instances when "killing" is not "murder"—doing murder is properly what the commandment forbids, as the Church has always understood, and, indeed, as modern Biblical scholars have shown us by analysis of the meaning of the original Hebrew.[29] The prohibition of murder does not admit of any exceptions.

What Dr. Callahan calls the exceptions—killing in self-defense, in a just war, or through the imposition of capital punishment for proportionate cause—are cases when killing is permitted in order to *uphold* the principle that life may not be wantonly taken by an individual aggressor or murderer or by a general military aggression. They are not in the least purely arbitrary exceptions to a rule, but are pretty generally admitted by the informed moral conscience of mankind, as abortion (except to save the mother's life) has never been. They constitute excellent examples of how the human conscience actually does operate within the framework of an objective, independent and (faith holds) God-given moral law. What, in the case of killing, is really left to the human conscience to decide is not, as Dr. Callahan holds, "under what conditions man has the right to control human life." God has already determined that for us: man may not do murder in the course of exercising over human life whatever physical control he has the power to exercise. What is left to man's reason and conscience to decide is the question of *when* the conditions that constitute murder in fact obtain. The human mind and conscience make a *practical* judgment about the morality of given acts; they do not themselves construct the moral rule in accordance with which this practical judgment is made. The rule is already there.

Moreover—to return to Dr. Callahan's ideas about simplicity versus complexity in moral decisions—the moral rules which are given in human experience are uniformly simple and straightforward. There is nothing in the least complex about a commandment to eschew false gods or to love our neighbor as ourselves. The complexity arises when these rules are applied to concrete situations. Who or what are the false gods which we must not worship? Perhaps the modern idol of "the quality of life" which conveniently does not lay down any "rigid rules" about taking the life of others? What is the proper way to love and serve our neighbor? Perhaps give her the abortion she has decided upon? Would not a more *complex* understanding of what any person's true good consists of persuade us that we would help and serve her better by helping her to carry the child she has conceived and not encourage her to resort to an evil act, whatever the circumstances?

The ultimate principle by which Daniel Callahan finally justifies abortion on request under certain conditions is this: "Man is responsible for everything to do with man, including control over life and death."[30] It is thus perfectly clear that his viewpoint is profoundly alien, not only to Catholic teaching on abortion, but to any moral viewpoint which holds that there is a moral law independent of the human will. Dr. Callahan has discovered no original new principle here, however. His viewpoint is identical to that of the original Greek Sophists: "Man is the measure of all things."

It is with perfect consistency, therefore, that Dr. Callahan explicitly rejects God's moral dominion over human life at the same time that he asserts man's dominion. "It is often said that man can't 'play God' with human life," he writes, "and that certain natural processes must be left entirely to God's providence. The trouble with that kind of moral reasoning is that it fails to see that God Himself does not 'play God' as that phrase is usually understood. God does not directly and miraculously intervene in natural processes. He does not directly 'bring' human beings into life or 'make' them die, just as He doesn't 'make' them sick or 'cure' them of illness."[31]

It is Dr. Callahan who completely misunderstands what the average person understands perfectly about the meaning of the phrase "playing God." He seems to think God's dominion over human life entails a direct divine intervention in natural processes. Nothing could be further from the truth. It is obvious that God normally allows "nature" to take its course; man is placed in nature with the freedom to exercise powers which he naturally has; at the same time, man is enjoined by God to exercise those powers only in certain ways, morally speaking.

The "dominion" that God retains over human life has reference to God's moral commandments and to man's duties every bit as much as it has to the fact that God created the world and keeps it in being. If in the course of nature human beings get sick or die, God assuredly does not normally intervene in a miraculous fashion each time to bring it about. At the same time no human being does wrong or incurs moral guilt because other human beings naturally get sick or die. If thousands die in an earthquake or a flood, what we judge to be a great natural evil occurs; still no human being is to blame for it. Such natural evils are "acts of God," in the picturesque phrase, not because God directly intervenes to cause them but because, as Creator, God is ultimately Lord of all that happens naturally.

But if we as human beings directly *cause* someone to get sick or die, we *are* to blame, we *do* do wrong, we *do* transgress the moral law. This point may seem to be no more than a truism. Nevertheless Daniel Callahan doesn't perceive the significance of it. In a conflict of interest between mother and child, Dr. Callahan denies the proposition that two natural deaths ("acts of God") are a lesser evil than one murder (the free act of a human being in contravention of the moral law). "Even if one assumes that the killing of the child would be 'murder,' one has to ask why this 'murder' would be a greater evil than the death of both," Dr. Callahan wonders.[32]

The theory that Daniel Callahan has so elaborately spun out in order to provide pluralistic America with an "abortion policy" is, then, a theory which does not discern any moral difference between *dying* and *killing!* In an earlier chapter we quoted words of his about a "right to die" when in fact he was talking about an alleged "right to kill." We now see the reason for his confusion—this confusion is actually the same as Fr. Curran's (though he reaches it by a different route). Fr. Curran, as we observed above, could similarly discern no moral distinction between what naturally happens and what we, as moral human persons, do. Much bioethical speculation today is simply useless because it similarly does not make any distinction between dying and killing. Proponents of euthanasia speak of "death with dignity," when they really mean killing. Even Catholics must favor *death* with dignity, but could never admit *homicide* "with dignity."

The fact is that all of us, including the mother who is given a temporary reprieve by the killing of her child, will in the course of nature eventually die. Our death may be a natural evil (though, as St. Francis noted, it is also the means of our entry into eternal life); but any natural evil whatever is simply not commensurate with the deliberate moral wrong of taking the life of another human being. A woman who dies naturally in childbirth is, as surely as if she were to die of a stroke, "called by God"—as the popular phrase has it ("Thou hast hidden all this from the wise and the prudent and revealed it to little children"). From any serious theistic perspective whatever, two natural deaths are necessarily a lesser evil than one murder. To attempt to avert a natural death by committing murder is to deny God's dominion. To deny God's moral dominion over human life is simply to deny God, period.

It has been necessary to investigate at length the theories of both Daniel Callahan and Fr. Curran in order to show that, though both are among the better known Catholics prepared to justify abortion under certain circumstances, neither has based his conclusions on any position or principle properly discernible as "Catholic." The fact that they are commonly identified as Catholics does not in any sense mean that there is now a new or optional Catholic position on abortion.

There remains the position of those Catholics who do see the frightful immorality of abortion but nevertheless deny that the practice should be prohibited or regulated by the civil law. Perhaps the best-known exponent of this school of thought has been Fr. Robert F. Drinan, S.J., the former Dean of the Boston College Law School, who, more recently, has become famous as the first Catholic priest ever to be elected to Congress. Fr. Drinan seems to come out for something close to abortion-on-demand himself. This is not, apparently, because he does not see the evil of abortion; it seems to be rather that he sees a greater evil in the explicit determanation by the state that certain categories of innocent human life are expendable. We have seen that the liberalized abortion laws based on the American Law Institute pattern do in fact establish categories of expendable human beings.

For Fr. Drinan, removing abortions entirely from the control of the criminal law "would not mean that the state approves of abortion but only that it declines to regulate it.

If one assumes that the law teaches minds as well as regulates conduct, the potential teaching impact of a law which exalts the superiority of a mother's health over her child's right to be born and of a legal system which specifically permits the annihilation of predictably deformed or retarded children can hardly be exaggerated. Such a system creates a new and revolutionary hierarchy of rights in which the rights of the living to happiness transcend the rights of the unborn to existence. A law which is silent about the abortion of non-viable fetuses says no such things."[33]

While we must certainly appreciate the heart-piercing dilemma Fr. Drinan so exactly describes, we must disagree with his conclusion that abortion-on-demand is the solution to it. No such dilemma would be created if abortion laws still in force in many states—allowing abortion only to save the life of the mother—were simply retained. The medical, legal, social, psychological, and moral considerations which we have covered up to this point all indicate rather insistently that the retention of such restrictive laws is, after all, the best minimum solution to the abortion problem. Fr. Drinan, however, seems to assume that permissive abortion will necessarily gain further victories in accordance with the Abortion Imperative, and that what Catholics must do is to rationalize the situation as best they can. He seems to be saying further that he, at least, is not prepared to do anything to resist the trend (though he has shown himself in Congress to be pugnacious enough in a number of other political battles, for instance, in his opposition to the constitutional amendment which would have allowed prayers in the public schools).

Can we even begin to calculate the "teaching effect," as he calls it, of allowing abortion-on-demand laws to go on the books? It is plain that, even if it were shown that there is truly a new democratic consensus in favor of abortion-on-demand—and it has not been shown—we would still be obliged to resist these laws with all the strength we can command. The passing of Jim Crow laws in many American states in the latter half of the last century surely seemed to be the wave of the future at the time. Did this make these laws right, or the trend to pass them a healthy one? No more is the trend towards legalized abortion right or healthy today. Legalized abortion amounts to an official declaration by society that it is all right to kill a child if he is unborn, and thus innocent and defenseless.

Catholics, as citizens, have both the right and the duty to work for and vote for moral convictions in the political sphere. The proponents of abortion press for *their* moral convictions, and with self-righteous zeal. They want their maximum demands translated into the law of the land. It is a strange brand of pluralism when they demand that the laws reflect their views—laws which regulate the lives of all of us—while we must hide our lights under a bushel. Thousands of unborn children are being slaughtered without even the pretense of a justification, and, according to one interpretation of the rules of pluralism, Catholics are supposed to go on nodding agreement about how "compassionate" the motives of the abortionists are.

Yet, in practical terms—unless the American system becomes drastically altered in the next few years—it is unlikely that any law or public policy can be maintained or continued in the face of massive and determined opposition by this country's Catholic citizens. Catholics can *stop* the abortion scourge—once they convince the politicians that one fourth of the American electorate will simply not tolerate legalized abortion. All that is required for the politicians to get this message is the active exercise by Catholics of political rights which they, along with other Americans, enjoy. No politician wants to alienate a per-

manent bloc of voters on an issue such as abortion; but the
politicians must be made to understand that support by
them for the relaxation of abortion laws *means* the alienation of the votes of Catholics.

This does not mean that abortion should be made into a
"Catholic" political issue. On the contrary, the public
stance of Catholic opponents of abortion should include a
refusal to concede that abortion is in any way a religious,
theological, or "Catholic" issue. The Constitution of the
United States already provides a sufficient basis for the
defense of the rights of the unborn; and it is on the Constitution that public, political, and legal opposition to abortion should be based. The support of Americans of any
religion or no religion prepared to agree with this constitutional stand should be welcomed; but at the same time,
it is imperative that Catholic political weight should be
felt. The Catholic bishops have spoken unmistakably on
abortion, but Catholic opposition should not be limited to
statements by the bishops; laymen working in their own
proper sphere should defend the basic moral issue of the
right to life by means of effective action in the political
sphere.

Professor Germain Grisez has reminded us that a favorite tactic of the pro-abortionists has been to maintain that
opposition to abortion comes *only* from Catholics, and we
have seen plenty of examples of that tactic. At a forum of
the Association for the Study of Abortion in 1967 several
speakers consciously adopted the slogan: "Public health in
proposition; Roman Catholic in opposition."[34] The idea
was that abortion should be sold to the American public as
primarily a "health" measure; everybody is in favor of
health. At the same time Catholic opposition to abortion
would be exclusively emphasized. It is perfectly clear that
this line has been consistently followed by the abortion

lobby. To admit that abortion was an issue of special concern of Catholics would thus seem to be falling in with the calculated plans of the opposition.

But to refuse to stand up and be counted in favor of the rights of the unborn because, as Catholics, we are vulnerable to charges of "religious prejudice" would represent an even more astounding victory for the tactic of the abortion lobby! Can we suppose that labor or management would similarly refrain from support of legislation favorable to its interests on the grounds that it could be accused of bias? Yet this is the kind of stand some Catholics are taking on abortion; they will not speak out, apparently, *because* they are Catholics!

This strange reluctance of some Catholics to take a stand on a moral issue as basic as the right to life seems to be motivated by a desire not to transgress any of the supposed rules of the new ecumenical spirit. In the general euphoria after Vatican Council II, when Catholics were supposed to be emerging from the isolation of their "ghettos" to take a more active part in American life, it has been too often forgotten that the Council never taught that we should automatically applaud *any* course of action our secular, pluralistic society should decide to embark upon. In the case of abortion, we must set ourselves resolutely against what our society is doing.

The experience of New York and elsewhere has already proved that neither the state nor the law will be neutral once abortion-on-demand has become established. However opposed we may be to abortion on moral grounds, we will not escape the scourge by "neutrality." We will not be spared the duty of paying for abortions with our tax monies; we are paying for them now. Once abortion has become just another medical procedure, and a desirable population and social control measure into the bargain, we will enter the era of *compulsory* anti-life measures: we will have to fight then, if we do not fight now, and the battle will be harder.

There is no alternative to a vigorous Catholic stand, in the political arena, against legalized abortion. It is not a question of "imposing" our morality but of whether our nation will continue to recognize any fundamental morality at all. The true problem originates with those who would legalize killing as the solution to anything. In trying to oppose this "solution," *we* may be blamed for our trouble, as the Prophet Elijah was blamed for "troubling Israel." (I *Kings* 18:17) We are being blamed anyway. Meanwhile "the voice of thy brother's blood crieth to Me from the earth." (*Genesis* 4:10)

X

God, Not Man, Is the Master of Human Life

CHARLES E. RICE, Professor of Law at Notre Dame University, has recounted the following hypothetical anecdote in his excellent book *The Vanishing Right To Live*: "About the termination of a pregnancy, I want your opinion. The father was syphilitic. The mother tuberculous. Of the four children born, the first was blind, the second died, the third was deaf and dumb, the fourth also tuberculous. What would you have done?" "I would have ended the pregnancy." "Then you would have murdered Beethoven."[1]

This anecdote may serve as the starting point for a concluding discussion of modern man's grasping efforts to control a destiny which, in actual fact, is essentially out of his hands—in spite of his most arduous efforts to manage it.

We did not make ourselves. We did not set the terms of

our existence on this earth. Our condition is given to us; and it is not uncommon for this condition to include, in the lives of each of us, any number of intractable difficulties. We have no earthly guarantee that the problems we face even *have* solutions. No amount of talk about the quality of life and the realization of human potential can change this human condition in its essentials. Neither science and technology nor modern medicine can change it.

At the very beginning of written history, Herodotus echoed what was already the ancient wisdom of the Greeks when he said: "Call no man happy till you know the nature of his death." In the Bible Job cried: "Let the day perish wherein I was born, and the night in which it was said, there is a man-child conceived." (*Job* 3:3) "Few and evil have the days of the years of my life been," lamented the Patriarch Jacob (*Gen.* 47:9).

The testimony of a Shakespeare echoes that of the ancients: "How weary, stale, flat and unprofitable seem to me all the uses of this world," Hamlet tells us. "You see me here, you gods, a poor old man, as full of grief as age: wretched in both"—this is the testimony of King Lear. "Nothing can we call our own but death," cries King Richard II, "and that small model of the barren earth which serves as paste and cover to our bones."

Closer to our own day, an A. E. Houseman concludes:

"Therefore since the world has still
Much good, but much less good than ill,
And while the sun and moon endure
Luck's a chance, but trouble's sure,
I'd face it as a wise man would,
And train for ill and not for good."

All this is not the whole of life, to be sure, especially for the Christian; but nobody who has lived for very long will fail to understand the almost universal testimony about the sufferings inherent in the human condition, in spite of the most laudable efforts we can exert to alleviate suffering.

Comes the World Health Organization in our day, however, and decrees that "health is a state of complete physical, mental and social well-being, and not merely the absence of disease or infirmity."[2] And at the same time we suddenly find people willing to justify abortions—the deliberate destruction of human lives—simply because a given mother or family may not enjoy this standard of health! Herodotus is turned up on his head; if we think a man might not be happy, we think we can *decide* the nature of his death!

"Pregnancy poses many threats to the mother which are outside the traditional realm of medical practice but well within this expanded concept [of health]," according to Dr. Kenneth J. Ryan, Chairman of the Department of Obstetrics and Gynecology at Western Reserve University in Cleveland. "These pregnancy 'threats' are variously the consequences of: poverty, the broken or unstable family, illegitimacy, rape, incest, social and religious pressures, age, psychic disturbances, conflicts regarding the use of contraceptives, chronic illness, and fear for the welfare of the unborn child. Although none of these may be life-threatening, they are life devastating."[3]

Obstetrician-gynecologist Dr. Arther J. Mandy has written in much the same vein: "There might be some justification for this insistence upon carrying patients to term if the same degree of concern was evidenced for the newborn infant whose life it seemed only a few months earlier so terribly important to maintain. Once it is born, however, few doctors can answer for its later welfare, either physically or emotionally."[4]

Who has *asked* the doctor to answer for the child's later welfare, or appointed him Lord of Life and Death? A

child's total welfare is something no doctor *can* answer
for. Not even the World Health Organization can guarantee (to any of us) "a state of complete physical, mental and
social well-being." Failure to enjoy such a state can hardly
be grounds for extermination, or most of the human beings who have ever lived on this earth would surely have
qualified for extermination, at least at some point in their
lives.

Although society can and should do more for those who
are less fortunate, can killing their offspring really be the
answer to their problems? Rather, will not acceptance of
abortion as the "solution" to social problems mean that
society will stop searching for better—and more moral—
solutions? The idea that we cannot legitimately oppose
abortion unless we have some "positive" solution to all the
problems which some propose to solve by killing is another favorite theme of the abortion lobby. But it is a totally inadmissible idea. We must oppose killing because it
is killing, regardless of what other "solutions" we may
have. If society terminates enough of their pregnancies,
the numbers of the less fortunate will assuredly diminish.
But is not the turning to a solution as violent as abortion
really a symptom of desperation, a gigantic loss of nerve?

As a society, we have apparently convinced ourselves
that we ineluctably *could* solve all human problems and
misfortunes by the application of purely technical solutions—generally programs involving the expenditure of a
lot of money. In fact, to consider most human problems
susceptible of solution by purely technical means is to
misconceive radically the true nature of most human
problems, which always and inescapably have a moral
dimension. Once it became apparent that we were really
not controlling much of anything—"without Me you can
do nothing" (*John* 15:5)—and that all the afflictions
enumerated by Dr. Ryan above remained all too rife,

many have apparently been prepared to abandon objective morality in their ever more desperate search for "solutions." Once the products of our technology and medicine showed that progress had been ambiguous at best—with pollution and overpopulation suddenly identified as the "worst" problems in the history of mankind—some could manage no better reaction than to succumb to the massive death wish represented by the Abortion Imperative. The strain of being human and of trying to cope with the human condition has proved to be too overwhelming for them.

Professor Garrett Hardin, whose ideas we have already encountered several times in these pages, appears to believe that the way to cope with the human condition is to *change* it to suit ourselves. In a guest editorial in *Science* magazine, he has written about the 500,000 people who were killed in the cyclone which struck the Bay of Bengal in November, 1970: "What killed those unfortunate people? The cyclone, newspapers said. But one can just as logically say that overpopulation killed them. The Gangetic delta is barely above sea level. Every year several thousand people are killed in quite ordinary storms. If Pakistan were not overcrowded, no sane man would bring his family to such a place. Ecologically speaking, a delta belongs to the river and the sea; man obtrudes there at his peril . . .

"Were we to identify overpopulation as the cause of a half million deaths," Professor Hardin's editorial continues, "we would threaten ourselves with a question to which we do not know the answer: *How can we control the population without recourse to repugnant measures?* Fearfully we close our minds to an inventory of possibilities. Instead, we say that a cyclone caused the deaths, thus relieving ourselves of responsibility for this and future catastrophes. 'Fate' is so comforting."[5]

What seems to be the real basis of Dr. Hardin's concern over a half million deaths in a cyclone? It cannot be that he is concerned about the deaths as such, since he is apparently prepared to see a great many more than 500,000 people *killed by abortion*—in order to achie 'e the control over our own population which he thinks is desirable. ("Pakistani parents repaired the loss in just 40 days, and the world turned its attention to other matters.")

Rather, the basis of his concern seems to lie in the fact that we were not *responsible* for these deaths; a cyclone was. "Fate" is not the least bit comforting for Dr. Hardin; it means there are things outside human control. If a half million people are killed in a cyclone, it is indeed a matter completely out of our control. If an equal or greater number are efficiently dispatched in sterile clinics, it is population control, the desired goal of today's enlightened.

What Dr. Hardin and his learned colleagues are really calling for is a world different from the real one; they want a world which can be managed and from which unknowns and uncertainties can be banished—a world where "sane" men can keep out of the paths of cyclones. It is intolerable to such "sane" men that we should be subject to what Dr. Hardin calls "fate," or that questions should exist to which we truly do *not* know the answers. Instead, a scientific élite should be in charge. As simple as that. We have seen earlier that the essence of Dr. Hardin's *moral* position is that man is in charge of human life; here we see the ultimate absurdity of this position, namely, that man should also be in charge of "fate"!

This overweening passion for control, especially evident among scientists but in fact almost pandemic throughout American society today, is clearly one of the most powerful motives behind the Abortion Imperative. We have regularly encountered this passion in the course of our review of some of the phenomena connected with the

Abortion Imperative. For the Christian, such a passion and even frenzy to get people and their problems under control can only appear to be a particularly aggravated kind of usurpation of God's dominion over human life. It is an attitude which, in fact, is precisely the antithesis of what Christians mean by *faith*. The question posed to every Catholic at his Baptism—"What do you ask of the Church of God?—has, as its answer, "Faith."

It is the Creator Who has set the terms of our existence on this earth; it is the Creator in Whom we must finally trust—otherwise we *are* subject to "fate," as Garrett Hardin sees, though what he does not see is that we *cannot* escape from it by "population control"—*his* faith!—or by any of the other panaceas which man has regularly devised in an attempt to escape from the consequences of his real condition—*the condition of a finite, sin-prone creature dependent upon the grace of God.*

It is perfectly clear that the terms God has set for our existence on this earth do not always necessarily include "a state of complete physical, mental and social well-being," as understood by the World Health Organization. Indeed "the Lord reproves him whom He loves, as a father the son in whom he delights," as we read in the Book of *Proverbs* (3:12).

The Christian is morally obliged to accept the suffering which comes to him. "Did not Christ have to suffer these things before entering into His glory?" (*Luke* 24:26) Nevertheless, the Christian's faith will continue to affirm the goodness of creation, whatever happens. Both the depth and beauty of life are often revealed through pain. Most difficult always to endure is the pain or loss we may be suffering *now*. Faith teaches that, whatever the pain, it has meaning, even if we cannot yet discern that meaning. We do not, and cannot, know the answers to all questions, but we must persevere anyway.

Faith teaches that, in the profound words of the Portuguese proverb, "God writes straight with crooked lines." The crooked lines are mostly of our own doing, but God ultimately brings good out of our evil. Joseph's brothers sold him into slavery and God made it the instrument of their own salvation. Man crucified the Lord of Glory (I *Cor.* 2:8) and God made the Cross the instrument of man's salvation. We cannot *know* how the deaths of 500,000 Bengalis in a cyclone can properly fit into the moral scheme of things, or how a woman's death in childbirth can be turned into good. We cannot fathom the value in God's sight of a "defective" or "retarded" human child (though we may imagine that God wants to see what kind of people *we* are in allowing the birth of such children); we cannot *know* how they might ultimately "shine forth as the sun in the kingdom of their Father." (*Matt.* 8:43)

But faith teaches us to look beyond what we see only "in part." (I *Cor* 13:13) Faith teaches us that there *is* a moral scheme of things in spite of some appearances (as we know anyway by looking into our own hearts); and it is in the perspective of faith that we apprehend the moral truth that we cannot attempt to bring about good ourselves by doing acts which we know to be evil; we cannot find solutions to human problems, however truly tragic, by killing the innocent.

Although man has been given many wonderful powers by his Creator, he has also been enjoined to exercise those powers only in accordance with a moral law which enlightens the conscience of every human being. It is true that man can disregard the moral law, stultify his conscience, and attempt to exercise his human powers autonomously; that is because man is *free.* Many today have chosen to exercise their freedom by opting for abortion. There is, however, nothing new in the human situation today which suddenly makes this choice either right or acceptable. Man has always enjoyed the same awesome power of choice. "I have set before you life or death, a blessing or a curse: therefore choose life that both thou and thy seed may live." (*Deut.* 30:19) Though man does have the power of choice, he can only rightly exercise it by choosing the good. It does not require profound reflection to realize that the law of God which we are asked to choose is in fact given to us for our own good. Given the miserable record of man's history on earth, who *wants* man in control of life? We need Somebody to set moral limits on our conduct if only to save us from ourselves.

"The law of the Lord is perfect," sings the Psalmist, "reviving the soul; the testimony of the Lord is sure, making wise the simple; the precepts of the Lord are right, rejoicing the heart; the commandment of the Lord is pure, enlightening the eyes; the fear of the Lord is clean, enduring forever; the ordinances of the Lord are true and righteous altogether. More to be desired are they than gold, even much fine gold; sweeter also than honey, and drippings of the honeycomb." (*Psalms* 18:8-11)

A society which can take abortion for granted is a society which has rejected the idea that God, not man, is the Master of human life. That our society has moved towards this rejection we have discerned not only in the cry for easy abortion, but in the current widespread acceptance of contraception. The contraceptive mentality also arises out of the modern obsession with control, similarly ignoring the possible demands of morality, which we have discovered at the heart of the Abortion Imperative. The very term "birth control" suggests this. Birth, like Professor Hardin's "fate," is something many in our society have found intolerable except on their own hedonistic terms. At the same time, few, if any, are prepared to renounce the sexual activity which, in the course of nature, can lead to "birth." The last thing so-called birth control ever entails is self-control! The will to "control" births is in fact, much more than abortion, the principal manifestation of the modern moral claim to control human life; in this perspective, abortion becomes merely another "method."

A Protestant observer, Professor Ralph B. Potter, has well expressed the intimate connection between contraception and abortion: "When a new habit of mind now attributes new life to 'rotten luck' in the practice of contraception rather than to the purposeful will of a merciful God, neglect of the countermeasure of abortion becomes irrational and superstitious retreat from the possibility of exercising control of one's destiny. Denial of accessibility to abortion comes to be seen by many as a violation of civil liberty."[6] We have encountered precisely this attitude in our examination of abortion; it is manifest that it is engendered by the typical outlook of a contraceptive society which had asserted its power and authority to control human life before the subject of abortion ever arose.

One of the things Pope Paul VI is saying when he reminds us that the Catholic Church "teaches that each and every marriage act must remain open to the procreation of human life"[7] is that God, and not man, ultimately is Master of human life—in the physical sense because God created all of the elements out of which human parents are able to generate life, and in the moral sense because he retains dominion over it. This is why, in marriage (as in every other area of our lives) we must remain "open" to the possible intervention of God, as the encylical *Humanae Vitae* has prophetically reminded us. People have managed their lives without effective contraceptives throughout all the generations of human history up to the present. Suddenly contraceptives have become absolutely indispensable!

The thought seems to have occurred scarcely to anybody that the alternative to "birth control" is not necessarily a child every year, but rather the use of the sexual faculty in marriage in harmony with the reason and will with which human beings have been richly endowed—if only they would use them as God intended (to know the truth and to choose the good) and rely on the abundant help in using them through the grace of God and the Sacraments of the Church. The contraceptive mentality substitutes mechanical or chemical control for the rational, voluntary, and grace-inspired control. But it is this latter kind of "control" which is called for in sex as in every other human activity. In a strict sense, the contraceptive outlook denies not only that man is free but that man lives under a moral law.

The self-indulgence of the contraceptive mentality can hardly be placed on the same *level* as abortion, of course. Abortion is the taking of a human life already in existence. Contraception is the deliberate prevention of life; its use constitutes an assertion that one indeed controls human life. Many, however, having made their initial assertion of control over human life, do not seem to be having too much trouble over abortion as one of the methods for making that control effective. We can only regard with utter dismay the ease and even the nonchalance with which our contraceptive society is now passing over from the prevention to the destruction of human life.

For example, the "perfect" contraceptive, the "once-a-month pill," which researchers are avidly striving to develop right now, is itself an abortifacient—a drug which will cause any child who *may* have been conceived during the month to be evacuated from the mother's body on a regular schedule. That is to say, it is a chemical method of abortion. The difficulties of developing this new pill are yet said to be so formidable that the commercial drug companies may never be able to manage the job; hence it is more and more insistently repeated that millions of the taxpayers' dollars will be required.[8] Hardly anybody thinks of asking why such a powerful drug, with wholly incalculable effects on a woman's body (and perhaps on any embryos that *are* allowed to gestate), has to be developed at all; it seems to be taken for granted that, of course, we need abortion-inducing drugs in today's world (as, apparently, we are coming to need drugs for practically everything). Indeed, some of the contraceptive pills already in use may work as abortifacients, as the intrauterine device (IUD) almost certainly does.[9]

The Catholic Church, for her part, will not cease to condemn the whole usurpation of God's dominion represented by both contraception and abortion, as she has unequivocally and expressly condemned abortion by name from the time of the *Didache*, which dates from 80 A.D. up until the present day. Vatican Council II linked abortion with infanticide and labeled both "unspeakable crimes."[10]

It was the late Pope Pius XII who probably best expressed the contemporary mind of the Church when he wrote: "Now the child, even the unborn child, is a human being in the same degree and by the same title as his mother. Moreover, every human being, even the child in his mother's womb, receives his right to life directly from God, not from his parents, nor from any human society or authority. Therefore, there is no man, no human authority, no science, no 'indication,' whether medical, eugenical, social, economic, or moral, that can show or give a valid juridical title for a deliberate and direct disposing of an innocent human life . . ."[11]

Pope Paul VI has reiterated the same teaching: "Faced with campaigns of opinions that severely test the very fundamentals of human morality, and this in the name of sensitivity and what is supposed to be common sense, we have to repeat this clearly: *nothing except legitimate self-defense ever authorizes a man to take the life of another man, or his own life.* The commandment is formal and absolute: *Thou shalt not kill.* Abortion has been considered as homicide since the first centuries of the Church; *nothing* today allows it to be considered otherwise."[12]

This is the constant teaching of the Church. No amount of religious pluralism, ecumenism, deference to the wishes of some of our fellow citizens—no amount of what used to be called "human respect"—can nullify the moral law which forbids the taking of life by abortion—or nullify the moral obligation of Catholics to oppose laws of civil society which attempt to incorporate contrary principles into the statute books of what is, after all, our country too.

In opposing abortion, we are not attempting to judge persons, whom we are expressly forbidden by Christ to judge lest we be judged ourselves. We are condemning *principles,* and the acts which proceed from them and doing all in our power to prevent our common society from being taken over by those principles.

For those who have already accepted such principles, our prayer must always be, "Father, forgive them for they know not what they do." (*Luke* 23:34) But we must nevertheless work against their principles by every political and legal means.

The acceptance of the practice of abortion in America, under whatever pretext, means, as we have now abundantly seen, the dethronement of God from any place in the governing of our commonwealth; and the abrogation of the moral law. It means the denial of those "self-evident truths" which the Declaration of Independence proclaimed. It means the abdication by the state of its responsibility for protecting all human life. It means the undermining of our legal and constitutional system. It means the corruption of the medical profession. It means the degradation of the women who consent to and undergo the operation. It means the usurpation of the father's rights over his children. It means the callous sacrifice of thousands upon thousands of helpless, dependent human beings. It was over the death of one single human being that the Evangelist has recorded in the Gospel: "Jesus wept. See . . . how He loved him." (*John* 11:35)

Epilogue:

Turning of the Tide?

"How long shall I take counsel in my soul, having
sorrow in my heart daily? How long shall mine
enemy be exalted over me?"
—*Psalms* 13:2

EVEN as the year 1970 brought abortion-on-demand in
four states and relaxation of the abortion laws in several
others, signs of a reaction against the Abortion Imperative
were nevertheless already appearing. As we have noted, a
number of court cases in late 1970 began to reassert the
constitutional rights of the unborn in opposition to the
earlier shallow court decisions which had voided some
restrictive laws on the grounds that they were "unconstitutionally vague" or that they violated a woman's "right to
privacy" in controlling her own reproductive life.[1] (For
those who still doubt the connection between contraception and abortion, we should emphasize that these courts
were basing their arguments from "privacy" largely on
the Supreme Court decision in the case *Griswold* vs. *Connecticut* which guaranteed to the practice of contraception the right of privacy; the lower courts, however, saw no

217

contradiction whatever in extending this "right" to abortion—the killing of a living child).

By mid-1972, the reaction against the Abortion Imperative was becoming a trend. Anti-abortion groups had "sprung seemingly from nowhere," according to *Newsweek* magazine,[2] and they proved to be remarkably effective in combatting legalized abortion in the legislatures of state after state. Up to June, 1972, no further bills to liberalize or legalize abortion had been enacted in any state, except in Florida where, constrained by an unfavorable court decision, the legislature enacted an ALI-type law; and such bills had been *defeated* in the legislatures of no less than 26 states.[3] Right To Life groups were also beginning to intervene effectively in a number of court cases.

Significantly, too, legislation was being introduced into the legislatures of a number of states which would *tighten up* some existing abortion laws: by acknowledging the constitutional rights of the unborn, protecting the rights of the father, prohibiting the advertising of abortions, and limiting the use of public funds to pay for them.[4]

Little of this pro-life legislation had passed up to May, 1972, when, in a stunning reversal of the Abortion Imperative, the legislatures of both Connecticut and New York *re-enacted* restrictive abortion statutes allowing abortion only to save the life of a mother. In New York, the votes of the Assembly and the Senate reinstating the previous New York abortion law were 79 to 68 and 30 to 27 respectively[5]; these favorable votes were the culmination of nearly two years of sustained efforts by pro-life forces. For weeks prior to the votes the halls of the Capitol in Albany had been "clogged" with opponents of abortion, according to the New York *Times*[6]; the *Times* itself ran three pro-abortion-on-demand editorials in less than a week,[7] but all to no avail. The pro-life drive in Albany was given tremendous impetus in its closing days when a letter was made public from President Nixon to Terence Cardinal Cooke, Archbishop of New York, indicating that the Chief Executive himself favored the efforts of the pro-life forces.[8]

The victory was short-lived, however, and came temporarily to naught when Governor Nelson Rockefeller vetoed the new restrictive legislation as resolutely as he had signed abortion-on-demand into law two years earlier. "I can see no justification now for repealing this reform and thus condemning hundreds of thousands of women to the dark ages once again," the governor said in his veto message.[9] Nevertheless, the fact that majorities in both houses of the New York Legislature had been persuaded to reverse their action of two years earlier augured well for an eventual return to moral sanity in New York.

In Connecticut, where neighboring New York's disastrous record with abortion-on-demand seemed to be a constant reminder, the General Assembly was called into special session by Governor Thomas J. Meskill expressly to pass a restrictive abortion law. The familiar three-judge federal court, in another incredible decision similar to the one we examined in Chapter IV, had voided Connecticut's abortion law after concluding that the state's interests were "insufficient to take from a woman the decision after conception whether she will bear a child. . .she, as the appropriate decision maker, must be free to choose."[10] Neither the Governor nor the General Assembly of Connecticut could agree, however, with such a manifest travesty of reason and law: the new Connecticut law, passed virtually within days by the special session, differed from the previous law which the court had voided only in its preamble which explicitly affirmed the right of the fetus to life.[11]

One of the particularly heartening things in both these instances is the evidence they provide that the futility of compromises or half measures, where the Abortion Imperative is concerned, is becoming well understood. The New York Legislature refused to consider a compromise offered by Governor Rockefeller which would merely have reduced the time limit past which abortion-on-demand would no longer be permitted under the present convenience law; similarly, the Connecticut General Assembly failed to include any modifying amendments, even one providing for the rape "indication." There was no talk in either state about the familiar "mental health" subterfuge.

Thus, with breakthroughs in two such states as these, a Right To Life movement in opposition to the Abortion Imperative now seems firmly launched on the realistic basis that only strict laws which forbid abortion except to save the life of the mother can provide adequate protection for the rights of the unborn. Coming in the very part of the country which has suffered most from the ravages of the Abortion Imperative, this evidence of respect for the sanctity of life may signal a "turning of the tide." It is too early to tell.

The new trend, if it is a new trend, could never have established itself in the path of the seemingly inexorable lava-flow of the Abortion Imperative, without the really extraordinary energy, selflessness, and dedication of the groups and individuals that, with often pitifully small resources, have stood up for life and for the rights of the unborn both in the legislatures and the courts. If adequate documentation were available, the story of their efforts in state after state would richly deserve telling; but it cannot be told here. (In an Appendix, we will review briefly the experience of Maryland, which may or may not be typical).

Moreover, considering only the phenomena we have chronicled in these pages, we cannot be too sanguine about the future, given the present state of our public morality on abortion. The bedrock fact of the matter is that abortion is widely accepted today, and is being carried out in hospitals by regular medical practitioners, often in spite of laws that happen to be in force. In a very real sense, those who are seeking the legalization of abortion are really seeking recognition and sanction for *what is already being done.* Restrictive abortion laws must be retained or re-instated, therefore, in order to uphold the *principle* of the sanctity of life in the face of this widespread and growing contempt and indifference. It may not be possible to legislate morality, as is often repeated, but it should be possible to retain laws against killing the innocent!

Those who are motivated by the Abortion Imperative are not going to be comfortable with the fact that the legislative and court battles are no longer going almost exclusively their way. They are likely to redouble their efforts, and, where they have already achieved all or part of what they want, they will ferociously resist "turning back the clock" ferociously. In general, the proponents of the new morality want to get abortion out of the way as a matter that is already "settled"—so as to get on with other favored schemes such as human "quality control," genetic engineering, mercy killing, and the like. So long as sex as pure enjoyment and utilitarian ethics are promoted by the press and media, and actually taught, as is increasingly the case, in the universities and schools of America, the proponents of abortion are likely to find continued support for their aims.

Moreover, even if they cannot succeed in gaining their maximum demands through the courts or the state legislatures, a "compromise" which will give them most of what they want may already be in sight. We caught a glimpse of it in considering what has happened in Washington, D. C., since the Supreme Court "upheld" the D.C.

abortion law in the Vuitch case.[12] In this case the Supreme Court did not rule either on the rights of the unborn or on the alleged "rights" of women not to be obliged to carry a given pregnancy to term. The question before the court was simply whether the D.C. law was too "vague" in its definition of health to be enforced. The court ruled that the law was *not* too vague, and that the law's definition of "health" included everything normally understood by that term, including "mental health." The court also held that the burden of proof rested on the prosecution to show that a given abortion was *not* performed on "health" grounds.

The result of this decision has been, in practice, something close to abortion-on-demand. Any abortion performed in the mass-production abortion clinics now operating in the nation's Capital is *claimed* to be for health reasons: let the prosecution try to prove otherwise in the face of a doctor's assertion that health reasons are involved. Who *decides* on health questions if not doctors? In this way, abortion virtually on demand continues unchallenged in Washington, D.C., under a law which supposedly restricts the procedure to *bona fide* medical cases. The same is true in other areas where the existing law allows abortions on "health" grounds.

What is to prevent other states from achieving abortion-on-demand merely by modifying their laws to admit legal abortion to preserve the mother's "health"? As indicated in the polls we cited in Chapter V, a majority of Americans, although they disapprove of simple abortion-on-demand, probably *do* approve of abortion to preserve a mother's health. Legislators would find it easier to vote for "reformed" abortion laws admitting only this single additional indication.

It is clear, therefore, that convincing the American public that there are few, if any, valid health reasons for an abortion must remain a priority objective of the opponents of abortion for convenience. We cannot allow the American people to remain in ignorance regarding the true medical status of "therapeutic" abortion.

Moreover, where the law allows, efforts must be made to have *prosecuted* the physicians who are openly performing most of today's abortions. The bonanza which abortion has represented for some physicians will no longer be quite so appealing after a few successful prosecutions. Many prosecutors are reluctant to move against licensed practitioners working in accredited hospitals. Physicians were almost never prosecuted under traditional abortion statutes; these laws were enforced primarily against illegal abortionists. Non-enforcement of the abortion laws in the case of physicians was perhaps tolerable when the vast majority of physicians refused to do abortions except for what they believed were valid medical reasons; but that situation no longer obtains today. Citizen pressure brought to bear upon prosecuting attorneys to enforce the law is as important as citizen pressure brought upon state legislators. It is scandalous that killing should be made respectable merely because it is done by doctors in hospitals; it is intolerable that the "body count" in the abortion mills should continue to mount, often in spite of what the law says.

In the long run, the existence and enforcement of laws restricting or prohibiting abortion will be only a partial answer to the Abortion Imperative. The real answer is a different moral outlook on life than the one that prevails in our affluent, hedonistic, and—what the Episcopal Bishop of Michigan has rightly called—*corrupt* society. We Christians will not see any significant improvement in the prevailing moral climate until we have made up our minds to abandon the bland philosophy of "getting along" at all costs and have begun to reassert the demands of a transcendent moral law—until, that is, we have begun preaching again, to all who will listen, the Gospel of Jesus Christ.

Appendix I*

The Experience of Maryland

ABORTION today is viewed by many not as the solution to any medical problem but as an answer to "overpopulation" or to a variety of social, economic and personal problems. Although the drive to gain acceptance for and legalize the practice is nationwide in scope, efforts to remove the existing legal restrictions have necessarily been focused on the various states, since American statutes which restrict or regulate abortion happen to be state laws.

Maryland's experience with abortion "reform" is particularly instructive. The state has been a center for agitation in favor of the practice and against the legal restrictions placed upon it. Maryland was also among the

*This narrative was prepared separately from the foregoing pages and includes a number of minor repetitions of material covered earlier.

first of the states to see its law on the subject amended (in 1968). And, in both 1970 and 1971, the virtual removal of abortion from the very province of the state's law was only narrowly averted—first by a governor's veto, and the following year by a hard-won majority vote in the state House of Delegates.

Although simple abortion-on-demand has failed, the 1968 Maryland law is one of the most liberal and permissive abortion laws in the country; it replaced the traditional statute in force in Maryland for one hundred years. This traditional statute, now off the books, permitted "the production of abortion by a regular practitioner of medicine when, after consulting with one or more respectable physicians, he shall be satisfied that the fetus is dead, or that no other method will secure the safety of the mother."[1]

Thus, even before the drive for legalized abortion began, the Maryland statute was already a very liberal one—especially when compared to the laws in force in a majority of American states. These laws specifically permitted abortion only to save the mother's *life* (and, in a very few cases, also her "health"). The traditional Maryland law, however, permitted abortion to secure her "safety." Moreover, the physician only had to be "satisfied" that her "safety" was in jeopardy, provided he had consulted another physician. With such a law as this, it seems pretty clear that any doctor could perform an abortion in almost any conceivable circumstances he believed called for one on truly medical grounds, without fear of prosecution.

A Maryland attorney has commented that "the Maryland law was so relatively permissive that, to my knowledge, there was never a prosecution, let alone a conviction, of a physician who actually conferred with another physician prior to performing an abortion. The only prosecutions that occurred were those of persons who could be characterized as professional abortionists operating on a wholesale basis or the non-physician abortionists."[2]

A favorite argument heard in the drive to legalize abortion is that it should be a "purely" medical matter. It is not, of course, and cannot be, a purely medical matter; but it seems clear that physicians in Maryland have always enjoyed the widest possible autonomy in making truly medical judgments about the termination of pregnancies. Nevertheless, serious agitation for a change in the Maryland law began as early as it began anywhere in America. Given the attention which abortion now commands in the public life of the country, it is hard to believe that the *first* American state to liberalize its abortion laws in any way, Mississippi, did so as recently as 1966. By the following year, 1967, a bill to liberalize the Maryland law had already been introduced into the Maryland State General Assembly.

The molding of attitudes which prefigures the acceptance of abortion, both by physicians and by the general public, had begun in the state long before. As early as 1954, Dr. Harold Rosen, a psychiatrist on the staff of the Johns Hopkins University Hospital in Baltimore, edited a book which promptly became something of a handbook for the pro-abortion movement throughout the country. The book's original title was *Therapeutic Abortion*. Ostensibly an objective treatment by a variety of experts on all aspects of the subject, the book was actually an elaborate plea for a more permissive attitude towards abortion. Expanded and re-issued in 1967 under a new title, *Abortion in America*, the book's foreword proudly notes the use made of it by Maryland Delegate Allen B. Spector (D.-Baltimore) the principal advocate and sponsor of legalized abortion during the period of his service in the House of Delegates. (It is significant that the word "therapeutic" was dropped from the book's title when it was re-issued thirteen years after its original publication. By then the pro-abortion forces were not really arguing for abortion on the basis of any kind of "therapy" whatever; they were arguing frankly for abortion-on-demand.)

The principal assumption underlying the essays in *Abortion in America* is that the fetus simply has no rights at all to be considered among other factors related to abortion; abortion is reduced to a medical *technique,* on the same footing as an appendectomy. "At the Johns Hopkins Hospital it is felt that this analogy to an appendectomy is valid," Dr. Rosen wrote in his introduction. "The procedure is the same as for any other medical problem."[3] This theme has been constantly reiterated in arguments to state legislators.

If Dr. Rosen's views correctly reflect the philosophy and practice at Johns Hopkins before any change in the Maryland abortion law, it is little wonder that pressures were not long in coming to change the law to sanction the existing practice. Although other doctors and hospitals were also active in promoting a new approach to abortion in Maryland, it is nevertheless difficult to exaggerate the role which the Johns Hopkins Hospital and its staff have played. Obstetrician-gynecologists Dr. Allan C. Barnes and Dr. Irvin M. Cushner, like Dr. Rosen, are well known nationally for their advocacy of easy abortion; but they have not neglected their home state for all of that. They have spoken widely throughout the state, and have always been ready with a team of expert witnesses on any appropriate occasion. In February, 1970, Dr. Barnes told a House committee in Annapolis: "We did over half the abortions in the state, but we did not do enough."[4] Personal lobbying efforts by Johns Hopkins doctors and their wives were a daily occurrence in Annapolis during the entire, prolonged debate on abortion which took place in the Spring of 1971, according to some members of the House of Delegates.[5] One delegate, John J. Gallagher (D.-Baltimore), publicly called for picketing the Johns Hopkins hospital.

Nevertheless it was hardly one small group of doctors from one hospital which could succeed in gaining for liberalized abortion the successes it has seen in Maryland to date. Once abortion had become a subject of public debate, it was both astonishing and dismaying to see the number and variety of people and organizations prepared to come forward to champion it. One expected pro-abortion activity from avowed anti-life groups such as Zero Population Growth, which has become quite active in the state in the past year or two; but one must wonder at the state of public morality when groups such as the state Medical and Chirurgical Society, the Maryland Council of Social Welfare, or the Maryland Psychological Association frankly come out for abortion-on-demand. Other groups as diverse as the Maryland Council of Churches and something called the Woman's Democratic Club of Montgomery County added their voices to the cause, as did prominent citizens who had been active in such organizations as the League of Woman Voters. Even official state entities such as the Department of Health and Mental Hygiene and the Department of Employment and Social Welfare turned out to be active in promoting abortion-on-demand.[6] The latter Department actually sent out a letter on official stationery congratulating the members of the House of Delegates who voted for the abortion repeal bill in 1971.[7]

Thus, as far as Maryland is concerned, abortion has truly seemed to be "an idea whose time has come," as one prominent pro-abortion lawyer has expressed it in an article in *The Atlantic*.[8] No one, contemplating a possible pro-life stance in the public life of America today, can ignore the fact that among the educated and the "élite" in America today there scarcely exists the recognition that abortion is a basic *moral* issue; rather, there seems to be a kind of amnesia among the leaders of society today regarding just what a truly moral issue might be. In this atmosphere of widespread acceptance of a practice that "people want," it is not surprising that the forces working for legislative change in Annapolis were quickly successful. A "reform" bill introduced in 1967 failed to pass in the House of Delegates that year, and thus Maryland did not immediately join California, Colorado, and North Carolina, the states which liberalized their abortion laws that year. In 1968, however, another bill liberalizing the state's century-old statute passed both houses of the General Assembly by comfortable margins—82 to 42 in the House, and 28 to 11 in the Senate.[9]

Even then, the pro-abortion forces did not get a bill as liberal as the one they wanted. At a time when Catholics and other opponents of abortion were generally asleep, there was nevertheless determined and intelligent opposition which succeeded in amending the 1968 bill drastically before it finally passed.[10] In general, the opposition at that time was mobilized by the Maryland Catholic Conference. What emerged as a result of the legislative process—to be signed into law by Spiro T. Agnew, then Governor of Maryland—was a liberal law patterned to a large extent on a "model" abortion law which the American Law Institute had included in its suggested revised "Code," published in the early 1960's.[11] The new Maryland law was similar in many respects to the liberalized laws already passed in three states—and subsequently passed in ten additional states between 1968 and 1972. But the Maryland version of the American Law Institute's "model" law contained some unique special features.

Basically, the 1968 law, which is still the law in Maryland, permitted what it called the "termination of a human pregnancy" by a licensed physician in an accredited hospital under the following conditions:

—If the mother's life is threatened.
—If there is "substantial risk" that continuation of the pregnancy would "gravely impair" the mother's physical or *mental* health.
—If there is "substantial risk" of the birth of a child with "grave and permanent physical deformity or mental retardation."
—If the pregnancy has resulted from forcible rape.[12]

Significantly, the law also removed abortion from the province of the *criminal* law, and placed it under the state Medical Practices Act.[13] This means that abortion is no longer a *crime* in Maryland unless performed outside a hospital and/or by a non-licensed physician (even then, the crime is only a misdemeanor, not a felony).

In opposing this bill, the anti-abortion forces worked hard to see that the act contained procedural safeguards. They did not consider permissive abortion to be in any sense desirable; nevertheless a relaxed law without procedural safeguards was considered even less desirable. Indeed Father David Granfield, a lawyer and author of one of the best recent books on abortion, called the 1968 Maryland statute "an outstanding example of the effective use of procedural safeguards. Despite the enactment of [this] moderately liberal law, the Executive Director of the Maryland Catholic Conference, Joseph G. Finnerty, Jr., could say, 'In evaluating the impact of this bill, it must be viewed in the light of existing conditions in this state prior to its enactment. When one considers the uncertain state of the present law, it is rather difficult to determine the extent of the relaxation, if any, that the new law will cause.' "[14]

In the event, Mr. Finnerty was to be proved wrong. Perhaps he could not have foreseen that the mental health clause of the liberalized Maryland law would come to be employed, in the permissive atmosphere which followed the passage of this 1968 law, as a justification for abortion virtually on demand. Nevertheless the effort to have procedural safeguards included in the law was not entirely in vain. Fr. Granfield enumerates the ones included in the 1968 Maryland law which really did tighten up some of the vagueness in the original Maryland statute:

"All abortions must now take place in an accredited and licensed hospital or the abortion is criminal. No abortion can take place after twenty-six weeks of gestation except to save the mother's life. Prior authorization must be granted by a hospital review board which is appointed by the hospital. Previously all that was required was prior consultation with one or more respectable physicians. The hospital review authority must report to the Joint Commission on Accredition and the State Board of Health, the number of requests, authorizations, performances, the grounds, and the medical procedures used. This report will be made public. The penalties for violations of this bill have been increased. A conscience clause, which may well become a model for other jurisdictions, was included."[15]

However, Professor Germain Grisez of Georgetown University, author of another recent book on the abortion issue, was probably closer to the mark when he characterized this Maryland law as the "most radical" of the state laws liberalized along the lines of the American Law Institutes' "model" statute. Professor Grisez points to the crucial importance of removing the "medical abortionist who works in a hospital from the scope of the criminal law." "It is hard to believe," he adds, "that the state Board of Medical Examiners will suspend or revoke a license for the performance of an act in itself not criminal unless the medical abortionist ignores procedural requirements or makes a regular practice of abortion without any reference to the conditions specified in the law."[16]

In practice the law has proved to be extremely permissive. The number of abortions performed in Maryland hospitals in the first year after its enactment rose by 159 per cent; hospitals performing abortions reported one for every seven live births compared to one for every nineteen live births in the same hospitals prior to the passage of the law.[17] During the fiscal year 1969-70, 3 maternal deaths were reported as a result of abortions; a total of 5,530 legal abortions were performed during the period, and 7,757 in the following fiscal year; some 96 per cent of all these abortions were done on so-called "mental health" grounds, confirming the experience of other states that the "substantial risk" that a pregnancy would "gravely impair" a mother's mental health seems to be simply assumed virtually any time a woman presents herself and announces that she does not want to carry the child. Around eighty per cent of all these abortions were performed in only six hospitals. Contrary to a persistent theme in the pro-abortion literature that most abortions are "needed" by married women living with their husbands, only 31.3 per cent of the women aborted under the new Maryland law in its first year were married.[18]

Given the extremely permissive nature of the 1968 law, and the startling increase in abortions which followed its enactment, it is difficult to imagine on purely rational grounds why any further relaxation of the law would be considered necessary by anybody. Nevertheless, in 1970, Delegate Allen B. Spector of Baltimore introduced a bill which would have provided for simple repeal of the very 1968 law which he himself had originally sponsored. A requirement that abortions be performed by licensed physicians in accredited hospitals was placed in the state

Medical Practices Act. With the passage of this legislation, abortion-on-demand, for any reason or for no reason, would have become the law of the state.[19]

The opposition was not prepared for this "repealer," so soon after the state had already relaxed its law; hardly anybody believed the bill would pass. No overt opposition was mounted; nobody even appeared to testify against the bill in committee. This was to ignore the whole wave-of-the-future mystique which has become associated with the subject of abortion. An effective tactic of the Maryland Committee for Abortion Law Repeal's paid lobbyist in Annapolis was to suggest to individual delegates that, "since the bill wasn't really going to pass," the delegate might as well get "credit" in some quarters by voting for it; it wouldn't cost him anything.[20]

In the event, in the closing days of the 1970 session, the bill did pass the House of Delegates—74 to 59. Attempts were then quickly mounted to try to block the bill's passage in the state Senate; but these attempts were successful only in restoring the "conscience clause" which protected doctors and hospitals refusing to perform abortions, after which the Senate too passed the bill, 23 to 18, in a dramatic vote that came after three o'clock in the morning.[21]

The bill thus accepted by both houses of the Maryland General Assembly would have permitted unlimited clinical destruction of the unborn by doctors in hospitals. Even then, as the legal Opinion on the bill prepared for the governor by the Attorney General pointed out,[22] the only penalty that presumably would have attached to a physician who failed to perform an abortion in a hospital would be a reprimand, or a revocation or suspension of his license to practice medicine.

No penalty at all, apparently, could have been imposed upon a physician who, say, delivering a full-term pregnancy, should decide to do away with a baby observed to be deformed or defective—always with the mother's consent, of course.

Again, according to the Maryland Attorney General's Opinion, "a physician could abort a pregnancy at any time up until the child was 'born alive' without incurring criminal liability. Presumably, the only crime which any other person, such as the mother, would commit for aborting a pregnancy at any time prior to the child's being 'born alive' would be the unlawful practice of medicine."[23]

While the Attorney General did not always bring out explicitly all of the bill's manifold defects, it will be clear to anybody who studies his Opinion carefully how many insoluble legal dilemmas House Bill 489, the abortion-on-demand bill, would have created for the state. For example, while the bill would have given any mother the absolute power of life or death over any of her unborn children, it would have denied to the same mother the right not only to prevent, but even to know about, an abortion performed on her minor daughter. Prescinding from the morality and legality of abortions for a moment, can a state simply decide to remove by the passage of legislation the real rights which parents have over their minor children?

The bill would have removed the father from the picture entirely, since the decision about the continuation of any pregnancy would be left to a woman and her doctor. How could a father then be held legally responsible for supporting his children, if he no longer had any say about whether they could even be born? (The legislators who voted for the bill in the misguided belief that it would help solve the state's burgeoning welfare problem were perhaps contributing to a potentially greater welfare problem than ever by establishing in the law the principle that a father has no rights over his children, and hence no responsibility for them either.) Finally, since the bill contained no residency requirement, Maryland would certainly have become one vast abortion mill. This became especially clear later, after New York State's experience with a similar law, when around 60 percent of all abortions were done on out-of-state women. With the prospect of a New York law real at the time the Maryland law was being considered, many argued that New York would attract the commercial abortion business. Al. Philip Kane, a prominent attorney in both Maryland and the District of Columbia, put this argument in perspective in his testimony against the 1970 bill when he asked: "Shall Maryland be Las Vegas or only Reno?"[24]

The real controversy over the 1970 bill began only after its passage by the Maryland General Assembly. There was a spontaneous public outcry as the shock at what the bill would actually do began to sink in. The Maryland Catholic Conference requested a special hearing on the bill, which Governor Marvin Mandel decided to hold. As it happened, more than in any other way the real depth of the opposition to the bill was articulated and publicized through this special hearing, held at the State House in Annapolis on April 23. The crowds which showed up at Annapolis for the hearing were overwhelmingly anti-bill, as their placards attested ("Kill the Bill, not the Baby!"). A very effective group of speakers was mobilized to speak against the bill—lawyers, doctors, mothers, and others. Although outnumbered by the speakers in favor of the bill who essentially reiterated the old arguments that abortion was a "purely medical matter" which a woman had a "right" to elect (as, of course, patients do *not* elect in the case of truly medical matters), the substantive case made against the bill in the presence of the governor was overwhelming. Moreover, as a result of the govenor's special hearing the opposition to abortion in Maryland was made publicly manifest. The press and media had consistently represented abortion as the coming thing, not having any significant opposition. As a result of the publicity generated by the hearing, however, more than 50 thousand letters, pro and con, were sent to Governor Mandel.

The governor waited for more than a month before finally deciding to veto the bill. In a letter dated May 26 addressed to the Speaker of the House,[25] he enumerated the reasons for his veto as follows:

"Immediately after the enactment of the bill to repeal all abortion laws, I expressed concern about its legal merits on three separate grounds.

"First, I noted that the bill contained no residency requirement.

"Second, I expressed concern that the measure made no provision for the knowledge of a husband prior to the performing of an abortion. Even the parents of an unmarried minor girl would not be required to give their consent to, or have knowledge of, an abortion under this measure.

"My third concern—and perhaps the gravest one— was that the bill repealing the present abortion law would allow an abortion even in the eighth or ninth month of a pregnancy.

"Since the Maryland General Assembly enacted the pending bill, three other states have adopted new abortion laws which are now being recognized as the most liberal in the nation.

"New York, Alaska and Hawaii have adopted new abortion laws, but each of them has some safeguard —a residency requirement, a limit on the period of time during which an abortion can be legally performed, or parental consent when a minor female is involved . . .

"While the existing Maryland law contains some safeguards—such as the ones I have illustrated—all would be repealed under the proposed law. Maryland would stand alone as the only state in the nation whose abortion law contained no safeguards."

Nobody believed that the issue was dead as a result of the governor's veto. Delegate Spector believed that the governor had given him "a complete campaign issue."[26] In the event, he was defeated in a bid to move up to the state senate. Abortion did become something of an issue in the 1970 elections, though not to the extent one would have imagined at the time of the fever pitch of interest which attended the governor's special hearing. Nevertheless the electorate did not lapse entirely into apathy. On the subject of the elections, the Baltimore *Sun* was to testify later, after the defeat of the 1971 bill:

"Some of the most effective lobbying against the bill, particularly in the Archdiocese of Washington headed by Patrick Cardinal O'Boyle, which includes Montgomery and Prince Georges Counties, began during the 1970 elections.

"More than 20 delegates who voted for the liberal 1970 abortion bill were defeated in the election and more than half of these were from areas of the state covered by the Washington Archdiocese."[27]

The expected 1971 abortion-on-demand bill was not long in materializing after the state's lengthened legislative session began in January. This bill would have allowed abortion on the request of the woman within the first 20 weeks of pregnancy, and thereafter if "deemed necessary" in the judgment of the treating physician. The bill was introduced by the two physician members of the House of Delegates, Dr. Arris T. Allen (R.-Anne Arundel) and Dr. Torrey C. Brown (D.-Baltimore).[28] Anyone talking to members of the House of Delegates found many of them very impressed with the bill's physician sponsorship: if doctors didn't know the whole story on abortion, who did? In actual fact, Delegate Brown's true understanding of the issue may perhaps be gauged by the fact that most of the questions he directed to witnesses during committee hearings were passed to him on slips of paper by the paid lobbyist of the Maryland Committee for Abortion Law Repeal who sat behind him during the hearings.[29] (This "committee" was never visible in the state except in the person of this lobbyist; it is uncertain what the true source of his salary was.)

In the beginning, the bill's proponents were confident of its passage. When it was approved by the House Committee on Environmental Matters in mid-February, the Washington *Post* reported that even its strongest opponents had "glumly predicted" or "grudgingly conceded" that the measure would soon successfully emerge from the House, probably within a week.[30] But the measure did not emerge from the House within a week. It was a full month before it was even cleared for a final vote. And, suddenly, the Baltimore *Sun* was reporting that the *opponents* of the bill had "the votes needed to defeat the measure in hand."[31] The following week the bill was, in fact, decisively defeated, 77 to 59.

What happened to this Maryland abortion-on-demand bill on its way to the inevitable victory abortion is supposed to be winning everywhere can be taken as one more proof that this victory is far from being won, if only people are prepared to resist "the wave of the future." The defeat of this legislation, in a state hitherto so favorable to the abortion mentality, did not just happen. It was managed, in the first instance, by a group of astute and dedicated delegates within the House who kept delaying the final vote on the measure by parliamentary tactics while citizen opposition to it was made overwhelmingly manifest.

The citizen opposition, in turn, was aroused in large part

by a small group of anti-abortion activists, chiefly doctors showing slides of aborted fetuses, who stumped many parts of the state impressing upon audiences the reality of abortion.

All the time the bill was being debated in the House, a convenient target existed against which citizen opposition could be aroused. The opponents in the House of Delegates continued to delay the final vote by the introduction of a new amendment each day, after which, according to House rules, the vote could be held over until the next day. After the vote on each amendment, another amendment would be introduced, and the vote held over again. "The daily abortion vote has become the session's most predictable and popular attraction, drawing packed galleries of abortion opponents and pulling staff assistants out of their offices," wrote the pro-abortion Washington *Post*. "Some freshman delegates, admittedly impressed by the parliamentary nimbleness of the opposition, credit the debate with offering them an unparalleled opportunity to learn all the tricks at once."[32]

The proponents of the bill initially seemed to dominate the voting on the bill. Only one of the many amendments offered, which would have prohibited the establishment of commercial abortion referral services, was finally adopted. All other amendments were defeated by the bill's proponents by fairly comfortable margins, except one lowering the abortion time limit to twelve weeks, which unexpectedly passed. The proponents of the bill regrouped their forces, came back the next day, and restored the twenty-week limit.

A few delegates were voting against each amendment in order to keep from having a *better* bill to defeat at the end; some of the House leadership, as the final vote proved, was apparently voting against the amendments introduced from the floor in order to uphold the committee system. It is perhaps noteworthy that the freely elected legislature of an American state actually *rejected* an amendment which would have required the physician to "make every effort to save the life" of any aborted fetus which showed any sign of life.[33]

While these parliamentary delaying tactics were going on, what Del. S. Frank Shore (D.-Montgomery County), one of the principal leaders of the opposition, called a "team effort" of doctors "blitzed the state speaking to groups everywhere to mobilize opposition."[34] This effort among the voters was the essential counterpoint to the tactics employed in the House of Delegates. As Delegate Shore told the Baltimore *Sun*, these tactics were used "until we could get to the voters," since the bill would simply have passed if it had been voted on when it first came to the floor.[34] Parliamentary maneuvers were essential, and they were brilliantly managed by such delegates as Andrew J. Burns (D.-Baltimore), Edward Dabrowski, Jr. (D.-Baltimore), and, especially, Paul E. Weisengoff (D.-Baltimore). In the parliamentary effort, freshmen delegates such as Samuel Dantoni (D.-Baltimore County) joined veterans who had been fighting and voting against abortion since 1967, such as Alexander Bolling Bell (D.-Montgomery County). But all the parliamentary maneuvers would have come to naught in the end unless the votes of enough delegates could be changed to effect the desired outcome. Almost alone among the delegates, S. Frank Shore (a freshman who had nosed out a pro-ZPG incumbent by only 49 votes after the absentee ballots were counted, and whose election was not even announced until a week after the votes were counted) realized the importance of mobilizing the people. He made himself the focus in Annapolis of the citizen opposition, as voters by the scores and then by the hundreds, sickened by the doctors' slides of aborted fetuses, began writing, wiring, and visiting Annapolis.

The efforts to mobilize the voters and motivate them to oppose the abortion bill actively had actually begun months earlier, before the 1970 elections. Dr. William F. Colliton, Jr., an obstetrician-gynecologist from Bethesda, Maryland, organized the first slide presentations. As chairman of the Maryland Human Life Committee, a small Catholic group working primarily in the Maryland counties of the Archdiocese of Washington, Dr. Colliton had already made his group a force to reckon with at the time of the elections. Assisted in the beginning primarily by Dr. Edward J. Connor of Prince Georges County and Dr. William J. Hogan, also of Bethesda, in Montgomery County, he had organized a group of more than a dozen additional physicians, as well as other speakers, who were giving presentations over a good part of the state by the time of the vote on the abortion bill.

Dr. Hogan presented the slides even to the House committee deliberating on the bill; the effects were visible on the faces of the committee members. Although the bill was ultimately voted out of committee by one vote, the tide that was beginning to run against it was already evident at the committee. A Baltimore group working against the bill turned up at the same hearings with a Protestant minister, the Reverend Robert T. Woodworth of the Open Bible Tabernacle to testify against it. A Black, Protestant lawyer from Baltimore, Mr. Thomas Curtis, decisively rejected the thesis that abortion-on-demand was primarily "needed" by Black ghetto women.[35] Mr. and Mrs. James Donahue of Glen Burnie were instrumental in organizing the initial citizens' effort in the Baltimore area.

What finally defeated the bill, then, was the rising citizen opposition. It became so obvious that even the press and media were forced to acknowledge its existence and even comment upon it. Speakers appeared on TV to "reply" to editorials favoring abortion. Spokesmen for human life were suddenly invited to be on panels hitherto reserved for Women's Lib' types. Letters to the editor began to be printed. Parish Right To Life Committees were formed in the three dioceses containing Maryland Counties, and, once formed, were responsible for getting out literally hundreds of voters. Priests such as Fr. Andrew Cassin of St. Bernadine's parish in Suitland worked tirelessly on these efforts. Fr. Charles D. Gorman of St. Jude's in Rockville mailed out thousands of pamphlets.

By the time of the vote on the bill, each delegate had received hundreds of letters and cables opposing the bill. The mail ran eight or ten to one against the bill. The galleries and corridors of the State House in Annapolis were packed almost daily by citizens wearing signs proclaiming "Life," "Abortion is Murder," or "Kill House Bill 100." Two housewives from one Catholic parish in Montgomery County, Mrs. Bridget Burkart and Mrs. Eileen Heim, managed to collect no less than 30,000 signatures on petitions against the bill, which were delivered to Annapolis prior to the vote. Another housewife, Mrs. Patricia Hurley of Sykesville, the weekend before the vote, organized a rally at a Baltimore hotel which was addressed by Delegates Shore and Gallagher, as well as by Dr. Hogan; Delegate Troy Braily (D.-Baltimore), who had voted for liberalized abortion in 1968, appeared unannounced to declare that this time his vote would be more pleasing to the opponents of abortion. It was. Two other housewives, Mrs. Mary Ann Egan and Mrs. Karen Helfert, organized an interdenominational Citizens Information Committee which was especially effective in helping to restore a prolife balance in the press and media.

In the middle of the Maryland debate on abortion, another housewife, Mrs. Jane Connelly, organized a local Birthright program,[37] a volunteer service staffed by women of all creeds, intended to provide an alternative to women with "problem pregnancies." The publicity which attended this effort also contributed to the increasingly pro-life atmosphere that was finally becoming manifest in Maryland by the Spring of 1971. The Archdiocese of Washington provided facilities to help the Birthright program get underway, as the Church generally provided the impetus and leadership necessary to insure the success of what, on the legislative front, was essentially an unfunded and unstaffed citizens' effort. Among Catholics, the moral issue of abortion was never allowed to be in doubt; this was the purpose of the Right To Life Sundays proclaimed in all three of the dioceses constituting portions of the State of Maryland.[38]

In the end, perhaps the remarkable thing is that more of the delegates in Annapolis didn't get the message, for fifty-nine were found to vote for abortion-on-demand.[39] It must be admitted, though, that the pro-life "victory" in 1971 was a victory for life only in a qualified sense. Maryland still has one of the most permissive abortion laws in America.

The experience of the state with abortion "reform" over the past five years suggests that the proponents of abortion and other anti-life "solutions" will keep on pressing as long as they do not encounter resistance. There seem to be no moral restraints which would prevent the implementation of the most radical kinds of "life control" schemes if the proponents of such anti-life measures are allowed to manipulate the political process without challenge.

The Maryland experience also suggests, however, that the anti-life forces can be stopped when effective resistance does materialize. It is to be hoped that the knowledge and concern about abortion and its spread, gained by so many Maryland citizens while the fight against it was going on, will be translated into a future effort to roll back some of the gains abortion has made.

Appendix II

Bernard J. Ransil, M.D., Ph.D., Discovers St. Thomas Aquinas

WHAT can we think about a Catholic doctor at Harvard University trying to justify the morality of therapeutic abortion from the writings of St. Thomas Aquinas? What next? we might wonder.

It is not as if Dr. Bernard J. Ransil, characterized as a "Catholic scientist-physician" (since otherwise we might not have guessed it), has seized upon the most characteristic features of the Angelic Doctor's thought, however. On the contrary, in composing a pamphlet which he has entitled simply *"Abortion"* (Paulist Press, 1969; $1.25), Dr. Ransil does not so much as hint at such basic Thomistic themes as:

—That the truth of reason is not opposed to the truth
of the Christian faith; or,
—That we must always do good and avoid evil.

Rather, he is quite sure that there are things which,
though they may once have been considered truths of the
faith, have fallen into conflict today with modern ideas:

—"Human knowledge at the active research fron-
tiers"; or
—"Advanced areas of specialization of which the
magisterium has only cursory knowledge."

Dr. Ransil seems completely unaware that Christian
morality is a question of the doing of good and the avoiding
of evil. He seems to think it is a matter of reaching psychological maturity and acquiring ever more experimental
knowledge— "the continuous acquisition of new data and
confrontation with divergent opinions," as he styles it.
"The transformation Christ calls upon each individual to
make," he further states, "deals primarily with ideas and
ideals which imply education, formation, growth and development . . ." Nothing about Christian morality here.
"Why seek you the living among the dead? He is not here."
(*Luke* 24: 5–6)

St. Thomas isn't here either, really. What Dr. Ransil
takes from St. Thomas is neither an essential nor even an
important part of the latter's thought. Rather, Dr. Ransil
takes merely St. Thomas' theory of human "ensoulment."
According to Thomistic thought, the rational human soul
is considered the "form" of the human body; hence a rational human soul can only be infused into a material body
capable of receiving it and being "formed" by it. Since
until very recently available biological knowledge
afforded scarcely a clue about the real nature of the human embryo, it was surely reasonable for St. Thomas to

conclude that the embryo was still unformed matter which had to be formed, first by a vegetative then by an animal "soul," before it could properly be animated by a rational human soul.

Hence the theory of St. Thomas—and Aristotle—that "ensoulment" takes place some time after conception—forty days for males and ninety days for females. Hence, too, the Angelic Doctor's mistaken opinion that although abortion before the "infusion" of the human soul was a grave sin, it was not equivalent to homicide. (Today there is more interest in St. Thomas' view that the embryo was not yet "human" at conception than in his view that destroying the embryo was nevertheless a "grave sin"; no more is Dr. Ransil apparently interested in this latter opinion of St. Thomas!)

We can be reasonably certain today that St. Thomas would have reached a different conclusion about the presence of true human life from the moment of conception if he had possessed our scientific knowledge. It is interesting that the Church, for instance, ascribes the immaculateness of Mary to the moment of her conception! In fact, the fertilized ovum, or zygote, though it is but a single microscopic human cell, is in itself a complete, integral, genetically unique vital organism with its own incredibly complex structure and function; within itself the zygote contains the ability and genetic "instructions" to subdivide into trillions of daughter cells, each with specialized structure and function. These cells eventually compose the adult human being. Moreover, a human being is the only thing this zygote *does* develop into—there is nothing "vegetative" or "animal" about it at any stage along the way; it is entirely human. Such is the evidence of modern biology. Would St. Thomas have doubted that such a—far from "unformed"—zygote was incapable of being infused with a human soul? For the eyes of faith, could not the soul be the very principle which animates this remarkable single human cell from the beginning?

However St. Thomas might have looked at it, Dr. Bernard Ransil, who does know all about the findings of modern biology, nevertheless doubts that the product of human conception is human. But then, on the evidence of his pamphlet, we could scarcely equate his thinking with what we are accustomed to find in St. Thomas!

As a matter of fact, Dr. Ransil doesn't appear to have *done* much thinking on the subject. Reasoned arguments showing that no human being is present until some undetermined time after conception, or *when* that time might be, are not his strongest point. To be sure he *asserts* that "the embryo, or fetus . . . is all promise; it is potential unrealized."

He also rehashes the arguments of St. Thomas—without, however, making it clear to what degree he accepts or rejects them. He seems more interested in using St. Thomas as a stick to beat the Church for her absolute prohibition of direct abortion; but surely he does not accept the metaphysical basis on which St. Thomas denied true human status to the undeveloped embryo. Hence we are entitled to know a little more about the basis on which Dr. Ransil thinks he is reviving the arguments of St. Thomas now. We get little enlightenment on this, beyond copious and imprecise references to Dr. Ransil's own "biomedical perspective."

But from the empirical, scientific standpoint it would seem to matter very little when the soul is infused, or indeed whether it is infused at all! What the scientific data do establish beyond doubt is that we are dealing with a new human individual from the moment of conception. Dragging the ideas of St. Thomas on "ensoulment" into this context merely serves to confuse the issue.

Dr. Ransil's own "scientific" arguments against full human status for the unborn child seem reducible to two: 1) the non-viability of the developing fetus outside the mother's body; and 2) the differences in the "morphology" of the fetus and that of a fully developed human person. "Beyond the time of uterine implantation, the embryo-fetus requires the circulatory system of the mother in order to survive," Dr. Ransil declares.

Well, Dr. Ransil requires the atmospheric system of the earth in order to survive! How does the nature of the environment he requires make him any less human? In fact, he requires different, specialized environments at different times and in different situations in his life, for example, the environment of a heated room or a warm bed in freezing weather, if he is to remain "viable."

Does the fact that an astronaut would perish outside the controlled environment of his spacecraft diminish his humanity? The fact that a fetus at two or three months of age would surely perish outside his mother's body is no argument against *his* humanity, either!

What Dr. Ransil's argument from "morphology" seems to amount to is that "the product of conception does not possess human form." (Incidentally, he regularly and almost exclusively refers to the unborn child as a "product of conception"; this clinical appellation effectively dehumanizes the child, until we reflect that we are *all* "products of conception.")

What the non-possession of "human form" seems to mean to Dr. Ransil, in turn, is that the human fetus doesn't (yet!) *look* like a human being. "No one seeing the fertilized egg and its immediate successive forms would *equate* (Italics added) it with a human being," Dr. Ransil says disingenuously. And: "In the absence of any other guide, we must accept the evidence of the senses" (i.e., the fetus is not a human being because it doesn't look like one). Perhaps we should similarly reject the atomic composition of matter because we can't see atoms with our own eyes.

But we do have another guide besides the senses in this matter. If Dr. Ransil had really delved into St. Thomas beyond his theory of "ensoulment," he might have discovered what this guide was; as it is, it does not seem to have occurred to him that his *reason* has to come into play at some point in interpreting the evidence of his senses. If an entity develops entirely according to its own nature how can we thereby conclude that it has *changed* its nature at some point (which point, however, cannot be specified)? One of the first rules both of sound philosophy and of the empirical sciences is that "appearances deceive."

What the non-human appearance of the fetus which Dr. Ransil has pointed to *really* proves is: that human beings *look different* at certain different stages in their development, not that they are non-human at any of these stages. Otherwise a quadruple amputee would lose his humanity along with his arms and legs!

Similarly, the use of terms such as zygote, embryo, fetus and the like no more indicates the non-humanity of the unborn at different stages in their development than does the use of terms such as newborn, infant, child, youth, or adult establish anything against the humanity of persons at one of *these* stages of a continuous human development.

So much, then, for the excursion of a "Catholic scientist-physician" into the writings of St. Thomas Aquinas. Why in the world did he bother? His own explanation, incredibly, is that he wished "to oppose and work to prevent or minimize error in Church teaching, [!] but also because," his explanation continues, "the veritable explosion of knowledge and technology in the domain of biomedical phenomena has provided man with the means of control over many specific processes of human life heretofore as-

cribed to the immediate watchful concern of Divine Providence."

In other words, because we now *can* control certain processes of human life, therefore we *should* control them
. . . We have already seen how Dr. Ransil tends to confuse
morality with mere knowledge and hence fails to see how
morality may still apply to those things which he thinks
have been "the immediate, watchful concern of Divine
Providence," regardless of our new knowledge and technology. Examples of this confusion abound in his pamphlet. Craniotomy—crushing of the fetal head to facilitate
delivery—is no longer *needed* with modern medical techniques, he remarks; presumably it would be all right if it
were needed, though. Masturbation may be *necessary* to
permit examination of sperm. And so on. Dr. Ransil seems
incapable of standing up and proclaiming that some
things are *wrong*—regardless of human power to do them,
or of their alleged need. Dr. Ransil seems here to have
accepted the rule of pure expediency which unfortunately
reigns in so many quarters of our society today.

In point of fact, his whole pamphlet seems to have developed out of his belief that therapeutic abortion—abortion
to save the life or health of the mother—is expedient and
necessary and justified today, whatever may have been the
Catholic condemnation of it in the past. Hence, since he
himself still seems to consider himself a Catholic, he
needs to produce some "Catholic" arguments which justify his stand and call into question the Church's absolute
condemnation of any direct abortive act. From his point of
view, then, the discovery that no less an authority than St.
Thomas Aquinas did not hold that human life was fully
present in the womb from the moment of conception was,
well, *we* can hardly call it a Godsend!—For we can too
easily imagine where else it may have come from! At

the very least, though, we have to admit that it fell conveniently to hand for Dr. Ransil's purposes!

We have seen, however, that his summoning of St. Thomas to the witness stand in this case will hardly help him in the court of Catholic opinion. Neither will his handling of the traditional Catholic moral principle of double effect. We will recall that this principle establishes that an action, good in itself and intended for a good effect, may be performed even though a second and bad effect which will follow from it is also foreseen, provided there is due proportion between the intended good and the permitted evil. (It was St. Thomas, of course, who first formulated the principle of double effect: we may wonder how Dr. Ransil failed to chance upon it in the course of his studies of St. Thomas.)

In accordance with the principle of double effect, for example, a physician could licitly remove a cancerous uterus which threatened the life of the mother even if he also indirectly caused an abortion thereby; but he could not directly destroy a fetus in the womb in order to stop, say, uncontrolled maternal vomiting even if it threatened the life of the mother.

Although it is a principle which manifestly arises from the application of right reason to human situations where real moral conflict exists, Dr. Ransil seems to think the Church holds to the principle of double effect in moral theology because she somehow prefers "new" life (the fetus) to developed, mature life (the mother). In his exact words: "If—constrained by the possibility of losing both lives—a choice must be made, the Catholic physician works for new life, tolerating but not willing the death of the mother if it occurs."

Since for Dr. Ransil the goal of life itself seems to be development to maturity (instead of development of moral character and eventual blessedness), he can only regard the Church's continued reliance on the principle of double effect, as he understands it, as profoundly mistaken. What he totally misses, however, is that in "choosing" the "new life," as Dr. Ransil styles it, a Catholic physician would merely be *permitting* the evil of the mother's death; he would not be *killing* the mother. There is quite a difference here!

In "choosing"—always in the sense Dr. Ransil means it —what he calls the "fully developed, flesh-and-blood, three dimensional person" of the mother, however, the Catholic doctor *would be* killing the child! Is there no moral difference between allowing someone to die, and killing someone? Dr. Ransil does not seem to perceive any, nor, we may add, do the proponents of permissive abortion generally seem to perceive any. But their blindness is no warrant for the Catholic Church to suspend her condemnation of the direct taking of any innocent life; and it has nothing to do with any supposed preference for "new" life.

The murk of Dr. Ransil's thought only deepens when he comes to consider the fact that natural miscarriages may be what he calls "natural ways of eliminating defective products of conception." He concludes from this observation about nature that "surgical removal of a defective product of conception is tantamount to *assisting nature* (Italics added) in performing a function which the body, left to itself, is unable to accomplish because of some defect in the natural abortion mechanism."

By this reasoning, pushing someone into a rent caused by an earthquake would apparently be "tantamount to assisting nature" in destroying him . . . Just because something may happen in nature hardly gives men the moral right to do it: that is what human morality is all about. A man might be struck by lightning, but that hardly gives us warrant to decide to electrocute him!

The pity of it is that, while a Catholic such as Dr. Ransil

spins out all these lugubrious sophistries trying to show that therapeutic abortion may be justified, the proponents of permissive abortion have already moved far beyond such niceties as the so-called medical "indications" for abortion. Even the moderate abortion "reform" which has taken hold in several states has already gone beyond mere therapeutic abortion and admits other grounds than maternal health (rape, eugenic considerations). What the pro-abortionists are now calling for goes much farther than these considerations: they don't think an abortion needs any reason at all!

While a Dr. Ransil deludes himself into thinking that there exists a "general consensus among mankind . . . [on] . . . the sacredness of life," bills for abortion-on-demand are being introduced into the legislatures of state after state. Some of these bills have already been voted into law, with slight variations or "safeguards" from state to state. And of course, abortion-on-demand is old hat in such countries as Japan and Hungary!

Meanwhile, a Dr. Ransil is still doubting that the "legalization of the principle of therapeutic abortion will inevitably lead to legalization of all forms of arbitrary killing, which in turn would lead to 'widespread moral decay.' " Not "will lead," Dr. Ransil. As the gasoline company ad has it, it's happening, right now . . . Commerce in live human fetuses for experimental purposes is reported in Britain . . . A noisy euthanasia lobby is meanwhile preparing to introduce killing-on-demand legislation into the Mother of Parliaments now that restrictions on abortion have been largely removed . . . A bill introduced into the Hawaii legislature, where most restrictions on abortion have also been lifted, would require the attending physician to sterilize any woman delivering her second child . . .

In Dr. Ransil's own scientific field, professional journals

such as *Science* and *Bioscience* have been tranquilly discussing population control measures of the most coercive and hair-raising kind for the past several years without a murmur of protest from their scientific clientele. Talk about "widespread moral decay"! Now the press and the mass media are starting to take up these themes; a couple of dozen population control bills have already been introduced into the U.S. Congress. One of them has already passed the U.S. Senate. With all of this, a Catholic doctor takes it upon himself to chide his Church and his fellow Catholics for opposing therapeutic abortion, and thinks he should call in St. Thomas Aquinas to help him do it!

What country and what century are you living in, Dr. Ransil? Back to your books! You can do better than that! May we particularly commend to your attention those chapters of St. Thomas Aquinas which explain the nature of *right* and *wrong* . . . And may we then not hope that your scientific and medical knowledge might be enlisted on the side of *right*?

SANCTE THOMA, ORA PRO NOBIS! AB INSIDIIS DIABOLI, LIBERA NOS, DOMINE!

Appendix III

Notes

I. The Reality of Legalized Abortion

1. "Newsletter"; National Right To Life Committee, December, 1970
2. "Report of Selected Characteristics on Induced Abortions Recorded in New York State, July 1, 1970-June 30, 1971." New York State Department of Health, October, 1971; also New York *Times*, February 20, 1972
3. Hyer, Marjorie. "Chaos Greets New New York Abortion Law." *The National Catholic Reporter,* July 24, 1970.
4. Peters, Doris Revere. "Some New York Nurses Quitting Over Abortion." NC News Service Report in the Washington *Catholic Standard,* November 19, 1970.
5. Scott, Lael. "Legal Abortions, Ready or Not." *New York* magazine, Vol. 3, No. 21, May 25, 1970.
6. *U.S. Medicine,* September 1, 1970.
7. National Association for Repeal of Abortion Laws, *NARAL News,* Summer 1970.
8. *Medical Tribune and Medical News,* August 10, 1970.

9.   Auerbach, Stuart. "Abortions: Now It's Big Business."
        The Washington *Post,* January 10, 1971.
10.   MacPherson, Myra. "The Everyday World of Abortion."
        The Washington *Post,* January 11, 1971.
11.   Arnold, Mark R. "New York Sharply Limits New Law for
        Abortions." *The National Observer,* October 26, 1970.
12.   Pollen, Richard H., M.D. Editorial in *Medical Bulletin,*
        Montgomery County Medical Society (Maryland), Febru-
        ary, 1970.
13.   Press Release, Office of the Administrator, New York City
        Health Services Administration, February 7, 1971.
14.   Personal communication with physicians practicing in
        Maryland and in New York City.
15.   The Washington *Post,* June 30, 1971.
16.   Quoted in Scott, *Loc. cit.,* Note 5 above.
17.   The Colorado experience is discussed in Droegmueller,
        Taylor and Dross. "The First Year Experience in
        Colorado with the New Abortion Law." Cited in Cava-
        naugh, Denis, M.D. "Reforming the Abortion Laws: A
        Doctor Looks at the Case." *America* magazine, April 18,
        1970. The results of the later study were reported in the
        Washington *Post,* December 14, 1971.
18.   The statement of the American College of Obstetricians
        and Gynecologists is dated May 9, 1968. Cited by Con-
        gressman John Dingell, *Congressional Record,* Vol. 116,
        No. 182, November 16, 1970, Page H10287.
19.   Quoted in Remsberg, Charles and Bonnie. "The Stormy
        Aftermath of Abortion Reform" *Good Housekeeping,*
        February, 1971.
20.   The Chicago *Tribune,* December 18, 1970; *The National
        Catholic Reporter,* March 5, 1971.
21.   "Newsletter," National Right To Life Committee, Janu-
        ary, 1971.
22.   Figure of 62 live births cited in *Serviam,* The Newsletter
        of Credo, No. 28, December, 1971; the 33 Oregon live
        births reported in the *Oregon Journal,* March 14, 1972.
23.   Peters, *Loc. cit.,* Note 4 above.
24.   The Washington *Post,* May 16 and 19, 1970, reported on
        the selling of live fetuses in England; for reports on fetal
        experimentation, see, for example, Morriss, Frank,
        "Aborted Fetuses used in Dental Experiments," *The*

Wanderer, March 2, 1972; and "A Thymus For Maggie," *Time,* February 28, 1972.

25.   NC News Service report by Tom Pawlick. The Washington *Catholic Standard,* April 9, 1970.

26.   The New York *Times,* October 17, 1970.

27.   Quoted in the Washington *Post,* March 23, 1970.

28.   "Report of Selected Characteristics on Induced Abortions Recorded in New York State," Note 2 above.

29.   For typical abortion referral service advertising see, for example, *Look's* issue of December 1, 1970; for accounts of abortion referral service activities on college campuses, see the Washington *Post,* January 17, 1971 and the Baltimore *Sun,* February 25, 1971. Actually the college newspaper which does *not* run abortion ads is probably the rarity these days. For accounts of travel agencies which have gone into the abortion business, see the Washington *Post,* February 19, 1970 and *The National Catholic Reporter,* June 28, 1970.

30.   NC News Service Report, "Abortion Is Big Business," in the Washington *Catholic Standard,* June 17, 1971.

31.   The New York *Times,* July 1, 1971; *Life In America,* June, 1971.

32.   Quoted in *Life In America,* July/August, 1971.

33.   *Medical Economics,* January 4, 1971.

34.   The Washington *Post,* March 15, 1970.

35.   *The Wanderer,* December 10, 1970; *NARAL News,* Summer, 1971.

36.   "Newsletter," National Right To Life Committee, December, 1970; Vanderhoeff, Kenneth D., Chairman, Voice for the Unborn in the State of Washington. Letter to the Editor, *National Catholic Reporter,* November 27, 1970.

37.   NARAL "Bulletin," January, 1972.

38.   Pastoral Letter of Patrick Cardinal O'Boyle, Archbishop of Washington, reprinted in the Washington *Catholic Standard,* April 16, 1970.

39.   For a perceptive account of some of the efforts of New York public officials to "implement" the new abortion-on-demand law, see Willis, Catherine B. "Abortion: Theory and Reality." *The Wanderer,* November 26, 1970.

40.   Greenhouse, Linda. "After July 1, an Abortion Should Be

as Simple to Have as a Tonsillectomy, But—" The *New York Times Magazine,* June 28, 1970.

41.   The Washington *Post,* July 2, 1970.

42.   *The Wanderer,* February 25, 1971.

43.   MacPherson, Myra. "Abortion Law Attack Gains." The Washington *Post,* November 11, 1969.

44.   Kilpatrick, James J. "Medi-Cal—Or Who Owes Whom a Living? The Washington *Evening Star,* February 11, 1971.

45.   San Francisco *Examiner,* July 22, 1971.

46.   The Washington *Post,* January 26, 1971. Colorado abortion statistics are quoted from *The Wanderer,* March 2, 1972; Maryland figures are from the State Department of Health and Mental Hygiene.

47.   For details on this Department of Defense abortion program, see *U.S. Medicine,* September 1, 1970. Copies of the actual exchange of memoranda establishing the program are in the possession of the writer. The program was established against the recommendations of the surgeons general of all three armed forces. For an authoritative discussion of the implications of the program, see Schmitz, John G. (Representative in Congress from California) "Abortion on Demand in U.S. Military Hospitals." *The Wanderer,* October 15, 1970. The DOD's public rationale for the program was revealed in replies to letters of protest about the program. The writer received such a letter through the office of Senator Charles McC. Mathias (R.-Md.) from Brigadier General C. J. Hayes, Principal Deputy to the Assistant Secretary of Defense for Health and Environment.

48.   The Washington *Post,* January 12, 1971.

49.   Quoted in the Washington *Post,* April 3, 1971. President Nixon's statement rescinding the Department of Defense abortion-on-request program is important enough to be reproduced here in full: "Historically, laws regulating abortion in the United States have been the province of the States, not the Federal Government. That remains the situation today, as one State after another takes up this question, debates it and decides it. That is where the decisions should be made.

"Partly for that reason, I have directed that the policy

on abortions at American military bases in the United States be made to correspond with the laws of the States where those bases are located. If the laws in a particular State restrict abortions, the rule at the military base hospitals is to correspond to that law.

"The effect of this directive is to reverse service regulations issued last summer, which had liberalized the rules on abortions at military hospitals. The new ruling supersedes this—and has been put into effect by the Secretary of Defense.

"But while this matter is being debated in State capitals, and weighed by various courts, the Country has a right to know my personal views.

"From personal and religious beliefs I consider abortion an unacceptable form of population control. Further, unrestricted abortion policies, or abortion on demand, I cannot square with my personal belief in the sanctity of human life—including the life of the yet unborn. For, surely, the unborn have rights also, recognized in law, recognized even in principles expounded by the United Nations.

"Ours is a nation with a Judeo-Christian heritage. It is also a nation with serious social problems—problems of malnutrition, of broken homes, of poverty and of delinquency. But none of these problems justified such a solution.

"A good and generous people will not opt, in my view, for this kind of alternative to its social dilemmas. Rather, it will open its hearts and homes to the unwanted children of its own, as it has done for the unwanted millions of other lands." Reprinted in The New York *Times,* April 4, 1971.

50.   *Medical World News,* June 12, 1971. An Air Force officer has informed the writer that military personnel and dependents can also obtain a "non-availability statement" at bases where abortion is illegal—this enables them to get an abortion from any civilian doctor or hospital at no cost except a small deductible.

51.   *U.S. vs. Vuitch,* 305 F. Supp. 1032 (1969).

52.   This entire account of the—ultimately successful—

efforts to force D.C. General Hospital to institute a program of abortions at public expense is taken entirely from the generally pro-abortion stories on the subject which appeared in the Washington daily press. See, notably, the stories appearing in the Washington *Post* for February 5, February 25, March 7, March 13, March 15, March 21, and April 29, 1970. The National Association for Repeal of Abortion Laws took credit for "initiating" the American Civil Liberties Union suit brought to force the issue; see *NARAL News,* Summer, 1970.

53. The Washington *Post,* March 13, 1970.

54. *Ibid.,* May 16, 1970.

55. *Ibid.,* May 7, May 23, May 26, May 30, and December 1, 1970.

56. Ibid., November 11, 1969; the Washington *Evening Star,* April 29, 1970.

57. The Washington *Post,* February 28, 1971.

58. *Ibid.,* January 15, 1971.

59. The Washington *Catholic Standard,* April 29, 1971; *Congressional Record,* Vol, 117, No. 57, April 23, 1971.

60. The Washington *Post,* March 12, 1971. Still another "abortorium," this one capable of doing about 15 abortions per day by the suction curettage method, was established in the nation's capital in May, 1971—*after* the Supreme Court overturned Judge Gesell's decision in the Vuitch case. See the Washington *Post,* May 20, 1971. By the fall of 1971, four clinics were openly performing abortions in the nation's capital. See *Washingtonian* magazine, October, 1971.

61. *Ibid.,* April 22, 1971.

62. Supreme Court of the United States, No. 84-October Term (1970-1971). *United States, Appellant vs. Milan Vuitch.* Mr. Justice Stewart, dissenting in part.

63. The Washington *Post,* April 22, 1971.

64. The Washington *Evening Star,* April 21, 1971.

65. The Washington *Post,* June 7, 1971.

66. *Washingtonian,* Vol. 7, No. 1, October, 1971; *Potomac* (The Washington *Post*), September 19, 1971.

67. *Redbook,* Vol. 137, No. 2, June, 1971.

68. *Pittsburgh Catholic,* July 23, 1971.

69.   *The National Catholic Reporter,* April 17, 1970.
70.   *NARAL News,* Summer, 1970; Alton *Evening Telegraph* (Illinois), March 17, 1971.
71.   *National Catholic Reporter,* February 19, 1971.
72.   The New York case is *Stewart vs. Long Island College Hospital,* 58 Misc. 2d 432 (Sup. Ct. King's County, 1968). This case cited by Pilpel, Harriet. "A Non-Catholic Lawyer's View." In Hall, Robert E., M.D. (Ed.) *Abortion In A Changing World,* Columbia University Press, New York and London, 1970. Volume I, Page 160. The Virginia case was reported in the Washington *Post,* November 23, 1971.
73.   See, for example, "Physician's Blue Shield Bulletin," dated January 25, 1971. Issued by Maryland Blue Shield, Inc., 7800 York Road, Baltimore, Md. 21203.
74.   *National Catholic Reporter,* September 10, 1971, reported the 18,000 figure. The estimate of 505,000 legal abortions is taken from *Population and the American Future: The Report of the Commission on Population Growth and the American Future,* Chapter 9, March, 1972.
75.   The Washington *Daily News,* October 8, 1970.
76.   Shelton, Elizabeth. "A Quick, Painless, and Uncostly Abortion Procedure." The Washington *Post,* September 26, 1970.
77.   "Letters," *Journal of the American Medical Association* , September 13, 1971, Vol. 217, No. 11.
78.   An Act Relating to the Right to Die with Dignity. Prefiled October, 1969, by Representative (Dr.) Walter Sackett. Report on the White House Conference in The Washington *Post,* November 30, 1971.
79.   The Washington Sunday *Star,* February 27, 1972.
80.   *Journal of the American Medical Association.* October 11, 1971, Vol. 218, No. 2

II. Is the Unborn Child a Human Being?

1.   Patten, Bradley M. *Foundations of Embryology,* McGraw-Hill, New York, 1964. Page 3.
2.   Byrne, Robert M. "Abortion On Demand: Whose Morality?" *Notre Dame Lawyer,* Vol. 46, No. 1, Fall, 1970. Pages 6-7. Byrne draws this scientific data from H.M.I. Liley,

Modern Motherhood (rev. ed., 1969) and Andre Hellegers, M.D., "Fetal Development." *Theological Studies* 3, 7 (1970).

3. Guttmacher, Alan F. Statement in "Symposium—Law, Morality, and Abortion," 22 *Rutgers Law Review* 415, 436 (1968). Quoted in notes to the majority opinion in *Rosen vs. Louisiana State Board of Medical Examiners,* U.S. District Court, Eastern District of Louisiana, Civil Action No. 70-1304, Section E.

4. The New York *Times,* May 22, 1967.

5. Montagu, Ashley. *Life Before Birth.* Quoted by Kindregan, Charles P. *Abortion, the Law and Defective Children.* A Legal-Medical Study. Corpus Books, Washington/Cleveland, 1969, Page 23.

6. Williams, Glanville, *The Sanctity of Life and the Criminal Law.* Alfred A. Knopf, New York, 1957, page 3.

7. Hardin, Garrett. Biology: Its Principles and Implications. Second Edition. W. H. Freeman and Company, San Francisco, 1966. Page 135.

8. The New York *Times,* March 3, 1967. Quoted by Callahan, Daniel. *Abortion: Law, Choice, and Morality.* The MacMillan Company, New York. Page 402.

9. Williams, Glanville. "Euthanasia and Abortion." 38 University of Colorado Law Review, 197-201. Quoted in Kindregan, *op. cit.,* Note 5 above.

10. Hardin, *op. cit.,* Note 7 above, Page 135.

11. Webster's Seventh New Collegiate Dictionary, G & C. Merriam Company, Springfield, Massachusetts, 1965. Page 487.

12. Ehrlich, Paul R. Interview in *Playboy* magazine. Vol. 17. No. 8, August, 1970.

13. Not only is the child a new human being from the moment of conception, he is *recognizably* human far sooner than commonly realized. By the end of the twelfth week of pregnancy (the time limit for "safe" abortions by the D & C or suction curettage methods), the baby's heart pumps 50 pints of blood a day, and he can move, kick, swallow, spread his toes, make a fist, turn his head, and frown, according to the *Marshall Cavendish Encyclopedia of the Human Mind and Body.* (Quoted in "Research Committee Report," Voice for the Unborn, 115 9th

Street, Vancouver, Washington.) Dr. H.M.I. Liley, who with her husband, A. William Liley, was a pioneer in developing techniques for blood transfusions in the womb[!], has written as follows: "Because the fetus is protected, warmed, and nourished within the womb, it was long thought that the unborn must have the nature of a plant, static in habit and growing in size. Recently through modern techniques of diagnosing and treating the unborn baby, we have discovered that little could be further from the truth.

"The fluid that surrounds the human fetus at 3, 4, 5, and 6 months is essential to both its growth and its grace. The unborn's structure at this early stage is highly liquid, and although his organs have developed, he does not have the same relative bodily proportions that a newborn baby has. The head, housing the miraculous brain, is quite large in proportion to the remainder of the body and the limbs are still relatively small. Within this watery world, however, where we have been able to observe him in his natural state by closed circuit x-ray television set, he is quite beautiful and perfect in his fashion, active and graceful. He is neither an acquiescent vegetable nor a witless tadpole as some have conceived him to be in the past, but rather a tiny human being as independent as though he were lying in a crib with a blanket wrapped around him instead of his mother." (Liley, H.M.I. *Modern Motherhood.* Random House, New York, 1959. Pages 26-27.) This same book points out what in fact should be obvious, namely, that the fetus *feels pain:* "When doctors first began invading the sanctuary of the womb, they did not know that the unborn baby would react to pain in the same fashion as a child would . . . By no means a vegetable as he has so often been pictured, the unborn knows perfectly well when he has been hurt, and he will protest it just as violently as would a baby lying in a crib." (Page 50) Both these passages are quoted by Congressman John Dingell, *Congressional Record,* Vol. 116, No. 182, November 16, 1970. Page H10289.

III. What Did We Do to Deserve Abortion On Demand?

1. *NARAL News,* Summer, 1970; Summer, 1971. The activist NARAL organization considers that even getting a bill introduced is a victory, whether the bill passes or not.

2. See *Life In America,* July, 1971. It is hard to see how Congress could enact Senator Packwood's bill without running afoul of the 10th Amendment to the Constitution which reserves legislative powers not specifically delegated to the federal government to the *states.*

3. Granfield, David. *The Abortion Decision.* Doubleday and Company, Garden City, New York, 1969. Page 79.

4. Quoted by Granfield, *Ibid.,* Page 73.

5. *Ibid.,* Page 76. The results of the new English law, which allows abortion virtually on demand, have been similar to what New York experienced two years later. London promptly became "the abortion capital of the world" (e.g., feature story in the Washington *Post,* July 10, 1969). As in New York, commercial abortion clinics sprang up outside the framework of the British National Health Service as soon as the law was passed. The cost of abortions rose fivefold; the maternal death rate from abortion rose 300 per cent. Patients needing medical care were denied beds given to abortion cases. Nurses revolted against handling the remains of the aborted children. By the end of 1970, nearly 250 members of Parliament had signed a petition calling for an inquiry into the law, although there had been only 83 votes against it when it passed. Abortion rates in Britain skyrocketed exactly as they have done in American States where the practice has been liberalized or legalized: 22,216 in 1968; 54,158 in 1969; 83,849 in 1970; 126,774 in 1971. (For documentation of these points, see NC News Service Reports printed *inter alia* in the Washington *Catholic Standard,* August 6, August 13, August 27, and November 19, 1970). Though most physicians favored the new abortion law when it passed Parliament, 92 per cent of physicians polled in 1970 had come to oppose it ("Consultants Report on Abortion," *British Medical Journal,* May 30, 1970).

6. See Granfield, *op. cit.,* Note 2 above, for text and discus-

sion of the American Law Institute's "model" abortion law. Pages 78-62, 186-193, and 238-239.

7. For the principal features of the current American abortion laws, see two leaflets published by the pro-abortion Association for the Study of Abortion, Inc., 120 West 57th Street, New York, N.Y. 10019. The leaflets are entitled "Checklist of Abortion Laws in the United States" and "Analysis of Abortion Laws in the United States."

8. Prosser, *Torts.* Quoted by Noonan, John T., Jr. "Amendment of the Abortion Law: Relevant Data and Judicial Opinion." *The Catholic Lawyer,* Vol. 15, No. 2, Spring, 1969. Reprinted as a pamphlet by the National Right To Life Committee. Professor Noonan includes a brief but convincing discussion of the legal status of the unborn child in both tort law and Constitutional law. See also the National Right To Life Committee's "Special Legal Report: Courts Defend the Unborn," March, 1971, obtainable from the Committee, along with a variety of other useful material, at P. O. Box 9365, Washington, D.C. 20005. For an excellent discussion of case law tending to establish the legal rights of the unborn, see Grisez, Germain. *Abortion: The Myths, The Realities, and the Arguments.* New York and Cleveland: Corpus Books, 1970. Pages 361-429.

9. E. g., *Who Shall Live?* A Report Prepared for the American Friends' Service Committee. Hill and Wang, New York, 1970. Page 28.

10. McCormick, Richard A., S.J. "Abortion and Moral Principles." In *The Wrong of Abortion,* Claretian Publications, Chicago, 1967.

11. According to the National Association for Repeal of Abortion Laws, the following are among the national organizations which have endorsed repeal of abortion laws, or abortion-on-demand:

American Association of Planned Parenthood Physicians
American Association of University Women
American Baptist Convention
American Bar Association
American Civil Liberties Union
American College of Obstetricians & Gynecologists
Americans for Democratic Action

American Ethical Union
American Friends Service Committee
American Humanist Association
American Jewish Congress
American Medical Women's Association
American Protestant Hospital Association.
American Psychiatric Association
American Psychoanalytic Association
American Psychological Association
American Public Health Association
Association for Voluntary Sterilization
B'nai B'rith Women
Church Women United, Board of Managers
Citizen's Advisory Council on the Status of Women
Clergy Consultation Service on Abortion
Episcopal Churchwomen of the U.S.A.
Federation of American Scientists
Group for the Advancement of Psychiatry
Izaak Walton League
Medical Committee for Human Rights
Moravian Church, Northern Province Synod
National Association for Repeal of Abortion Laws
National Committee for Children and Youth
National Council on Crime and Delinquency
National Council on Family Relations
National Council of Jewish Women
National Council of Obstetrics-Gynecology
National Council of Women of the U.S.
National Emergency Civil Liberties Committee
National Medical Association
National Organization for Women
Physicians Forum
Planned Parenthood-World Population
Population Association of America
President's Task Force on the Mentally Handicapped
Student American Medical Association
Unitarian Universalist Association
Unitarian Universalist Women's Federation
United Automobile Workers Union
United Church of Christ, United Church Board for Homeland
    Ministries
United Methodist Church, Board of Christian Social Concerns

United Presbyterian Church in the U.S.A., Board of Christian
    Education
White House Conference on Children and Youth
Women's Division of the United Methodists
Women's Liberation
Young Women's Christian Association of the U.S.
Zero Population Growth, Inc.

12. *Glamour,* August, 1971.
13. The Washington *Evening Star,* August 6, 1971.
14. Breslow, Lester, M.D., M.P.H. "Abortion: The Case for Repeal" Leaflet distributed by NARAL.

IV. Will the Courts Save Us?

1.   For a brief but excellent summary of the abortion issue in the courts, see "Special Legal Report: Courts Defend the Unborn," March, 1971, distributed by the National Right To Life Committee, P. O. Box 9365, Washington, D.C. 20005. See also, McKernan, Martin F. "Recent Abortion Ligitation." *The Catholic Lawyer,* Vol. 17, No. 1. Winter, 1971. For notices of the more recent Florida, Kansas, and Vermont cases, see "Newsletter," National Right to Life Committee, February, 1972, and the Washington *Post* December 12, 1971 and March 14, 1972. For Connecticut case, see the New York *Times,* April 19, 1972.
2.   Kummer, Jerome M. "Abortion Reform: A Successful Model of Social Psychotherapy." *Medical Tribune and Medical News,* August 24, 1970.
3.   Supreme Court of the United States, No. 84-October Term, 1970. *United States, Appellant v. Milan Vuitch,* April 21, 1971.
4.   See the summary of arguments presented in the Georgia and Texas cases in the Washington *Post,* December 14, 1971.
5.   On the Byrn case see especially the New York *Times,* February 26, 1972; see also NC News Service reports in the Washington *Catholic Standard,* December 16 and 23, 1971; January 13, February 3, and March 9, 1972.
6.   Steinberg V. Brown, 321 F. Supp. 741 (1970).
7.   Quoted in Detroit *News,* July 10, 1971.
8.   See NARAL 'Bulletin," January, 1972.
9.   The Washington *Post,* February 8, 1972
10.   *Babbitz vs. McCann.* 310 F. Supp. 293 (1970).
11.   See the National Right To Life Legal Report cited in Note 1 above.
12.   *Ibid.*

V. The Arguments for Abortion "Reform"

1. The Washington *Post,* November 30, 1969.
2. *Time* magazine, June 6, 1969; *Population and the American Future: The Report of the Commission on Population Growth and the American Future,* Chapter 9, March, 1972.
3. The results of this poll are cited in Shaw, Russell. *Abortion on Trial.* Pflaum Press, Dayton, Ohio, 1968. Pages 38-39. *The Milbank Memorial Fund Quarterly* poll is cited in Patrick Cardinal O'Boyle's Pastoral Letter on the 1970 Maryland abortion-on-demand bill, reprinted in the Washington *Catholic Standard,* April 16, 1970.
4. Blake, Judith. "Abortion and Public Opinion: The 1960-1970 Decade." *Science,* Vol. 171, February 12, 1971. Pages 540-549.
5. Quoted in O'Donnell, Thomas J., S.J. *Morals in Medicine.* The Newman Press, Westminister, Maryland, 1960. Fr. O'Donnell includes copious citations from the medical literature on each of the diseases or conditions once held to indicate therapeutic abortions. See especially pages 168-235.
6. Wilson, David C., M.D. "The Abortion Problem in the General Hospital." Included in Rosen, Harold, M.D., PH.D. (Ed.) *Abortion in America.* Beacon Press, Boston, 1967.
7. Also included in Rosen, *op. cit.,* Note 6 above, Page 12.
8. Dr. Guttmacher's book is published, appropriately enough, by the Diablo Press, Berkeley, California, 1967. The quotation from Dr. Guttmacher is on Page 9. Dr. Hall's statement is quoted in Lasagna, Louis, M.D. *Life, Death, and the Doctor.* Alfred A. Knopf, New York, 1968, Page 179.
9. Callahan, Daniel. *Abortion: Law, Choice and Morality.* The MacMillan Company, New York, 1970. Page 31. Professor Germain Grisez' summary of the medical situation is taken from his book Abortion: *The Myths, The Realities, and the Arguments,* Corpus Books: New York and Cleveland, 1970. Page 73. Many, many more citations from the regular medical literature could be quoted casting doubt on the question of whether abortion is ever called for on strictly medical grounds. For example:

(a)   Rovinsky, J.J. and Gusberg, S.B. *American Journal of Ob-stetrics and Gynecology.* Vol. 98. Pages 11-17, 1967. "The growing opinion that for most clinical conditions, the natural history of a disease is not influenced deleteri-ously by an intercurrent pregnancy."

(b)   Moore, J. and Randall, D.L. "Trends in Therapeutic Abor-tions: A Review of 137 Cases." *American Journal of Ob-stetrics and Gynecology.* Vol. 63, Page 28, 1952. "With the exception of a few cardiac cases, it might seriously be doubted that maternal diseases commonly offered as in-dications for therapeutic abortion would directly result in death if properly managed during pregnancy."

(c)   Ottoson, Jan-Otto. "Legal Abortion in Sweden: Thirty Years' Experience." *Journal of Biosocial Science*, Vol. 2. April, 1971, Page 191: "Purely medical reasons are no longer mentioned; instead, each case is considered from medical, social and psychological aspects. We no longer see clear-cut diseases so much as ill people whose situa-tion can be understood only by collaboration between physicians and social workers. Thus, abortions are no longer a purely medical problem either in the investiga-tion or in abortion-preventing measures."

10.   Overstreet, E.W., M.D. *Ob-Gyn News*, May 15, 1969. Cited in Connor, Edward J., M.D., F.A.C.O.G., and Aydinol, Or-han H., M.D., F.A.C.O.G., "Therapeutic Abortion-Wash-ington, D.C." *Medical Annals of the District of Colum-bia*, Vol. 39, No. 3, March, 1970. Page 134.

11.   Quoted in *Medical Tribune and Medical News*, August 10, 1970.

12.   Press Conference at Cathedral Latin School, Washington, D.C., December 9, 1969. Text printed in the Washington *Catholic Standard*, December 11, 1969.

13.   According to the Oregon State Board of Health in the case of the Oregon figure: cited in "Research Committee Re-port," Voice for the Unborn, 115 9th Street, Vancouver, Washington. The Maryland figure was cited in the Bal-timore *Sun*, February 19, 1971.

14.   The Colorado figure is taken from *Promoting the Health of Mothers and Children*, Maternal and Child Health Service, Department of Health, Education, and Welfare, 1971; the California figure is from Cavanaugh, Denis, M.D. "Reforming the Abortion Laws: A Doctor Looks at the Case." *America*, April 18, 1970; the result in Virginia was reported in the Washington *Post*, March 13, 1971; for the results of the ten-state study, see Kahn, James B.,

M.D., Boume, Judith P., R.N., M.S., Asher, John D., M.D., and Tyler, Carl W. Jr., M.D. "Surveillance of Abortions in Hospitals in the United States," 1970. *HSMHA Health Reports*, May, 1971, Vol. 86, No. 5.

15. These New York figures are summarized and commented upon by Dr. Pisani in a personal communication to the writer.

16. NARAL "Bulletin," January, 1972.

17. Quoted in *The Wanderer*, January 8, 1970.

18. Arbuse, D., M.D. and Schedtman, J.M.D. "Neuropsychiatric Indications for Therapeutic Abortions." *American Practitioner*, I, 1069, 1950. Quoted in O'Donnell, *op. cit.*, Note 5 above, Pages 223-224.

19. Wilson, *Loc. cit.*, Note 6 above, Page 195.

20. Ottoson, Jan-Otto, "Legal Abortion in Sweden: Thirty Years Experience." *Journal of Biosocial Science*, Vol. 3, N. 2. April 1971, Page 181. See also, Ekblad, Martin. "Induced Abortion on Psychiatric Grounds: A Follow-up Study of 479 Women." *Acta Psychiatrica et Neurologica Scandinavica, Supplementum* 99-102, Stockholm, 1955. Cited by Callahan, *op. cit.*, Note 9 above, Page 68.

21. Ford, Charles V., M.D., Castelnuovo-Tedesco, Pietro, M.D., and Long, Kahlila, MSW. "Abortion: Is It a Therapeutic Procedure in Psychiatry?" *Journal of the Medical Association*, November 22, 1971, Vol. 218, No. 8.

22. Quoted by McCarthy, Colman. "Worst Form of Birth Control Hurts Woman's Psyche." The Washington *Post*, February 28, 1971.

23. See *The Right To Abortion: A Psychiatric View*. Formulated by the Committee on Psychiatry and Law, Group for the Advancement of Psychiatry. Charles Scribner/s Sons, New York, 1970. Especially Page 44.

24. The American Psychoanalytical Association's Study is cited in *U.S. Medicine,* September 1, 1970; Dr. Hellman is quoted by the Washington Post, November 25, 1971.

25. Buck, Pearl S., Foreword to *The Terrible Choice: The Abortion Dilemma*. Bantam Books, New York, 1968.

26. Lasagna, *op. cit.*, Note 8 above, pages 186-187. Another parent of a Mongoloid child, New York State Senator William T. Conklin (R. -Brooklyn), was described by the New York *Times* as a "long-time opponent of abortion re-

form"; in the debate on the New York abortion-on-demand legislation, Senator Conklin too spoke of the "special joy these 'special children' bring to parents" and voiced his deep-seated opposition to those who argued that abortion was justified to avoid the birth of retarded children.

27.   See, for example, the discussion in Callahan, *op. cit.*, Note 9 above, pages 91-95.

28.   *Ibid.*, Pages 104, 106.

29.   Friedman, Theodore, M.D. "Prenatal Diagnosis of Prenatal Disease." *Scientific American*, Vol. 225, No. 5, November, 1971.

30.   Quoted in Simpson, R.S.J. *Abortion-A Matter of Life or Death*. H.C.T.S. Publications, Melbourne, Australia, 1969. Page 27.

31.   See "Research Committee Report," Note 13 above.

32.   See *The Terrible Choice*, Note 25 above, page 70.

33.   Cited in *The Educator*, September/October, 1971.

34.   Diamond, Eugene F. "A Pediatrician Views Abortion." In *Child and Family*, Vol. 7, 1968.

35.   Cavanaugh, *loc. cit.*, Note 14 above.

36.   Granfield, David. *The Abortion Decision*, Doubleday and Company, Garden City, New York, 1969, Page 192.

VI. The Arguments for Abortion on Demand

1.   Potter, Ralph B., Jr. "The Abortion Debate." In Cutler, Donald R. (Ed.) *Updating Life and Death*. Essays in Ethics and Medicine. Beacon Press, Boston, 1969. Pages 85-134.

2.   *Statistical Abstract of the United States*, 1970. Page 141.

3.   Callahan, Daniel. *Abortion: Law, Choice and Morality*. The MacMillan Company, New York, 1970. Page 246. See especially Chapters VI and VII for a discussion of these points.

4.   *Ibid.*, Page 256.

5.   *Ibid.*, Page 260.

6.   "The Abortion Act (1967)." Findings of an Inquiry into the First Year's Working of the Act Conducted by the Royal College of Obstetricians and Gynecologists. *British Medical Journal*, May 30, 1970. Pages 532-533. For the

report of the later "boom" of illegal abortions in Britain, see *Parade* Magazine, June 27, 1971.

7. For Northern European figure, see Callahan, *op. cit.*, Note 3 above. Page 204; for the English figure, see *Medical Tribune World-Wide Report*, May 4, 1970.

8. *Statistical Abstract of the United States*, 1970. Page 55.

9. *Life*, February 27, 1970; *Newsweek*, April 13, 1970; *Pageant*, May, 1970; *New York Times Magazine*, June 28, 1970; *Ramparts*, August, 1970. Senator Tydings quotes the 1.2 figure for illegal abortions on page 43 of his book *Born To Starve*, William Morrow Company, New York, 1970.

10. *South Dakota vs. Munson*; dissenting opinion of Judge Cassibry in *Rosen vs. The Louisiana State Board of Medical Examiners*.

11. Weinberg, Roy D., B.A., LL. B. *Laws Governing Family Planning*. Legal Almanac Series No. 18. Oceana Publications, Dobbs Ferry, New York, 1968. Page 50.

12. Niswander, Kenneth R. "Medical Abortion Practices in the United States." In Smith, David T. (Ed.) *Abortion and the Law*. Western Reserve University, Cleveland, Ohio, 1967. Page 59.

13. Quoted in Shaw, Russell. *Abortion on Trial*. Pflaum Press, Dayton, Ohio, 1968. Page 31.

14. *Statistical Abstract of the United States*, 1970. Page 58.

15. Cited in Callahan, *op. cit.*, Note 3 above, Page 134.

16. Cavanaugh, Denis, M.D. "Reforming the Abortion Laws: A Doctor Looks at the Case." *America*, April 18, 1970.

17. Related by Congressman John Dingell, *Congressional Record*, Vol. 116, No. 182, November 16, 1970. Page H10288.

18. Atkinson, Ti-Grace. Speech reported in the Washington *Catholic Standard*, March 18, 1971.

19. Although the more scholarly of the pro-abortionists admit the fallaciousness of the usual inflated estimates of illegal abortions—and of the maternal mortality and morbidity which allegedly result from illegal abortions— activist organizations such as the National Association for Abortion Law Repeal (NARAL) continue to trot out the "one million illegal abortions per year" in their current publicity. See "Abortion: Questions and Answers"

and "Abortion: The Case For Repeal," by Lester Breslow, M.D., M.P.H., both leaflets distributed by NARAL. A representative of the Women's Abortion Action Coalition cited the one million figure on national TV on November 21, 1971.

20. Ramsey, Paul. "Feticide/Infanticide Upon Request." Condensed in the *Medical-Moral Newsletter*, Vol. VII, Nos. 3 & 4, November and December, 1970.

21. Quoted in *The Wanderer*, May 28, 1970.

22. *Time*, August 3, 1970.

23. Quoted in *The Terrible Choice: The Abortion Dilemma*. Bantam Books, New York, 1968. Page 73.

24. Callahan, *op. cit.*, Note 3 above, page 454.

25. "Newsletter," National Right To Life Committee, September, 1971.

26. The Washington *Post*, April 1, 1970.

27. WMAL Radio, Washington, D.C., November 18, 1971.

28. Ashe, Christy. "Abortion . . . Or Genocide?" *The Liberator*. Vol 10, No. 8, August, 1970.

29. The Washington *Post*, October 22, 1971.

30. See Callahan, *op. cit.*, Note 3 above, especially pages 221-226 and 235-237. See also Endres, Richard J., M.D. "Abortion in perspective." *American Journal of Obstetrics and Gynecology*. Vol. III, September-December, 1971.

31. Wilson, David C., M.D. "The Abortion Problem in the General Hospital." In Rosen, Harold, M.D., Ph.D. (Ed.) *Abortion in America*, Beacon Press, Boston, 1967. Page 196.

32. Grisez, Germain G. *Abortion: The Myths, the Arguments, and the Realities*. Corpus Books, New York and Cleveland, 1970. Page 74.

VII. Is There a Population Explosion?

1. See, for example, Ehrlich, Paul R. and Holdren, John P. "Population and Panaceas: A Technological Perspective." In *Bioscience* magazine, Vol. 19, No. 12, December, 1969.

2. Bates, Marston. *Expanding Population in a Shrinking World*. American Library Association and Public Affairs Pamphlets, New York, 1963, page 1. Cited in Rushdoony,

Rousas J. *The Myth of Overpopulation*. The Craig Press, Nutley, N.J., 1969. Page 18.

3. See, for example, Howard, Walter E. "The Population Crisis Is Here Now." In *Bioscience*, Vol. 19, No. 9, September, 1969. Pages 779-784. Or see: Ehrlich, Paul R. *The Population Bomb*. Ballatine Books, New York, 1968. Chapter One, "The Problem."

4. Ederer, Rupert, Ph.D. "Overpopulation Mythology." In *Social Justice Review*, Vol. 63, No. 2, May, 1970. Page 44.

5. The Washington *Post*, October 28, 1970.

6. Ederer, *loc. cit.*, Note 4 above.

7. The percentages showing the declining birth rate are cited by Jermann, Thomas C. "It's Time To Defuse Population Explosionists." *The National Observer*, July 27, 1970. The Washington Center for Metropolitan Studies data is analyzed in two articles appearing in the Washington *Post*, September 7 and 26, 1971. See also "U.S. Birthrate at All-Time Low," Newsletter, National Right to Life Committee, February, 1972.

8. The Washington *Post*, August 13, 1970.

9. Ederer, *loc.cit.*, Note 4 above, referring to Clark, Colin, *Population Growth and Land Use*, St. Martin's Press, New York, Page 153.

10. Mayer, Jean. "Toward a Non-Malthusian Population Policy." *Columbia Forum*, Summer, 1969. Reprinted in *Effects of Population Growth on Natural Resources and the Environment*. Hearings before a Subcommittee of the Committee on Government Operations, House of Representatives, Ninety-First Congress. U.S. Government Printing Office, Washington, D.C., 1969. Pages 11, 115, and 118.

11. *Ibid.*, Page 116.

12. Broadcast, WGMS Radio, Washington, D.C., February 15, 1971.

13. Quoted from a story in *The National Observer*, October 26, 1970.

14. Brown, Lester R. "Human Food Production as a Process in the Biosphere." *Scientific American*, Vol. 223, No. 3, September, 1970. Page 163.

15. *Ibid.*, Page 162.

16. *Statistical Yearbook of the United Nations*, 1968.

17.   Clark, Colin. "The Earth Can Feed Its People." In McCormack, Arthur (Ed.). *Christian Responsibility and World Poverty*. A Symposium. The Newman Press, Westminster, Maryland, 1963. Page 132.

18.   Ehrlich, Paul R. Holdren, John B. "Impact of Population Growth." *Science*, Vol. 171, March 26, 1971.

19.   Mayer, *loc. cit.*, Note 10 above, Page 114.

20.   Figures on densities taken from *Statistical Yearbook of the United Nations*, 1968.

21.   Clark, Colin. "Starvation or Plenty?" *Triumph* Magazine, Vol. VI, No. 2, February, 1971. This particular issue of *Triumph* is devoted to "exploding the population explosion," and is an excellent source of both facts and arguments.

22.   Enumerated in Rushdoony, *op. cit.*, Note 2 above. Page 3.

23.   Granfield, David. *The Abortion Decision*. Doubleday and Company, Garden City, New York, 1969. Page 79.

24.   Shrag, Peter. "Who Owns the Environment?" *Saturday Review*, July 4, 1970. Page 8.

25.   Bundy, William P. "The Tortuous Road to Population Control." The Washington *Post*, August 9, 1970.

26.   Domville, Fred. "The Depopulation Bomb." *Triumph*, Vol. VI, No. 2, February, 1971; *The Geography of Survival*, booklet distributed by the American Trucking Association.

27.   Chapman, William. "Rural America: The Exodus Continues." The Washington *Post*, March 21, 1971. Professor Joachin F. Wohlwill, Department of Psychology, Clark University, Worcester, Mass., wrote to *Science* magazine apropos of some of the drastic population control measures advocated from time to time in its pages and pointed out that "between 1950 and 1960 the population increase of 820,000 in Pennsylvania was accounted for entirely by the two major metropolitan areas of Philadelphia and Pittsburgh, with the remainder ot the state actually decreasing by 40,000." *Science*, Vol. 167, No. 23, January, 1970 (letters column).

28.   Misra, R. "The Role and Scope of Ecology in India." Address delivered to the First Indian-American Ecology Symposium at the Indian National Academy of Sciences in New Delhi, February 24-27, 1971.

29. Bundy, *loc. cit.*, Note 25 above.
30. Coale, Ansley J. "Man and His Environment." *Science*, October 9, 1970.
31. The Washington *Post*, November 30, 1971.
32. Von Kuehnelt-Leddihn, Erik. "Population Explosion?" *National Review*, November 5, 1971.
33. The Washington *Post*, October 4, 1971.
34. Even the current Director of the U. S. Office of Child Development, Dr. Edward F. Zigler, fears that with comprehensive day-care schemes such as recommended by the Rockefeller Commission "this nation may set up a network of 'warehouses for children' instead of supporting the family." San Francisco *Examiner*, February 10, 1971.
35. *Population and the American Future: The Report of the Commission on Population Growth and the American Future*, March, 1972.

VIII. The Inroads of the New Morality in America Today

1. Eichhorst, Calvin J. Quoted from the *Lutheran Standard* in *The Wanderer*, October 22, 1970.
2. *Time*, July 6, 1970; Arnold, Mark R. "New York Sharply Limits New Laws for Abortions." *The National Observer*, October 26, 1970.
3. The New York *Times*, January 4, 1971. In addition to NARAL and the *Times*, the wife of New York City Mayor John Lindsay also figured among those who saw nothing wrong with the first year's experience with New York's abortion-on-demand law. In May, 1971, fearing that there was a "real threat from backroom politicians" to amend the law, Mrs. Lindsay came out with what was described as a "rare public statement" in favor of it: "I think it would be criminal to repeal this law when it hasn't even been given a chance," she said. "It took a lot of courage to put in on the books—let's leave it there." (The Washington *Post*, May 13, 1971.) Taking a leaf from the book of Oregon's Senator Robert Packwood, Mayor Lindsay advocated a *national* abortion-on-demand law while speaking before a woman's group during the Florida presidential primary. (New York *Times*, March 7, 1972)

Mayor Lindsay had earlier signaled his active support of abortion-on-demand in a letter to the National Association for Abortion Law Repeal (NARAL), as did presidential candidate Rep. Paul McCloskey. Among other active presidential candidates, former Vice President Hubert Humphrey and South Dakota Senator George McGovern have indicated they think abortion is a matter between a woman and her doctor. Maine Senator Muskie has in the past expressed doubts about abortion but finally came out with the statement that he would favor the liberalization of state laws to permit therapeutic abortions, i.e., "abortions sought as a result of rape, incest, danger to the mother's life and so forth." ("Newsletter," National Right to Life Committee, February, 1972)

4. Morriss, Frank, "Abortion Drive in High Gear." *The Wanderer*, October 5, 1970.

5. Dr. Duncan Reid's plan for abortion centers was outlined at the 1970 meeting of the Planned Parenthood Physicians and reported by Dr. Frank J. Ayd, Jr. in *Medical-Moral Newsletter*, Vol. VII, No. 1, September, 1970.

6. Halberstam, Michael J., M.D. "Abortion: A Startling Proposal." *Redbook*, April, 1970. Dr. Halberstam's companion article in *Ob-Gyn News* (5/5/70) is cited by Dr. Frank J. Ayd, Jr. *loc. cit.*, Note 5 above.

7. *Medical Tribune and Medical News*, August 10, 1970.

8. Kummer, Jerome M., M.D. "Abortion Reform: A Successful Model of Psychotherapy." *Medical Tribune and Medical News*, August 24, 1970.

9. Quoted in Hyer, Marjorie. "Chaos Greets New York Abortion Law." *The National Catholic Reporter*, July 24, 1970.

10. Cited by Congressman John Dingell in *The Congressional Record*, Vol. 116, no. 182, November 16, 1970.

11. The New York *Times*, February 10, 1971.

12. Letter of Dr. Hall to the Editor of the *Saturday Review*, March 1, 1969.

13. Editorial, *California Medicine*. Official Journal of the California Medical Association. Vol. 113, No. 3, September, 1970. Pages 67-68.

14. See Note 10, Chapter III for a partial listing of organizations which have endorsed repeal of abortion laws, or abortion-on-demand.

15. *Time*, September 19, 1969. Dr. Egeberg later resigned as HEW Assistant Secretary to become a special consultant on health to President Nixon. Also, the California Supreme Court, in *People vs. Belous, did* declare the California law unconstitutional, but in the meantime the legislature had passed a liberal, ALI-type law.

16. Quoted in the Washington *Post*, May 6, 1970.

17. *Hall vs. Lefkowitz*, 305 Fed. Supp. 1020 (S.D.N.Y., 1969).

18. See "Population Control: U.S. Aid Program Leaps Forward," *Science*, Vol. 159, February 9, 1968, Pages 611-614; the Washington *Post*, July 2, 1969.

19. See "Birth Control: U.S. Research Advances Despite Papal Edict." *Science*, Vol. 162, November 1, 1968; the Washington *Post*, July 2, 1969.

20. Quoted in the Washington *Daily News*, October 8, 1970.

21. See the Washington *Post*, April 3 & 4, 1971.

22. McCarthy, Colman. "Worst Form of Birth Control Hurts Woman's Psyche." The Washington *Post,* February 28, 1971.

23. Novak, Franc, M.D. "Experience with Suction Curettage." In Hall, Robert E., M.D. (Ed.) *Abortion in a Changing World*. Columbia University Press, New York and London, 1970. Volume I, Pages 74-79.

24. See, for example, Edwards, R.G., and Fowler, Ruth E. "Human Embryos in the Laboratory." *Scientific American*, Vol. 223, No. 6, December, 1970.

25. Glass, H. Bentley. "Science: Endless Horizons or Golden Age." AAAS Presidential Address, December 28, 1970. Reprinted in *Science*, January 8, 1971, Page 28.

26. See, for example, the article "AAAS Convention: Radicals Harass the Establishment" in the same issue of *Science* as the address of Dr. Glass.

27. Glass, *loc. cit.*, Note 25 above.

28. For Dr. Handler's 1970 statement, see "Science Can Make Our Dreams Come True." An address reprinted in *Nutrition Today*, Vol. 6, No. 1, January/February, 1971. His 1971 statement is quoted in *The National Review*, November 19, 1971.

29. The Washington *Post*, March 17, 1970.

30. Lader, Lawrence. *Breeding Ourselves To Death*. Ballantine Books; New York, 1971. page 6.

31.   Rockefeller, John D. III. "Abortion Law Reform—The
       Moral Basis." In Hall, Robert E., M.D., *op. cit.*, Note 23
       above, pages xv-xx.
32.   *Ibid., Page xvi.*
33.   *Fletcher, Joseph. Situation Ethics.* The Westminster
       Press, Philadelphia, 1966. Pages 26, 136.
34.   Fletcher, Joseph and Bard, Bernard. "The Right to Die."
       The Atlantic, Vol. 221, Number 4, April, 1968. Page 63.
       We may note that, for all his frankness, Prof. Fletcher (or
       the editors of the *Atlantic*) still persists in using the eu-
       phemism "the right to die." What he is asserting, of
       course, is a presumed "right to kill."

IX. Can We Impose Our Morality On Others?

1.   Breslow, Lester, M.D., M.P.H. "Abortion: The Case for
      Repeal." Leaflet distributed by the National Association
      for Repeal of Abortion Laws (NARAL), 1970.
2.   Pilpel, Harriet. "The Right of Abortion." *The Atlantic*,
      Vol. 223, No. 6, June, 1969.
3.   The Catholic moral teaching on abortion is based on the
      divine commandment which forbids the direct killing of
      an innocent person under any circumstances. This com-
      mandment is also accepted by Protestantism and Juda-
      ism which, however, have historically recognized
      abortion to save the life of the mother as an exception to
      the rule; their position has been traditionally embodied
      in the Anglo-American legal system. The Catholic
      Church does not admit this "exception," but the Church's
      teaching does admit "indirect abortion," i.e., the sacrifice
      of fetal life as a result of some other medical procedure
      which is not intended to kill the fetus but which in fact
      results in his death. The rules justifying this indirect
      taking of fetal life have been formulated in the well-
      known principle of double effect.

         The principle of double effect, according to the moral
      theologian Fr. Francis J. Connell, "means that under cer-
      tain conditions a person may perform an action even
      though he foresees that one of the effects will be evil,
      either physical or moral. Four conditions must be
      fulfilled in order that one be justified in acting thus:

"1) The action which is to be performed by the agent must be morally good, or at least morally indifferent by its nature.

"2) The bad effect may be only permitted; it may not be willed in itself.

"3) The good effect must be caused at least as directly as the bad effect. In other words, the bad effect may not be a means to produce the good effect. Sometimes this condition is expressed by the phrase that the good effect must be at least equally immediate with the bad effect. But this immediacy refers to the order of *causality*, not the order of *time*. In the order of time the bad effect may precede the good effect.

"4) The good effect must be sufficiently beneficial to compensate for the permitting of the bad effect. Many factors must be considered in determining this condition. Thus, a greater good is *per se* required to compensate for the permitting of a *morally* bad effect (the sin of another) than for the permitting of a *physically* bad effect; a greater good is required only when the bad effect is injurious to the *common* good than when it is harmful only to an individual." (Connell, Very Rev. Francis J., C.S.S.R., S.T.D., LL.D., *Outlines of Moral Theology*. The Bruce Publishing Company, Milwaukee, 1958. Pages 22-23.)

As applied to abortion, Fr. David Granfield has described three situations which help to clarify the meaning of this principle of double effect: "First, a woman has an operable cancer of the cervix. If the womb is removed before metastasis, in accord with accepted medical practice, the woman will live but the child will die. The abortive action may be performed, however, since the destruction of the child is indirect and unintended, is not caused by the good effect, and has a proportionately grave reason. Next, a woman has an ectopic pregnancy with a nonviable fetus in the Fallopian tube. The tube will certainly rupture and hemorrhage long before viability, thereby gravely endangering the lives of both mother and child. In such a case, the removal of the tube to prevent the hemorrhage is considered licit since the sacrifice of the child is only indirect. Finally, a pregnant woman has a serious kidney, lung, or heart disease and will die before she can bear her child to term. Although such a case would be a medical rarity nowadays, if it did occur, no abortion of the child could be permitted, since the killing would be direct.

"In all three cases, the child's life is sacrificed to save the mother. In the first case, the womb happens to be cancerous—a fact not related to the child. In the second case, the child is the cause of the harm to the mother owing to its misplaced nidation. In the third case, the child's presence puts a lethal burden on the mother's already weakened condition. But the decision to permit the sacrifice of the child in the first two cases but not in the third is not because of the degree of danger to the mother or because the child is the cause of the danger to the mother, but primarily because the causality involved is only indirect. The child cannot be killed directly for any reason—even to save the mother from imminent death. The child may be killed indirectly as the result of a licit operation for a proportionately good reason. Although the intention of the aborter is significant, the physical causality is primary. The doctor may not intend the death of the child; but even if his primary intention or motive is directed toward saving the mother, that fact does not make the killing of the child indirect if the child's death is the means whereby the mother is saved." (Granfield, David. *The Abortion Decision*. Doubleday and Company, Garden City, New York, 1969. Page 135.)

4.   Connery, John R., S.J. Review of *Abortion: Law, Choice, and Morality* by Daniel Callahan. *The National Catholic Reporter.* August 7, 1970.

5.   The Detroit *News*, May 10, 1971.

6.   Potter, Ralph B. "The Abortion Debate." In Cutler, Donald R. (Ed.) *Updating Life and Death*. Essays in Ethics and Medicine. Beacon Press, Boston, 1969. Page 88.

7.   Quoted by Shaw, Russell. *Abortion on Trial*. Pflaum Press, Dayton, Ohio, 1968. Page 174. Mr. Shaw also quotes the unambiguous judgment on abortion of the famous Lutheran anti-Nazi theologian, Dietrich Bonhoeffer: "Destruction of the embryo in the mother's womb is a violation of the right to live which God has bestowed upon this nascent life. To raise the question whether we

are here concerned already with a human being or not is merely to confuse the issue. The simple fact is that God certainly intended to create a human being and this nascent human being has been deliberately deprived of his life. And that is nothing but murder." (Page 175. Cited from Bonhoeffer's *Ethics*, ed. Eberhard Bethge, New York, 1965; paperback edition.)

8. Quoted in *Medical-Moral Newsletter*. Edited by Frank J. Ayd, Jr., M.D., Vol. VII, Nos. 3 and 4, November and December, 1970.

9. Quoted in *AMA News*, October 5, 1970.

10. According to Rabbi Bertrand Fink of the Baltimore Rabbinical Council in public statement in opposition to the 1970 Maryland abortion-on-demand bill later vetoed by Governor Marvin Mandel. Quoted in the Washington *Catholic Standard*, April 30, 1970.

11. Quoted in the Baltimore *Catholic Review*, March 26, 1971.

12. *National Review*, Vol. XXIII, No. 15, April 20, 1971.

13. Herberg, Will, in the *National Review*, Vol. XXIII, No. 7, February 23, 1971.

14. Quoted in "Newsletter," National Right To Life Committee, December, 1970.

15. All quotations are from Curran, Charles E. "Natural Law and Moral Theology." In Curran (Ed.), *Contraception: Authority and Dissent*. Herder and Herder, New York, 1969. Pages 160-163.

16. Callahan, Daniel. *Abortion: Law, Choice, and Morality*. The MacMillan Company, New York, 1970. Page 318.

17. *Ibid.*, Page 316.

18. *Ibid.*, Page 326.

19. *Ibid.*, Page 18-19.

20. *Ibid.*, Page 327.

21. *Ibid.*, Page 18.

22. *Ibid.*, Page 9.

23. *Ibid.*, Page 493.

24. For an account of Medical euthanasia in Nazi Germany, see Wertham, Frederick. *A Sign for Cain*. The MacMillan Company, New York, 1966.

25. See Novak, Franc, M.D. "Experience with Suction Curettage." In Hall, Robert E., M.D. (Ed.) *Abortion in a Chang-*

ing World. Columbia University Press, New York and London, 1970. Volume I, Pages 74-75.

26.   Callahan, *op. cit.,* Page 312.

27.   *Ibid.,* Page 339.

28.   *Ibid.,* Page 339.

29.   See, for example, Cazelles, Henri. *"Les Origines du Decalogue."* In *Eretz-Israel,* Archeological, Historical, and Geographical Studies, Volume Nine. Israel Exploration Society, Jerusalem, 1969. Page 17. According to Cazelles, the murderer is *"celui qui verse du sang innocent."*

30.   *Ibid.,* Page 341.

31.   *Ibid.,* Page 340.

32.   *Ibid.,* Page 425.

33.   Quoted in *The Terrible Choice: The Abortion Dilemma.* Bantam Books, New York, 1968, Page 102.

34.   Grisez, Germain. *Abortion: the Myths, the Realities, and the Arguments.* Corpus Books, New York and Cleveland, 1970. Page 347.

X. God, Not Man, Is the Master of Human Life

1.   Rice, Charles E. *The Vanishing Right To Live.* An Appeal for a Renewed Reverence for Life. Doubleday and Company, Garden City, New York, 1969. Page 46.

2.   Quoted in *The Terrible Choice: The Abortion Dilemma.* Bantam Books, New York, 1968. Page 46.

3.   *Ibid.,* Page 70.

4.   In Rosen, Harold, M.D., Ph.D. (Ed.) *Abortion in America.* Beacon Press, Boston, 1967. Page 209.

5.   *Science* magazine, February 12, 1971.

6.   Potter, Ralph B., Jr. "The Abortion Debate." In Cutler, Donald R. (Ed.) Updating *Life and Death.* Essays in Ethics and Medicine. Beacon Press, Boston, 1969. Page 88.

7.   Pope Paul VI, *Humanae Vitae,* #11.

8.   See, for example, Djeressi, Carl. "Birth Control After 1984." Talk presented at a symposium of the California Institute of Technology entitled "Technological Change and Population Growth," May 6, 1970. Reprinted in *Science,* Vol. 169, No. 3949, September 4, 1970. Pages 941–951.

9.   See discussion in Grisez, Germain. *Abortion: The Myths,*

the Realities, and the Arguments. Corpus Books, New York and Cleveland, 1970. Pages 106-116.

10.   Quoted from Abbott, Walter M., S.J., General Editor. *The Documents of Vatican II.* Herder and Herder Association Press, New York, 1966. Page 256. The full text of Vatican II's statement is as follows: "From the moment of conception life must be guarded with the greatest care, while abortion and infanticide are unspeakable crimes."

11.   Pope Pius XII, "Allocution to Midwives" (October 29, 1951) 43 *Acta Sancta Sedis* 835.

12.   Pope Paul VI. From a letter dated 10/11/70 reprinted in a leaflet on abortion, "The Church Speaks Out," distributed by Catholics United for the Faith, 222 North Avenue, New Rochelle, New York 10801.

Epilogue: Turning of the Tide?

1.   See Chapters II and III.
2.   Newsweek, May 3, 1971.
3.   See summary of legislative action in *NARAL News,* Summer, 1971.
4.   See "Newsletter," National Right to Life Committee, March, 1971.
5.   New York *Times,* May 10 and 11, 1972.
6.   *Ibid.,* May 10, 1972.
7.   *Ibid.,* April 29, May 1, and May, 5, 1972.
8.   *Ibid.,* May 8, 1972.
9.   *Ibid.,* May 14, 1972.
10.   *Ibid.,* April 23, 1972.
11.   *Ibid.,* May 24, 1972.
12.   See Chapters I and IV.

Appendix I: The Experience of Maryland

1.   Maryland Annotated Code, Article 27, 3 (1957).
2.   Finnerty, Joseph G. "Legal Considerations Concerning Abortion Law." Unpublished paper dated March 2, 1971.
3.   Rosen, Harold, M.D., Ph.D. "A Case Study in Social Hypocrisy." Chapter in *Abortion in America,* edited by Dr. Rosen. Boston: the Beacon Press, 1967. Page 312.
4.   The Washington *Post,* February 25, 1970.
5.   Personal Communication.

6.   For news stories reporting on some of the groups which have regularly supported liberalized abortion in Maryland, see the Washington *Catholic Standard,* April 30, 1970; February 4, 1971; the Washington *Post,* April 24, 1970, January 29, 1971; the Washington *Evening Star,* April 24, 1970, January 29, 1971; the Baltimore *Sun,* January 29, 1971.

7.   The Washington *Catholic Standard,* April 24, 1971.

8.   Pilpel, Harriet. "The Right to Abortion." *The Atlantic,* Vol. 223, No. 6, June, 1969.

9.   *Journal of Proceedings of the Maryland General Assembly,* 1968. Pages 1443, 1672.

10.   Grisez, Germain. *Abortion: The Myths, The Realities, and The Arguments.* New York and Cleveland: Corpus Books, 1970. p. 247.

11.   For text and summary of the American Law Institute's "model" abortion law, see Granfield, David. *The Abortion Decision.* Garden City, N.Y.: Doubleday and Co., 1969. Pages 78-81, 238-39.

12.   Maryland Annotated Code, Article 43, Section 149E (1969 Supplement)

13.   *Who Shall Live?* A Report Prepared for the American Friends Service Committee. New York: Hill and Wang, 1970. Page 27.

14.   Granfield, *op. cit.,* Note 11 above, pp. 198-199.

15.   Ibid., pp. 199-200.

16.   Grisez, *op. cit.,* Note 10 above, pp. 249-250.

17.   Cited by Jacobsen, Richard K., President, St. Thomas More Society, Baltimore, in testimony before the Environmental Matters Committee of the Maryland House of Delegates.

18.   "Abortion Surveillance Report, Maryland: July 1, 1968-September, 1970." Prepared by the National Right to Life Committee, P. O. Box 9365, Washington, D.C. 20005.

19.   The Washington *Post,* February 25, 1970.

20.   Personal Communication from a member of the House of Delegates.

21.   The Washington *Post,* April 1, 1970.

22.   Opinion of the Attorney General of the State of Maryland, dated May 13, 1971. Text published in full in the Baltimore *Daily Record,* Monday, May 18, 1970.

23.   *Ibid.,* Reply to the Tenth Question.
24.   Kane, Al. Philip. Statement before the governor's hearing on House Bill 489, Annapolis, Md., April 23, 1970.
25.   Sent out by the governor's office in response to a query regarding his stand.
26.   The Baltimore *Sun,* May 27, 1970.
27.   *Ibid.,* March 25, 1971.
28.   House of Delegates, No. 100. By Delegates A. T. Allen and Brown-Environmental Matters. By the House of Delegates, January 21, 1971; see also the Washington *Evening Star,* January 21, 1971.
29.   Personal Observation by the writer.
30.   The Washington *Post,* February 20, 1971.
31.   The Baltimore *Sun,* March 19, 1971.
32.   The Washington *Post,* March 3, 1971.
33.   For a list of some of the amendments introduced, see the Washington *Catholic Standard,* February 25, 1971.
34.   The Baltimore *Sun,* March 25, 1971.
35.   On the Committee hearings, see the Baltimore *Sun,* the Washington *Post,* and the Washington *Evening Star,* all for January 29, 1971; the Washington *Catholic Standard,* February 4, 1971.
36.   The Washington *Catholic Standard,* April 22, 1971.
37.   *Ibid.,* February 4 and 11, March 11, 1971.
38.   *Ibid.,* March 4, 1971.
39.   On the final vote, see the Baltimore *Sun,* March 25, 1971, for the most complete single analysis of why the 1971 Maryland abortion-on-demand bill failed.

Index

289